The Poverty of Our Freedom

The Poverty of Our Freedom

Essays 2012–2019

Axel Honneth

With translations by Gabriel Borrud, Mitch Cohen, Blake Emerson, Alex Englander, Felix Koch, Arvi Särkelä, and Daniel Steuer

polity

Originally published in German as *Die Armut unserer Freiheit. Aufsätze 2012–2019*
© Suhrkamp Verlag Berlin 2020. All rights reserved by and controlled through
Suhrkamp Verlag Berlin.

This English edition © Polity Press, 2023

Polity Press
65 Bridge Street
Cambridge CB2 1UR, UK

Polity Press
111 River Street
Hoboken, NJ 07030, USA

ISBN-13: 978-1-5095-5632-8 – hardback
ISBN-13: 978-1-5095-5633-5 – paperback

A catalogue record for this book is available from the British Library.

Library of Congress Control Number: 2022948167

Typeset in 10.5 on 12 pt Palatino
by Fakenham Prepress Solutions, Fakenham, Norfolk NR21 8NL
Printed and bound in Great Britain by TJ Books Ltd, Padstow, Cornwall

The publisher has used its best endeavours to ensure that the URLs for external
websites referred to in this book are correct and active at the time of going to press.
However, the publisher has no responsibility for the websites and can make no
guarantee that a site will remain live or that the content is or will remain appropriate.

Every effort has been made to trace all copyright holders, but if any have been
overlooked the publisher will be pleased to include any necessary credits in any
subsequent reprint or edition.

For further information on Polity, visit our website:
politybooks.com

Contents

Acknowledgments

"The Depths of Recognition: The legacy of Jean-Jacques Rousseau." First published in: Avi Lifschitz (ed.), *Engaging with Rousseau: Reaction and Interpretation from the Eighteenth Century to the Present*, Cambridge: Cambridge University Press, 2016, pp. 189–206.
First published in German as: "Untiefen der Anerkennung: Das sozialphilosophische Erbe Jean-Jacques Rousseaus," in: *WestEnd. Neue Zeitschrift für Sozialforschung*, 9 (2012), no. 1/2, pp. 47–64.

"On the Poverty of Our Freedom: The greatness and limits of Hegel's doctrine of ethical life." Published in: Paul Dumouchel and Reiko Gotoh (eds.), *Social Bonds as Freedom. Revisiting the Dichotomy of the Universal and the Particular*, New York/Oxford: Berghahn, 2015, pp. 109–24.
First published in German as: "Von der Armut unserer Freiheit: Größe und Grenzen der Hegelschen Sittlichkeitslehre," in: Axel Honneth and Gunnar Hindrichs (eds.), *Freiheit: Internationaler Hegelkongress 2011*, Frankfurt am Main: Vittorio Klostermann, 2013, pp. 13–30.

"The Normativity of Ethical Life." First published in English in: *Philosophy and Social Criticism*, 40 (2014), no. 8: Special issue: Freedom's Right: A Symposium on Axel Honneth's Political Philosophy. Guest Editor: Eduardo Mendieta, pp. 817–26.
First published in German as: "Die Normativität der Sittlichkeit: Hegels Lehre als Alternative zur Ethik Kants," in: *Deutsche Zeitschrift für Philosophie*, 62 (2014), no. 5, pp. 787–800.

"Hegel and Marx: A reassessment after one century." First published in English in: Banu Bargu and Chiara Bottici (eds.), *Feminism, Capitalism, and Critique: Essays in Honour of Nancy Fraser*, Basle: Springer International, 2017, pp. 185–207.
First published in German as: "Hegel und Marx: Eine Neubewertung nach 100 Jahren," in: *WestEnd. Neue Zeitschrift für Sozialforschung*, 13 (2016), no. 2, pp. 53–74.

"Economy or Society? The greatness and limits of Marx's theory of capitalism."
First published in German as: "Wirtschaft oder Gesellschaft? Größe und Grenzen der Marxschen Theorie des Kapitalismus," in: *WestEnd. Neue Zeitschrift für Sozialforschung*, 15 (2018), no. 2, pp. 3–27.

"Three, Not Two, Concepts of Liberty: A proposal to enlarge our moral self-understanding." First published in English in: Rachel Zuckert and James Kreines (eds.), *Hegel on Philosophy in History*, Cambridge: Cambridge University Press, 2017, pp. 177–92. Delivered as the *Dewey Lectures* on January 1, 2014.
First published in German as: "Drei, nicht zwei Begriffe der Freiheit: Zur Reaktualisierung einer verschütteten Tradition," in: Olivia Mitscherlich-Schönherr and Matthias Schloßberger (eds.), *Internationales Jahrbuch für Philosophische Anthropologie. Die Unergründlichkeit der menschlichen Natur*, Berlin: de Gruyter, 2015, vol. 5, pp. 113–30.

"The Diseases of Society: Approaching a nearly impossible concept." First published in: *Social Research: German Perspectives on the Social Sciences*, 81 (2014), no. 3, pp. 683–703.
First published in German as: "Die Krankheiten der Gesellschaft: Annäherungen an einen nahezu unmöglichen Begriff," in: *WestEnd. Neue Zeitschrift für Sozialforschung*, 11 (2014), no. 1, pp. 45–60.

"Education and the Democratic Public Sphere: A neglected chapter of political philosophy." First published in English in: Odin Lysaker and Jonas Jakobsen (eds.), *Recognition and Freedom: Axel Honneth's Political Thought*, Leiden: Brill, 2015, pp. 17–32.
First published in German as: "Erziehung und demokratische Öffentlichkeit: Ein vernachlässigtes Kapitel der politischen Philosophie," in: *Zeitschrift für Erziehungswissenschaft*, 15 (2012), no. 3, pp. 429–42.

"Democracy and the Division of Labor: A blind spot in political philosophy."
First published in the German edition of the present volume as: "Demokratie und soziale Arbeitsteilung: Noch ein vernachlässigtes Kapitel der politischen Philosophie."

"Childhood: Inconsistencies in our liberal imagination."
First published in German as: "Kindheit: Unstimmigkeiten unserer liberalen Vorstellungswelt," in: Monika Betzler and Barbara Bleisch (eds.), *Familiäre Pflichten*, Berlin: Suhrkamp, 2015, pp. 147–74.

"Denaturalizations of the Lifeworld: On the threefold use of the humanities."
First published in German as: "Denaturierungen der Lebenswelt: Vom dreifachen Nutzen der Geisteswissenschaften," in: Atenea Panteos and Tim Rujek (eds.), *Zur Theorie der Geisteswissenschaften*, Stuttgart: Reclam, 2015, pp. 283–315.

"Is there an emancipatory interest? An attempt to answer critical theory's most fundamental question." First published in English in: *European Journal of Philosophy*, 25 (2017), no. 4, pp. 908–20.

"A History of Moral Self-Correction: Tracing European solidarity."
First published in the German edition of this volume as: "Eine Geschichte moralischer Selbstkorrekturen: Auf den Spuren europäischer Solidarität." *Marc Bloch-Lecture*, delivered on June 11, 2019 at the Sorbonne, Paris.

Previously published texts have been checked and, where necessary, revised or expanded in line with the arrangement of the present volume.

I would like to thank Daniel Steuer for his excellent work on the translation of the remaining articles in this volume that had not yet been published in English.

Preface
Of the Poverty of Our Liberty

Most of the essays collected in the present volume are attempts to fill gaps in my book *Freedom's Right*, gaps I recognized only in hindsight.[1] When the first substantial responses to the original German edition of the study appeared in 2012, pointing to certain shortcomings in my reflections, I began to clarify the questions that had been left unanswered, and to expand on theses that had not been worked out in enough detail. Looking back over these pieces, written over a period of seven years, I decided to bring them together in a volume arranged around the notion of "social liberty." In almost all of the essays, I attempt to shed further light on the meaning of this concept of liberty, whether by engaging with its tradition, pointing out areas in which its normative content has yet to be sufficiently developed, or, finally, tracing the impulses that continue to emanate from it. The title of the resulting volume, *The Poverty of Our Freedom*, is a minor variation on the title of one of the pieces it contains. In that essay, I try to use Hegel's conception of "ethical life" to illuminate the idea of social liberty. The claim that we suffer from a poverty of liberty refers to the fact that our efforts at putting the normative promises of modern society into practice have not been successful in realizing the principles of social liberty where they are needed most.

Readers of *Freedom's Right* will know that Hegel's doctrine of ethical life forms its backbone, and the doctrine is also at the center of the essays that form part I of the present collection. This part further elaborates the notion of social liberty chiefly through an engagement with the philosophical tensions between Hegel and Marx. The intellectual constellation between Hegel and Marx is of particular relevance for the project of a critical theory of society. But beyond this, a look back at this crucial nineteenth-century debate is of particular importance because it was taken for granted, back then, that the idea of social liberty was an independent approach to understanding what it means for us to be free. Hegel and Marx were both convinced that the individual's freedom can exist only in the context of successful intersubjectivity, for without affirmative recognition by the other, an individual is not able to realize her intentions and impulses without constraint. The difference between the two thinkers lies in the very different ideas they went on to develop about the social institutions that make this kind of successful intersubjectivity possible. All the essays in part I, except the last, examine the alternatives developed by Hegel and Marx, and try to establish their value for our social self-understanding today. The last essay, however, tries to sketch the systematic core of the idea of social liberty through a discussion of competing concepts of liberty in the modern philosophical tradition, although I am still not fully satisfied with the results of these reflections.

The title of part II, "Deformations of Social Freedom," is meant to indicate that the essays in this part, except the first, are attempts to work out why there is such a lack of social opportunity to realize this kind of liberty today. The first essay is a renewed attempt to outline a key concept in my analysis of the contemporary situation, "social pathology," in a way that departs from the concept as it appears in *Freedom's Right*.[2] The attempt treads new paths that, if they were explored further, would lend some of the thoughts in *Freedom's Right* a more radical edge. The other essays discuss three social areas in which the lack of any serious effort to promote social – as opposed to mere "negative" – liberty is particularly blatant. The first deals with a social institution of "ethical life" whose significance I completely overlooked when writing the book, possibly because of an overly strong adherence to Hegel's model. Like Hegel – who fell behind Kant in this regard – I almost entirely disregarded the enormous significance of public education and its institutions for the stabilization of democratic (in Hegel's terms "civic") attitudes and dispositions.[3] The essay on the role of schooling in the democratic process, which draws on Kant, John Dewey, and Émile Durkheim, is an attempt to compensate for this unfortunate omission. The final two pieces of part II have a more experimental character, but also pursue the question of how our ideas about central areas of social life would need to change if we seriously wanted to transform them into spheres for the realization of social – and not just "negative" – liberty. The essay on the social role of work explains, in far more detail than *Freedom's Right*, why a crucial condition of democratic will-formation is a fair, inclusive, and transparent division of labor. In the essay on childhood, I tentatively try to uncover the deep-seated premises that inform our liberal ideas about children, and ask which of them might be preventing children from developing voices of their own and thus acquiring democratic autonomy.

The title of part III, "Sources of Social Freedom," might at first seem somewhat artificial, for the section brings together three essays that not only derive from very different occasions but also pursue questions that do not appear to have a lot in common. However, although they set out from very different starting points, they all concern individual or collective experiences that, properly understood, reveal the need to move on from a notion of liberty couched in purely individualist terms to one that is grounded in non-coercive mutual social relations. The first of these essays uses the logic of the humanities disciplines to show that our engagement with the cultural-intellectual conditions of our social world compels us to see ourselves as members of an active community that advances its own interpretations in a struggle against forms of dependence that only seem to be naturally given. The second essay takes up the old question of whether there is such a thing as an emancipatory interest.[4] It argues that repressed groups can begin to liberate themselves only through a cognitive mobilization against a naturalizing understanding of the existing social order that rests on frozen hegemonial patterns of interpretation. The final essay of part III is a reminder to Europeans: that we can recover solidarity only if we come to terms with the global injustice and harm caused by European states right up to the very recent past. We must do so in the spirit of social liberty, and with the aim of creating normative mechanisms that prevent us from perpetrating similar offenses. This text may seem to lie outside of the bounds of the present volume, but to me its inclusion was important, for it points to the political actuality of some of the ideas set out in the other pieces.

Once again, I have to thank Eva Gilmer, who accompanied me on the way toward the publication of this collection of essays with her characteristic diligence, circumspection, and helpfulness. My thanks are also due to Jan-Erik Strasser, who read and corrected the final manuscript with great expertise.

Axel Honneth, January 2020
Translated by Daniel Steuer

Part I

Forms of Social Freedom

1

The Depths of Recognition
The legacy of Jean-Jacques Rousseau

In 1932, when Ernst Cassirer published his long essay *The Question of Jean-Jacques Rousseau*, he must have been certain that he had finally found the key to an integral understanding of the philosopher's fissured work.[1] Today, however, some eighty-five years later, Cassirer's suggestion is almost forgotten; scholars continue to puzzle over where, if at all, unity can be sought in the seemingly contradictory writings of the great thinker. No other modern philosophical author, with the exception of Nietzsche perhaps, has elicited more starkly opposed interpretations of his work; no other author has therefore remained so constantly the eternally young, always provocative and disturbingly contemporary. Depending on the reader's attitude and the contemporary historical context, one could discover in Rousseau the anthropologist invoking a model of human nature, a theorist who stresses feeling and emotion like the English moral philosophers, or a progenitor of democratic self-determination who paved the way for Kant. When the times called for different philosophical emphases, one could also find in Rousseau the pioneer of a totalitarian conception of democracy, the fervent defender of republican equality, or the advocate of an ideal of personal authenticity. As heterogeneous as they might appear, all these interpretations of Rousseau have had to struggle with the same great problem of being able to refer only to some parts of his work while sweeping other, contradicting parts under the rug. Only a few have succeeded, like Ernst Cassirer, in suggesting a reading that could interpret the philosopher's disparate writings and thoughts as stages in the realization of a single basic idea.

Cassirer saw this convergence point of Rousseau's work in the idea of the human will's capacity for self-determination in spite of all social and political hazards.[2] And yet Cassirer's interpretation soon faced many emphatic challenges from ongoing research. Not only did such a reading, making Rousseau the direct precursor of Kant, seem to place too little emphasis on the collectivist tinge in Rousseau's *Social Contract*, it also seemed to ignore what can be read in Rousseau's other writings on the mutual dependence of subjects, indeed on their being at the mercy of each other.[3] This element of his work, rooted in the notion of *amour propre* or self-love (which is constitutive both for Rousseau's *Discourse on Inequality*[4] and his *Emile*),[5] came increasingly to the fore in more recent interpretations. This, however, did not offer a key to the underlying idea of the whole of Rousseau's work as long as it remained unclear how Rousseau's pessimistic diagnosis of the ever-increasing dependence of the modern subject on the esteem of others could be brought together with the more confident lines of thought developed in the *Social Contract*.[6] After all, where the notion of *amour propre* was the theme in the early writings, it was only in the context of the danger of the complete external control of the subject. However, in the *Social Contract* – the constructive part of Rousseau's work – the same subjects are suddenly conceived as having an irreducible capacity for self-legislation. The breakthrough to a connection between these two elements and thus to an integral interpretation of Rousseau's oeuvre did not emerge in the research literature until the concept of *amour propre* was fanned out to include a positive variant as well as the negative. With this suggestion, which we probably owe to the ground-breaking study of N. J. H. Dent,[7] it became possible to conceive of Rousseau's idea of the constitutive dependence of the subject on the other as the fundamental hinge between the two parts of his work by spelling out the negative form of the notion of *amour propre* in his cultural critique and the positive version in drafts of the *Social Contract*.

However, Dent's reinterpretation probably achieved more than he himself originally intended. Giving only a little twist to his interpretation, it was easy to develop from it the thesis that, with his bipolar notion of *amour propre*, Rousseau had become the founder of the whole tradition of recognition theory. The step toward this thesis – which is of downright subversive significance in the history of ideas – was probably first taken by Frederick Neuhouser in a major study.[8] Neuhouser asserts that the idea that human subjects owe their social agency to the recognition granted by other subjects was not Hegel's invention, as had been assumed hitherto, but can be traced back to Rousseau. The significance of this reformulation and the degree to which it relocates Rousseau's oeuvre become clear only in light of its distance from Cassirer's overall reading. While for Cassirer Rousseau stands as a lone precursor to Kant because he is seen as engaging in a lifelong effort to elaborate the active, self-legislative aspect of the human will, those who follow Dent's interpretation see the unifying thread in Rousseau's work in precisely the opposite thesis – that for good or evil, the human will is dependent on the affirmation and esteem of other subjects.

In what follows I would like to elaborate on this second thesis, first showing where it is justified and then highlighting its limits. As I would argue, throughout his life Rousseau was too uncertain about the real significance of intersubjective recognition in the structure of social life to be able to clearly make this intersubjectivity the foundation of his entire theory. Specifically, the first section of the chapter addresses Rousseau's intellectual development to the point where he becomes aware of the necessity of a socially sustainable, egalitarian form of mutual recognition against the harmful forms of *amour propre*. From here it will be easy to survey the enormous influence Rousseau's bipolar conception of social recognition has had on modern philosophical discourse. In the second section I discuss how the negative aspect of this conception, that is, the human need to surpass one's fellow creatures in social esteem, is reinterpreted in Kant's writings on the philosophy of history as a driving force of human progress, and how Fichte and Hegel further develop its positive variant of mutual respect among equals in the direction of a recognition theory of law and an ethical social life. Not until the third section of the chapter will I proceed to address the skepticism that Rousseau always exhibited (increasingly toward the end of his life) toward the dependence on others inherent in *amour propre*. In his late writings, as earlier in the *Discourse on Inequality*, he plays again with the idea that it might be advantageous for people's peace of mind if they became fully independent of intersubjective recognition. In this respect, Rousseau's works exhibit two fundamental philosophical motifs that stand in constant conflict with each other: the Stoic idea of personal independence from all external attachments and the intersubjective idea of a deep-seated dependence on others.

I

The motif from which Rousseau initially draws his central concept of *amour propre* emerges more clearly in his early critique of theater than anywhere else. Already in the *First Discourse*, he subjects what he derogatorily refers to as "play-acting" to an extremely negative analysis;[9] this critique matures in his *Letter to d'Alembert*. For Rousseau, the theater is not merely one cultural institution among others, in which an enlightened audience learns through the contemplation of or engagement with works of art. He regards the stage and the theater hall as a special instance where the behavior of actors can infect the audience with the virus of "mere appearance." In contrast to the museum or the concert hall, where the viewer might at least imagine in the presented work of art the authentic intention of the artist, Rousseau regards the theater-going audience as initially confronted solely with a form of behavior through which the actor wants to reveal his skill at "putting on another character than his own."[10] But the still-innocent audience is thereby encouraged to practice gestures and expressions that serve no other goal than disguising their true character. From such critical observations, Rousseau draws the far-reaching conclusion that the creation of theaters does great harm to any republican commonwealth because the arts of disguise presented in the theater undermine precisely those attitudes and behaviors that are necessary for political institutions built on the will of the people – duty, honesty, and civic pride. As Rousseau puts it in the *Letter to d'Alembert*, the actor develops "by profession the talent of deceiving men."[11]

Admittedly, Rousseau believes that the danger of infection from the playacting on the stage merely reinforces a cultural tendency already powerfully operative in a wide variety of places. Four years before the *Letter to d'Alembert* was published, Rousseau, in his *Discourse on Inequality*, already sought to analyze the genealogy of those new behaviors of pretentious disguise and the craving for social esteem he experienced so intensively in Parisian society. In searching for the anthropological roots of the individual affectation with prestige that the theater merely intensifies, he found in his *Discourse* a specific form of the human relation to the self. While he did not regard it as being of natural origin, its cultural proliferation still seemed to establish it as a kind of second nature. Rousseau named this form of behavior *amour propre*. This concept not only forms the basis of his entire critique of society; it is also the key to understanding what he will contribute to the development of a theory of intersubjective recognition.

In the genealogical logic of the *Discourse on Inequality*, *amour propre* does not play as prominent a role as its importance for the overall design of that study actually demands. Certainly, Rousseau uses the term now and then when identifying the causes underlying the emergence of social inequality,[12] but he restricts his attempt to clarify its meaning to a single long note whose weight, however, can hardly be overestimated. Here, in note XV of the text, Rousseau outlines the significance of *amour propre* in contrast to *amour de soi-même*, drawing distinctions between the two on the basis of the standard of evaluation that each presupposes.[13] For Rousseau, *amour de soi* is a natural human disposition – a form of self-interestedness that contributes to human self-preservation by letting each human being rely solely on his own individual, vital criteria of the right and the good. In the later and thus somewhat artificial phenomenon of *amour propre*, by contrast, the normative standard of self-interestedness shifts to take the opinion of others as the yardstick of opportune behavior. Rousseau explains this difference most trenchantly in a remark where he takes from Hume's moral theory the formulation already prefiguring Adam Smith's notion of the impartial spectator: in the feeling or striving of *amour de soi* the subject is the sole spectator of himself, whereas in *amour propre* the subject regards others as judges of his actions and omissions.[14]

If the differences between the two kinds of self-interest are explicated in this way, it initially remains completely unclear why the second attitude, that of *amour propre*, should be at all tied to a tendency toward the negative or problematical. On the contrary, from Adam Smith's perspective, it could be said that, in terms of consideration and appropriateness, orienting one's actions toward the internalized judgment of initially merely external others is far superior to an act that is purely self-referential.[15] But in his commentary, Rousseau focuses on a different aspect of this intersubjectively mediated self-assessment that no longer seems compatible with the wholesome effects of Smith's impartial spectator as described in the *Theory of Moral Sentiments*. For Rousseau, the other who has become the judge of one's actions is not an instance for correcting one's own judgment, not a power fostering cognitive and moral decentralization, but rather a source of constant urging to prove oneself superior to one's fellow citizens.

What the *amour propre* of the *Discourse on Inequality* becomes, then, is a form of self-interestedness that transforms into a spur to social esteem, thereby making the activity needed for self-preservation dependent on assessment by others.

Yet even upon closer observation, it is not at all easy to accurately identify where Rousseau's account of the status of the internalized spectator deviates from the description Smith provided only a few years later. This difficulty arises because both authors initially aim at a similar assertion, that the socialized human being usually judges the appropriateness of his actions in terms of a presumed evaluation by a generalized spectator. However, one difference in their readings, serious in its consequences, consists in Rousseau's expansion of this bilateral relationship between the subject and his internalized spectator by adding another, second kind of relationship. This relationship emerges because real, empirical others observe the subject in his attempt to orient his actions toward his intersubjective judge. According to Rousseau, when a subject is confronted with these two perspectives, he is driven to present his action to his internal observer in such a way that it seems superior or nobler than those of the other persons present. Thus, *amour propre*, in contrast to self-assessment by imagining the perspective of an impartial spectator, is the expression of a tripartite set of relations of the socialized human being: once the individual has learned, as an effect of ever denser social interactions, to orient his behavior toward the judgments of generalized others, he will strive to present himself as favorably as possible in relation to these judgments so that he can expect also to be positively evaluated by those contemporaries. For Rousseau, as he repeatedly notes, what is perfidious about this dependence on others' judgment is not the mere fact that someone pretends to have properties that he does not believe he has; what is disastrous here is that *amour propre* permits individuals to deceive themselves, because they must not only be able to present themselves externally to their fellows, but also to their internal judge, as persons with the best possible attributes. What an individual driven by *amour propre* desires is not just social affirmation, but self-affirmation – that is, a consciousness of his own worth.[16]

All the social pathologies that Rousseau discusses in the *Discourse on Inequality* have their roots, he argues, in the craving for social esteem arising from *amour propre*. In bourgeois society, people are restlessly at work developing the attributes that might make them appear superior to their contemporaries in the eyes of their internalized spectator. Once set in motion, this "petulant activity of our *amour propre*" knows no limit;[17] it exhausts every distinguishing trait due to its merely relative character, thus forcing the subject to make new efforts to plausibly demonstrate his superiority. And, as a result of its social spread, every quality of wealth or power or beauty that was the sign of individual superiority yesterday must be trumped today, so that every field of status competition is dominated by a tendency to spiral ever higher in the search for distinction.[18] As we have seen, in this cultural process the theater merely assumes the role of an institution that intensifies sophistication. The reason Rousseau despises the theater so much is that here citizens so convincingly learn to feign behaviors associated with status, that eventually they themselves believe in the authenticity of such performances.

Already in *Emile* – which Rousseau began drafting only a few years after publishing the *Discourse on Inequality* – it is obvious that Rousseau is not content with this merely critical diagnosis of *amour propre*. Here the same term appears repeatedly again, but without the same automatic and immediate derogation that was apparent in the context of the earlier cultural critique. If in addition to *Emile* we consider the *Social Contract*, which he was writing at about the same time and which does not speak directly of *amour propre* but does speak of related attitudes, we can make out a trajectory in Rousseau's thinking that reveals a growing effort to differentiate its guiding concept. Dissatisfied with his inability to find a way out of the pathologies of bourgeois society, from the early 1760s onward the philosopher wrestles with the possibility of asserting a beneficial, socially acceptable form of *amour propre*. But it is not easy for Rousseau to shift from a wholly negative presentation of *amour propre* to an account that suddenly sheds a favorable light on this concept. Necessary for such an achievement would be an account of the conditions under which the intersubjectively mediated self-assessment could escape the need to present oneself as superior to one's fellows. *Emile* has a number of formulations that clearly show how Rousseau first struggles with the difficult task of pinning down such conditions. In every instance where he begins to speak of the unavoidable development of *amour propre* in his tutee, he investigates at the same time (as if in an experimental setup) what measures could prevent the danger of the ensuing striving for prestige.[19]

The solution Rousseau finally offers to this problem is a suggestion that at first glance seems rather puzzling: "Let us extend *amour-propre* to other beings. We shall transform it into a virtue, and there is no man's heart in which this virtue does not have its root."[20] This formulation makes sense when one realizes that an extension of *amour propre* would mean seeing every other person orienting his own activity in the same way toward the judgment of a generalized observer. If such a change of perspective is carried out, Rousseau seems to say, we recognize all fellow subjects struggling in the same way for the approval of their internal judge; and then the drive to outdo them in reputation and status must vanish. This reasoning can be understood more clearly if, instead of an inner judge, we regarded subjects as equally depending on a generalized approval from the surrounding society. To speak of the extension of *amour propre* is, then, nothing other than suggesting to the subjects the insight that they reciprocally need each other's recognition and should thus forgo a competitive striving for higher reputation. Rousseau tries to prevent the poisoning of his pupil's *amour propre* by trying, given the need for social recognition that all human beings share, to teach him to be satisfied with social prestige that expresses precisely this mutual dependence. Respect among equals is the formula that expresses a form of social recognition tempered in this way, and that seems to reproduce adequately Rousseau's suggested solution.[21]

Summarizing this way the educational therapy of *amour propre* in *Emile* enables us, for the first time, to make sense of why Rousseau can appear today as a theorist of recognition. From its first introduction in the *Discourse on Inequality*, the concept of *amour propre* apparently meant more than mere human passion to prove oneself superior to others and to struggle for ever higher levels of social esteem. Beneath such forms of striving as a driving force lies the human desire to count as someone in the eyes of members of society in general and to enjoy a kind of social value. Before *amour propre* becomes the desire for prestige and special esteem, it therefore has the innocent form that it would assume in Adam Smith's internal spectator.[22] Its essence is to let us be dependent in our self-esteem and self-image on social recognition from the society around us. For Rousseau, this dependence on the generalized other acquires the negative form of a compulsive drive to compare oneself and feel superior to others only when we neglect the accompanying awareness that we all share the same basic need for social approval and affirmation. In such a case we lose sight of the fact that, together with all other members of society, we are part of that court of an inner judge from which we expect approval of our behavior. Thus it is only logical that, in his writings on education, Rousseau advises teachers to employ pedagogical measures that convey a sense of social equality to pupils from an early age. For only when an individual learns to understand himself as an equal among equals can he also grasp himself as a contributor to the generalized other, upon whose verdict the satisfaction of his own *amour propre* depends.

This last formulation is manifestly chosen in anticipation of Rousseau's design to solve the problem of *amour propre* in his *Social Contract*. In *Emile* we already find the thought that respect for and from one's peers satisfies the fundamental desire for social recognition, but not yet the much farther-reaching idea that this enables the individual subject to understand himself as the co-author of judgments on which his understanding of himself will thereafter depend. With the concept of the general will, with which Rousseau crowns his *Social Contract*, he clearly hoped to outline such an idea of a standard of judgment for social recognition, a standard created by those subject to it. The self-esteem of citizens in a republic is thus no longer subject to an external instance of the generalized other, because in a previous spontaneous act of consultation they have agreed on a common will – in whose light they now can recognize each other in a way that they collectively hold to be right.[23] Rousseau seems to think that in such a society all those uncontrollable standards of individual worth, forced upon each person and hitherto responsible for the corrupt influence of *amour propre*, will have vanished. Instead, only self-imposed and transparent sources of social recognition will remain. This would ultimately mean that the members of this society respect each other as free and equal persons.

And yet the final chapters of Rousseau's *Social Contract* also seem to imply that he was not entirely convinced that *amour propre* could be completely satisfied only through this mutual respect. His discussion of civil religion and republican patriotism seems to imply that the individual strives for a stronger sense of self-worth than recognition as a free and equal citizen can provide.[24] In *amour propre* – the need for other members of society to see one as worthy – excessive claims burgeon that are hard to satisfy, even when egalitarianism reigns. Therefore, Rousseau apparently seeks additional resources of social recognition even in a republican community.[25] These other sources must not provide a basis for the easily inflamed version of the craving for recognition; hence they must be sufficiently generalizable in society, but they should also permit individuals to enjoy special esteem for virtuous action. Democratic patriotism, civil religion, and indeed all forms of constitutional patriotism are, for Rousseau, sources of social recognition that supplement the general will. Like other well-known representatives of the republican tradition – for example, Montesquieu and Tocqueville, to name just two – Rousseau believes that even democratic societies always face the ceaseless task of establishing sufficient scope for the satisfaction of the individual's desire for reputation and esteem.[26] But before discussing this further complication of Rousseau's theory of recognition, I would like to briefly outline the enormous impact his thematization of *amour propre* had on subsequent discussions in modern philosophy, for later thinkers have independently taken up and further developed many of the aspects of Rousseau's key concept.

II

If we look at the very different aspects of Rousseau's *amour propre* so far discussed, it should be no surprise that the most diverse conclusions were drawn from it in the subsequent philosophical discussion. Depending on whether one based one's reading upon the negative pole of pure craving for recognition or the positive pole of egalitarian mutual recognition, the notion could support diagnoses with diametrically opposed interests. The great host of Rousseau's successors certainly subscribed to the political program of the *Social Contract* without seeing, however, that the latter resulted from a complicated reinterpretation of the initially negatively employed notion of *amour propre*. Other successors of the Genevan philosopher tied in exclusively with the *Discourse on Inequality*, whereby their pessimistic diagnoses of the times lacked any prospect of the therapeutic remedies developed only in Rousseau's later writings. But there were also thinkers who were intuitively aware of the whole spectrum of meanings of this notion that was so central to Rousseau's thought, and who could therefore probably envisage the internal connection in his writings – which are so difficult to read consistently. These rather rare exceptions in the history of Rousseau's reception may have included Immanuel Kant. In his work, depending on the particular philosophical interest pursued, the notion of *amour propre* appears either in its positive or in its negative meaning. The differences are already marked in his choice of terms. Whether Kant adequately comprehended the systematic connection of both aspects of the human need for recognition is less important in this context than the astonishing fact that he was familiar enough with both modes of *amour propre* to be able to employ them for his purposes in a targeted way.

Well known, of course, is how much theoretical inspiration for his moral philosophy Kant drew from Rousseau's notion that only those general laws that every individual can recognize as self-imposed may be regarded as valid. Kant even shared with his lifelong role model the ensuing consequence that such a common procedure of self-legislation leads to a relation of egalitarian recognition among those involved, summed up in the term "respect" (*Achtung*).[27] Less well known, however, is that Kant not only takes up Rousseau's positive reinterpretation of *amour propre* but also designates a precisely determined place for the use of the originally purely negative version of *amour propre*. Beyond many references to the anthropological role of comparative self-love, which clearly bear Rousseau's conceptual stamp, an idea of the social craving for recognition is at work particularly in the drafts for his philosophy of history.[28] The inspiration for this notion can have come only from an intensive reading of the *Discourse on Inequality*. The role assigned to this exclusively negative notion of *amour propre* in Kant's philosophy of history stems from the aim Kant has for this philosophy of history within his overall work: it has to protect us from despair in the face of the solely transcendental, and hence empirically ineffective, validity of moral laws by tentatively creating a picture of human history (with the aid of the faculty of judgment). This picture contains sufficient clues of progress toward betterment so as to motivate and spur our moral efforts in spite of everything.[29] To achieve this objective, however, Kant has to endow his hypothetical draft of the course of history with at least as many clues of real moral progress as are necessary to ensure that it does not lose all credibility for his contemporaries. Precisely at this point in his philosophy of history, where the empirical plausibility of a moral progression of history is at stake, Rousseau's negative conception of *amour propre* comes into effect in a downright paradoxical way. Entirely against the intention of the *Discourse on Inequality*, Kant attempts to give the craving for recognition (which he too regards as constitutive for humankind) a twist that will explain why moral betterment will arise from this desire after all.

Due to their "unsocial sociability," human subjects – so the train of thought goes in Kant's *Idea for a Universal History with a Cosmopolitan Purpose* – always strive to distinguish themselves by achievements for which they can find recognition within a social community. At a certain threshold in history, this vanity-motivated struggle for distinction reaches a point where the rivaling subjects retain no other potential for distinction than to attempt special achievements in the domain of moral behavior and the ability to discriminate.[30] Thus, for Kant, what was initially just a craving for public esteem leads eventually, in the longer run of human development, also to progress in moral relationships, so that we can summon the courage for further moral improvements despite our empirical reservations. Quite ingeniously, Kant has thereby unified the two poles of meaning of *amour propre*, whose internal connection in Rousseau's work he may not have even realized. The positive version of the notion, referring to reciprocal respect among equals, has the task of elucidating the normative aspect of morality, while its negative version has the function of yielding a hypothetical explanation of the path toward this moral standpoint. One could also take a step further and posit that Kant resolved the difficulties resulting from the double meaning of *amour propre* ontologically by relegating its divergent meanings to two different spheres: on the one hand to empirical reality, on the other hand to the noumenal. In the causal realm of history, human self-interest-edness appears in the shape of the craving for social recognition; in the rational realm of moral laws, by contrast, it takes the shape of moral respect.

Even Kant himself, however, could not have been entirely convinced by such a simple solution, for in his essays on the philosophy of history he endeavored to build a theoretical bridge between factual history and the ideal – in order to keep the gap between the two realms from widening. It thus seems more likely that Kant did not generally realize that, at least for Rousseau, both the craving for social recognition and the striving for moral respect could originate from one and the same motivational source, namely from *amour propre*. If Kant had known about this internal connection in Rousseau, he would not have bothered considering the causes for the shift in the underlying human need. Rather, he would have picked up two notions from the writings of his great role model Rousseau, each appearing, independently from one another, to possess such explanatory force that he would have attempted to draw upon them at different places in his work.

Even more difficult, however, is an appraisal of the dependence on Rousseau's notion of *amour propre* in the case of thinkers who wanted to transcend Kant's theory immediately after his death, with the aim of preventing from the outset the emergence of any gap between the two realms of empirical causality and noumenal reason. We can note that at least Hegel, though not Fichte, was intuitively aware of the origins of his own theory of recognition in the heritage of Rousseau's thought. Although Hegel, to my knowledge, does not mention the notion of *amour propre* and also takes his entire terminology of recognition more from Fichte than from Rousseau, many remarks in the *Philosophy of Right* allow the conclusion that Hegel conceived of *Sittlichkeit* along the lines of Rousseau's *volonté générale* – namely as the result of reciprocal recognition among individuals limiting themselves in their subjectivity.[31] If one considers that Hegel traces "vanity" and "hypocrisy" to the failure to recognize how the need for recognition binds subjects together, a contextual-notional dependence (if not a direct one) on Rousseau's horizon of thought seems plain. Like the great Genevan, so too the German philosopher perceives the subjective craving for recognition and mutual recognition, that is, vanity and equal respect, as two sides of the same human striving to be acknowledged as a person of social worth in the eyes of other people.[32] But, as in Kant's case, it is extremely difficult to make out the extent to which Hegel really understood the double meaning of *amour propre* in Rousseau's work; although the *Philosophy of Right* makes distinctions similar to Rousseau's between decadent and successful forms of the need for recognition, it is doubtful that Hegel's distinctions originate directly in an adaptation of the notion of *amour propre*. One reason why later generations had such difficulties seeing the whole range of meanings of Rousseau's key notion may be that Rousseau himself never shed a certain reservation concerning the relationship to the self thus designated. To the end of his life he struggled with the question whether, on the whole, it would not be more conducive to a good life to mentally overcome our dependence on others.

III

Looking back at what we have learned about Rousseau's theory of *amour propre* before this interim overview of the history of ideas, the enormous range of this concept is as striking as its inherent character of constant unease: *amour propre*, as opposed to mere *amour de soi*, is a self-interestedness mediated by others. For Rousseau it does not even lose its boundlessness and insatiability when, due to the insight of shared dependence, it has taken the form of a mutual respect among equals. As identified by Frederick Neuhouser, the anthropological realism of Rousseau's thought lies in the fact that, after the loss of contented self-love, the individual retains a constant craving to be recognized as an especially esteemed member of his social community. Thus a socialized individual cannot be satisfied merely by being acknowledged as an equal among equals in a republican community, but must strive beyond that for a social esteem that accrues to skills and attributes that differentiate him from all others.[33] Such an excess in the striving for recognition, which compels Rousseau to seek out additional sources of personal worth and reputation in the *Social Contract*, is itself grounded in the structure of the attitude to the self that is characteristic of *amour propre*. Taking up this relation, we have lost all standards of self-assessment that might have arisen from our natural needs, so to speak; hence we are now able to assess our merit only in the reflection offered by those who, taken together, form "public opinion" or the "generalized other." The uncertainty whether our accomplishments are actually honored appropriately by such public judgments remains even if, as co-authors of the *volonté générale*, we are involved in achieving universally binding standards of value. To preclude any possible misinterpretations of our personality, even under the condition of equal respect, we thus must still strive for a recognition that makes us stand out from all others. Unlike Adam Smith, who could imagine the external observer as so completely generalizable as to have lost any actual features of arbitrariness and even as identifiable with reason as such,[34] Rousseau cannot believe in the possibility of such a complete rationalizability of the general judge.[35] For him, the extrinsic judgment that the individual is exposed to in the relationship of *amour propre* to the self always contains the danger of remaining unrecognized to the extent that a pre-emptive pursuit of special esteem is not only widespread, but also culturally justified.

On the other hand, this risk of failure to be recognized, by which Rousseau means not simply a lack of respect for individual merits but the absence of their cognitive perception, is also a constant source of anxiety for Rousseau. He sees the tendency of the social environment to misjudge the true nature of the individual and fail to recognize his special talents as the real danger posed by the moment of civilizing transition from *amour de soi* to *amour propre*.[36]

This diagnosis, which may be easily overlooked but consequently emerges as the core of Rousseau's theory of recognition, imperceptibly shifts the reference points of social dependence upon the other from the moral to the epistemic. The internalized authority of public opinion, on which the individual's self-assessment depends, no longer presents itself as a moral but as a theoretical judge, who is to assess the qualities a subject actually possesses. With this transition, of course, there is also a change in how *amour propre* prompts a person to action. Just as a person should be able to demonstrate his social value and individual abilities as long as the generalized other is a moral instance, he must also be able to prove the merits and talents he actually has if he interiorizes an epistemic judge.

A look at Rousseau's writings makes it seem rather improbable that he gave a sufficient account of his own oscillation between a moral and an epistemic understanding of *amour propre*. Wherever he addresses the pathological desire for recognition and recommends as therapy the republican spirit of egalitarian respect, the normative notion of the generalized other predominates. Yet as soon as he begins speaking about the more fundamental harm of being dependent on the other, the epistemic model often presses imperceptibly into the foreground. In this shape of an internalized instance – not of moral evaluation, but rather of theoretical assessment – Rousseau's *amour propre* has had an enormous effect on the development of French philosophy. Up to Sartre and Lacan, we find remnants of the idea that dependence on social recognition is inevitably linked to the cognitive failure to recognize the core of one's subjectivity.[37] For Rousseau, however, the epistemic notion of an "inner judge" repeatedly provides the occasion to approach theoretically the radical alternative of overcoming as a whole the relationship of *amour propre* to the self. Rousseau's autobiographical writings, in particular, constantly revolve around the possibility of regaining an individual attitude in which the social recognition of one's own merits and capabilities has lost all existential significance. Such considerations exhibit a Stoic motif in Rousseau's thought and unmistakably contradict the view presented so far – that as socialized beings we inevitably need the recognition of our social value.

If we examine the works in which Rousseau discusses his own relationship to himself – less perhaps the *Confessions* than *Rousseau, Judge of Jean-Jacques*, whose title is already quite revealing, and the *Reveries of a Solitary Walker* – what is immediately apparent is how much they renounce any dependence on the judgment of others.

Here, the path to the good and proper life is characterized as a constant search for inner harmony that is accomplished only by ignoring the judgmental behavior of our social environment.[38] That the author Rousseau regards only himself as qualified to judge his alter-ego already shows that he sees a desirable goal in finding a position of independence from others' attributions and from judgments which one cannot affect. If I want to be at peace with myself, my self-esteem and my self-image should be based solely on characterizations of my person, whose author I can consider only myself. A threat to such an ideal of autonomous judging seems to lie not primarily in dependence on the moral judgment of public opinion, but in its judgments about our qualities and activities – for these lead us to deceive ourselves about our true nature and thus to fail to recognize the valuable talents we actually have. It is thus not surprising that, in the famous fifth walk of his *Reveries*, Rousseau describes as the epitome of existential happiness a state in which the author, through the mere passive observation of natural processes, learns about the qualities he truly possesses and about the worries that really drive him. Because nature cannot speak and makes no judgment of us, in it every impulse of *amour propre* is deprived of its nourishing substance: we become unconcerned with others, and thus can recognize ourselves.[39]

As his late writings make clear, Rousseau wavered all his life between a resolute endorsement and a radical rejection of existential dependence on others. On the one hand, his work enables a fundamental insight to prevail: the idea that human beings owe their self-esteem and their capacity for action to intersubjective recognition. But on the other hand, he also recognizes the hazards associated with being subjected to the judgments of one's social environment. Even if his own indecision may ultimately be rooted in the fact that he does not distinguish clearly enough between a moral and an epistemic understanding of recognition, he nonetheless initiated a philosophical debate that has not reached its conclusion to this day. There are always spirited partisans at hand of both of the positions he promulgated: the transformation of *amour propre* into symmetrical recognition and the rejection of any dependence on the "generalized other." The legacy that Rousseau left to the theory of recognition remains highly double-edged; as with a Trojan horse, those who try to take it up always invite the rival into their own home.

Translated by Mitch Cohen and revised by Avi Lifschitz

2

On the Poverty of Our Freedom
Relevance and limits of the Hegelian ethical system[1]

There is no normative guiding belief more implicit or attractive
today than the idea of individual freedom. If one follows the
journalistic coverage of world events even only periodically, like
Hegel did, one immediately sees just how important this value is
for the motivation or justification of social action: political party
manifestos are drawn up, structural changes to the labor market
are legitimized, legal reforms are publicly defended, and even vital
decisions in personal relationships are justified – all in the name of
individual freedom. Of course, such claims to freedom are almost
always accompanied by other values that are construed either as
a conducive condition for these claims or, more seldom, as that
"for-the-sake-of-which" (Worumwillen)[2] they are made: freedom,
in its accepted form, is only feasible among equals and presupposes a universal security, which is why a provision of equality
or political stability represents a necessary and enabling prerequisite; love, too, demands uncoerced and voluntary attention,
which is why individual freedom is cherished for the sake of love
and thus functions as its prerequisite. However, in such lines of
argumentation, freedom is always the key insofar as, without it,
the complementary values either completely lose their attractive
relevance or their attractiveness becomes normatively unintelligible. If we consider just how central a value individual freedom
is for our cultural and social self-conception, it can only amaze
us how obscure its conceptual meaning remains in contemporary
social usage. We speak openly of "freedom" as if it existed and
were implemented in only one way, although we certainly know,
and can even see formally, that there are vast differences between

the freedom of political representation, the freedom of entering into contractual agreements, and the freedom, as it were, of the spontaneous union of people in love. So far, all philosophical efforts to provide conceptual redress, namely by distinguishing between different forms of freedom, have failed in achieving their self-imposed objective. This applies most of all to Isaiah Berlin's famous distinction between negative and positive freedom (Berlin, however, speaks of two types of "liberty"),[3] which, while causing a storm in the world of philosophy, ultimately failed to deliver the necessary distinctions for our self-conception because, phenomenologically, its positive side remained too vague and lacked clarity.[4] In the following chapter, I will try to show that Hegel's concept of ethical life (*Sittlichkeit*) poses to this day a better and more persuasive alternative to such attempts. It offers a philosophical source that continues to provide the means with which we can articulate the conceptual distinction between differing forms of freedom, both those we practice and those we value. One of the main tasks of Hegel's conception of modern ethical life – in addition to many others to be discussed below – is that of educating the members of modern society about these necessary distinctions in their usage of "freedom." What is more, Hegel's theory of free will – developed in his *Outlines of the Philosophy of Right*[5] – can even be read as a kind of instruction manual on how to distinguish between the different forms of individual freedom, so as to give each its appropriate place in the institutional fabric of a society differentiated through the division of labor. In a first step, I will attempt to demonstrate the extent to which Hegel's concept of ethical life aims to distinguish between the different forms of freedom; even this is no simple task, however, considering that Hegel's idea of ethical life seeks first and foremost to define a sphere of institutional structures that is immune to the perpetual interrogation and reflection that emanate from modern, "free" subjectivity, such that the connection with human freedom at this initial stage is not yet present. In a second step, I will then attempt to show how Hegel proceeds from his theory of the will to those determinations (*Bestimmungen*) that allow him to distinguish between different forms of individual freedom within modern ethical life. Here we must establish whether we are justified in assuming that Hegel's concept can indeed classify on a conceptual level our different understandings of freedom and assign to each its own institutional position. Admittedly, Hegel's concept of ethical life falls short in some aspects, most of which are due to his failure to take his own intentions seriously enough throughout his articulation and development of the concept. I wish to turn to these limitations in a third and final step to raise once again the question of Hegel's contemporary relevance.

Hegel's Three Concepts of Freedom

As is characteristic of Hegel's *Realphilosophie*, i.e., the parts of his philosophical system tailored to the explanation of "reality" in his philosophy of right and the state (*Rechts- und Staatslehre*), i.e., his theory of "objective Spirit," concepts are introduced in a dialectic (*Doppelung*) of logical determinations and phenomenological characterizations, something which remains to the present day one of the most attractive attributes of his entire undertaking. As Dieter Henrich (2003: 65) has shown, one of Hegel's most outstanding talents is his ability – in the course of his efforts to achieve a formal-ontological blueprint (*Erschließung*) of reality – to define the respective equivalences in our natural and social environment with such concision and exactness that they are rendered intelligible even for readers unfamiliar with his science of logic (*Logik*).[6] This ability to think in a highly abstract yet still concretely diagnostic manner made Hegel a kind of sociologist *avant la lettre*; before the discipline even existed, he had already established himself as a modern social theorist – whose insights are perhaps still unmatched today.

In our attempt to comprehend the purpose and meaning of Hegel's conception of ethical life, we can avail ourselves of the dialectical meaning of all concepts used in his *Realphilosophie*. On the logical side, as is well known, Hegel's philosophy of right and the state attempts to define the process of realization – or self-realization – of the determinations of reason on the level at which these concepts manifest themselves in the objectivity of social reality. On the phenomenological or empirical side, however, Hegel strives to make us aware of those phenomena in our social existence that allow us to understand that we, as sons and daughters of modernity, are actively involved in the generation of the logical determinations of reason. If one were to draw up a contemporary program of social theory in order to illustrate this striving, one could perhaps claim that Hegel focuses exclusively on those "collective" assignments of status and function that harmonize with the organic attributes of overarching reason.[7] However, as we know, Hegel's dialectical analysis of modern society presupposes a protracted process of historical development that leads, for the first time around the turn of the nineteenth century, to institutional premises in which the determinations of reason are reflected. In order to understand the intention of Hegel's philosophy of right and the state one must therefore be constantly aware that it first attempts its explanation at a point in history when social reality – via previous processes of maturation – has already become so saturated with reason that social processes and institutions can be understood as embodiments of the logical determinations of Spirit.

This central premise of Hegel's entire *Philosophy of Right* arises from his assumption – which he regards as a virtually self-evident fact – that only upon the breakthrough of modernity are social institutions at last able to actively facilitate the realization of freedom. From now on, not only is the individual, with his/her distinct and independent ethos and beliefs, to understand himself/ herself as "free," but the institutions necessary for the function of society are also to be understood in this way – so that they can enable the freedom of outward social action. It is above all in his philosophy of history that Hegel makes clear why this exit of freedom out of mere inwardness and into the objective world of social institutions implies reaching a stage in which the logical determinations of Spirit first find their full application. He demonstrates there the extent to which each new stage in the process of historical development brings with it an advancement of social reality, which can be understood according to the model of the self-realizing, self-referential subjectivity of Spirit, because with each historical progression falls off a portion of impenetrable, still-spiritless objectivity, which prevented it from being understood with the help of logical determinations. It is only after freedom has become the organizing principle of all central institutions, in the "new era" of modernity, that such a complete rendering of social reality using the concepts of logic becomes possible, for only then are human beings in their social objectivation able to relate to themselves in the way necessitated by organic, contemplated Spirit in its self-referentiality. Using these historico-philosophical premises, Hegel is thus able to complete his *Philosophy of Right* – which, according to his systematic idea, represents a theory of the institutional realization of freedom in modernity – in the form of a formal-ontological explanation of social reality: everything that Hegel takes into consideration with regard to modern societies, in order to define the "reality" of freedom, must follow the concepts of a logic that ultimately attempts to describe Spirit in the process of its undiminished self-realization.

As point of origin of Hegel's *Philosophy of Right*, these presuppositions immediately give rise to the need for an explication of "freedom" – in its modern understanding – that allows one to identify within it the characteristics of the incrementally self-referential Spirit. If the freedom realized in modern societies were not comprehended according to such a model, the theory of these modern societies could not be developed throughout according to logical determinations. Hegel addresses the ensuing problem in his "Introduction" (to the *Philosophy of Right*), which constitutes a fascinating attempt at repudiating the dominant understanding of the concept of "freedom" and simultaneously drastically expanding the scope of any "philosophy of right." I wish to address here only a very rudimentary form of this extremely complex line of thought, which goes through several stages of logical determination, because I am solely interested in illustrating the application of Hegel's idea of ethical life. This concept emanates from a quite primitive, yet – for modern society – highly influential conception of freedom according to which the individual subject is "free" only insofar as it possesses an outer sphere of autonomy in which no other subject is allowed to intervene. Whether the specific desires and intentions that are realized in that sphere are "free" or not, i.e., whether they are motivated by reasons the subject deems "right" and not by mere natural causality, is irrelevant for such a concept insofar as its essence is the unhindered realization of any arbitrary purpose. This formulation alone suggests that Hegel is toying here with what Isaiah Berlin will later call "negative liberty."[8] Berlin's conception implies that individual freedom is granted to each subject insofar as he or she possesses the capacity to realize his or her own desires in an unobstructed fashion. It is not difficult to see why Hegel is forced to dismiss this conception of "freedom" as deficient; it comes nowhere near his own benchmark concept of "Spirit" because we aren't certain whether the desires realized here concern the "Spirit" in any way at all, i.e., whether or not they are simply contingent on mere causal relations (*kausal Bewirktes*). For Hegel it is utterly impossible to speak of "freedom" in a philosophically ambitious, rational sense amid the obscurity of whether the desires in question can even be designated as "free." Nonetheless, as we will see later on, Hegel will take up this primitive concept in his theory of social modernity and will assign to it a systematic position within the subsystem of "Abstract Right," because he is convinced that without it we cannot fully understand the freedom of our institutional practices.

The second concept of freedom, which Hegel also takes up in his "Introduction" due to its powerful relevance to our modern self-conception, is distinguished from the first "negative" form in that the emphasis is now shifted to the "freedom" of the desires that are to be realized in the external world. According to this second model, which Isaiah Berlin, presumably, would have added to his "positive" concepts of "liberty," we are only able to call human actions "free" insofar as they are based on desires and intentions determined outside of natural causality, i.e., self-imposed motives that are viewed subjectively as "right." It is self-evident to Hegel that this concept represents an important step beyond the merely outward concept of negative freedom; for the idea that freedom can only exist where the condition of rational self-determination is met already converges with the horizon of Hegel's Spirit, which is also to be conceived according to the model of a reflexive relation-to-self (*Auf-Sich-Beziehen*). However, this comparison with the structural characteristics of Spirit shows why Hegel must also dismiss as still deficient this second, and to a certain extent Kantian, concept of positive or reflexive freedom. It is lacking – to use Hegel's spiritual-philosophical (*geistphilosophisch*) termi-nology – that moment of objectivity required by Spirit in order to grasp the "other" of itself (*Andere seiner Selbst*), i.e., non-Spirit or object (*Nicht-Geist oder Objekt*), as a product of its own reflexive self-relation. If we translate the reservation hinted at here into the concrete and phenomenological language that Hegel consist-ently uses in order to make us aware of the equivalences between his logical determinations and our familiar social reality, then his criticism of the idea of freedom as "rational self-determination" reads as follows: individual freedom, as defined here, implies nothing more than the possession of rational intentions and desires, i.e., those based on reasons deemed subjectively "right"; however, freedom actually depends much more on whether or not we can also comprehend reality as "objectivation," as the embodiment of subjective self-determination.

In his "Introduction," Hegel is thus faced with the difficult task of formulating a third conception of freedom that bears resemblance to the structure of Spirit insofar as, within this conception, the objectivity of social reality can be comprehended in one way or another as the product of rationally self-reflexive subjects. Of course, it should come as no surprise that Hegel also expects his concept of ethical life to meet this demand. It is perhaps not a bad idea to turn first to Hegel's own formulations – concrete and based on perception (*anschauungsnah*) as always – in order to exhibit the translatability of his logical determinations into the commonplace phenomena that constitute everyday life. For instance, in connection with an explanation of freedom according to the model of a consciously autonomous, objectified subjectivity, he immediately turns to the concrete examples of "friendship" and "love": "Here we are not," Hegel writes, "inherently one-sided; we restrict ourselves gladly to relating ourselves to another, but in this restriction know ourselves as ourselves. In this determinacy a human being should not feel determined; on the contrary, by treating the other as other, it is there that he first arrives at the feeling of his own selfhood. Thus freedom lies neither in indeterminacy nor in determinacy; it is both of these at once.[9]

In the "self-restriction" mentioned here by Hegel, we can see first on the level of human sentience a pre-form of the rational self-determination that serves as criterion for all individual freedom according to our second, "positive" or Kantian model. If I choose to become friends with another person or to begin an intimate relationship, this is not the result of mere disposition or of my being led blindly by impulse; on the contrary, I am following here certain deliberations and reasons that, insofar as they convince me of the "rightness" of my action, can be understood as a source of rational self-determination and of the restriction of all my impulses to the person whose contact I seek. This notion of self-restriction resulting from autonomy, however, is misleading and one-sided – or so would Hegel perhaps argue – for in friendship or in love it is only through the other person that the realization of my own self-determination is enabled; instead of "self-restriction" (*Selbstbeschränkung*), we should perhaps speak of a "self-unchaining" (*Selbstentschränkung*). In such cases where the other person desires from me what I desire from him/her, this person, my opposite, must be understood as that which alone enables me to consummate my freedom.

If we now translate these concrete references back into the formal language of Hegel's conception of Spirit, we have the key element of his third, so-called "objective" definition of freedom. In the case of friendship or love, the subject relates to himself or to herself in such a way that he or she beholds, in the objectivity of the other, an objectivation of his or her own desires, insofar as he or she perceives in the other a reflection of this objectivation and thus sees there, in the "other," the other of himself or herself (*Andere seiner Selbst*). If we abstract further from the specific examples of "friendship" or "love," we can conclude that objective freedom is present wherever socially established institutions allow subjects to grasp the actions of their partners as objective embodiments of their own desires acquired in reflexive self-relation. Here, and only here, does the subjectivity of acting individuals take a shape resembling that of overarching Spirit, in that it allows them to perceive in the objectivation of institutionalized practices the product of their own reflexive self-determination. Hegel incorporates all the institutions that provide for the permanent enabling of such an experience into the section of social reality which he calls "ethical life." He views this concept as superior to other institutional entities, not simply because ethical life gives individuals a sense of relief and liberates them from the pressure of reflection, but also because it imparts a form of freedom that towers above the other forms – praised by modernity – for their degree of reality and realizable non-coercion (*Wirklichkeitssättigung*). One instance of this superiority – at this point, it almost seems superfluous to make separate note of this – can be seen in Hegel's demonstration that only "ethical life" can be fully reflected in the logical concepts of "Spirit," while the forms of agency which are connected with the other two conceptions of freedom still contain the remains of obscure, completely foreign objectivity, which make it impossible to interpret them entirely according to the model of Spirit. Such obstacles are surmounted in Hegel's conception of objective, ethically mediated freedom, because here the subjects perceive the object as the "other" of their self, i.e., as a product of their own self-relation.

From this intermediate conclusion, Hegel only requires one last small step to define the entire program of his *Philosophy of Right* and the particular conception of "right" it contains. It is this precise point that will clarify for us what Hegel actually intends to achieve with the distinction – merely outlined so far – between the different conceptions of freedom. Hegel proceeds in strictly immanent fashion by first demonstrating how, in the prevailing philosophy of his time, arguments for the rights to which citizens should be entitled invariably presuppose a concept of individual freedom on which they are based. Pursuing this line of argumentation, depending on whether the "negative" or "reflexive" conception of free will is presupposed, the extent and forms of subjective rights to be guaranteed by the state vary correspondingly. The ingenious move made by Hegel is that such a derivation of "right" forces us to relinquish the idea that merely subjective rights are implemented here, insofar as we now take the objective conception of freedom as our basis and not one of the deficient conceptions as before. As soon as we comprehend that the actual form of subjective freedom is defined neither as a space of mere individual caprice nor as a form of Kantian reflexive self-determination, but rather as active involvement in ethical institutions, the entire idea of "right" must be qualitatively re-expanded, because these institutions themselves now acquire a normatively grounded right to exist. We might venture to say that Hegel dispossesses conventional philosophy of its own concept of "right" by demonstrating that this concept must also contain social elements if it is to determine a more plausible basis for subjective individual freedom. In Hegel's words, the hitherto prevailing "definition of right ... involves that way of looking at the matter, especially popular since Rousseau, according to which what is fundamental, substantial, and primary is supposed to be the will of an individual in his own arbitrary self-will, not the rational will in and for itself, and [S]pirit as a particular individual, not [S]pirit as it is in its truth";[10] however, if individual free will is to be understood according to the model of Spirit, i.e., as a self-recurring will in the objectivity of certain practices in its self-relation, then the definition of "right" must also be amended correspondingly, because it must now encompass the institutionalized practices that provide for such self-relation.

Hegel's *Philosophy of Right* demonstrates the implementation of the program outlined here; it operates with a socio-ontologically expanded concept of "right" in order to show as legitimately given – as justified spheres of action, dictated by the demands of individual freedom – all institutional practices which help modern subjects attain the experience of objectively mediated self-relation. Hegel's next move is an attempt to split the idea of objective freedom into different forms and to assign each to its own particular position in the institutional fabric of society. I will try to show this in the following section, which will also serve as an explication of the contemporary relevance of Hegel's ethical system – i.e., its capacity to provide us with a normative vocabulary with which we can separate and evaluate the different forms of our practiced freedom.

The Fabric of Freedom in Our Modern World

Hegel intends with his concept of ethical life, as we have seen so far, to single out in the standard social apparatus those institutions that enable mutually communicative subjects to experience not only negative or reflexive freedom, but also freedom in the objective sense discussed above. "Objective" implies that form of individual freedom which allows each subject to recognize himself or herself in social institutions insofar as he or she can perceive in the habitual desires of fellow citizens a precondition – or perhaps even a product – of his or her own rationally attained desire. However, before Hegel can decorate such social institutions with the title "ethical" he must first solve a rather difficult problem, which arises from the ambition of his *Philosophy of Right* to deliver a universally valid analysis of the objective, institutional preconditions for the freedom of the individual. He therefore cannot allow himself to be content with a mere identification of rationally attained desires, but must provide the much more complicated proof that (1) all modern subjects, as stipulated by their rational self-awareness, share certain desires with one another that (2) can only be realized without coercion insofar as these subjects are actively involved in already historically established social institutions. It is (unfortunately) not the case, however, that Hegel goes to any great length to consecutively elucidate these two arguments. As always, the crux of his justification also here appears as a philosophical derivative within which we are unable to separate the arguments we are to follow from the logical determinations it expresses. If we nonetheless attempt to undertake such a separation *ex post*, we can perhaps discern the following with regard to the exoteric, concretely phenomenological side of Hegel's argumentation. In contrast to Kant, Hegel is convinced that the individual – as a product of his or her rational self-determination – orients him/herself around the normative rules introduced in the process of socialization as the code of behavior of surrounding institutions. It would therefore be erroneous for Hegel to presuppose an arbitrary pluralism of individual desires whose moral rightness the individual can only evaluate afterwards; as rationally self-determining beings, we reach rather a sense of universal agreement in that we adhere in our actions to the maxims of those mutual practices that provided the moral fabric within which we grew. This said, Hegel allows us to assume that the subjects of his time – as stipulated by their rational self-awareness – only share as many desires as there are institutions that serve as educational establishments for their individual Spirit, once they have gone through them, and as places of rationally consensual practices. In short, the crux of Hegel's ethical task is thus to identify the universal, motivation-inspiring institutions of his time that enable members of society to recognize in the actions of their fellow citizens the objectivation of their own freedom.

Given Hegel's outstanding sociological capacities, he is able to solve this task in a way that remains even today worthy of theoretical usage – which, though it is not applicable in all of its facets, certainly is applicable with regard to its structure. If one considers other social theories with similar ambitions that emerged much later, for instance those of Durkheim or Talcott Parsons, one immediately perceives the superiority of Hegel's distinction between forms of freedom as found in his *Philosophy of Right*. After he gave up the idea – pursued enthusiastically in his youth – according to which the integration of complex societies can take place through the mere extension of interpersonal relations (e.g., intimate relationships and friendship), Hegel came to the much more realistic understanding that the reproduction of modern societies depends essentially on the combination of three universal, motivation-inspiring institutions: In addition to the private relationships based on love and friendship – Hegel managed here to preserve elements of his original conception – he included the capitalist market economy and the political organs that make up a constitutional monarchy. However, despite his philosophical maturity, Hegel had not yet cast aside his original aspirations, and he again attempted to comprehend these three complex institutions according to that same model which he had previously used to interpret the reciprocal nature of intimate love. This, as we already saw in the example of "love and friendship" in Hegel's "Introduction," was tantamount to the task of identifying in these other institutions, the market economy, and the state, the same mechanism of reciprocal objectivation between self-determined actions that was introduced as the substance of "objective freedom." Hegel thus arrives at the conviction – central for his entire *Philosophy of Right* – that the institutions of romantic love, market economy, and constitutional monarchy represent spheres of modern ethical life. Raised within the moral fabric of these three institutional structures, modern subjects are to develop – through the cultivation of their capacity for self-determination

– rational desires and intentions, the realization of which they can understand as the uncoerced objectivation of their individual freedom.

However, it is of course not enough for Hegel to simply list these three forms of objective freedom next to each other; indeed, in order to introduce and categorically distinguish them from one another, he must first rank them normatively so that he can compare them and assess each with regard to its normative value. In the course of this assessment, Hegel once again makes use of his organic concept of Spirit, which he applies to the three institutional manifestations of freedom as he did before in his assessment of the prevailing conceptions of individual freedom. Accordingly, he must prove that the differing forms of objective freedom are all the more consummate, and thus valuable, the less they are determined by remnants of natural causality, so that when at their peak they can then be completely understood according to the model of Spirit that recognizes itself reflexively and free of coercion in its objectivations. Here, too, Hegel astounds with his masterful ability to use purely logical determinations to provide us with a technically lucid and empirically intelligible blueprint of social reality. Thus, the practices of reciprocal care and affection that constitute love, friendship, and family represent a subordinate level of objective freedom because, in them, only our socially interpreted nature is satisfied intersubjectively; the institutionalized practices (e.g., the capital-mediated exchange of goods and services) that constitute market economy possess by comparison a higher degree of objective freedom, because reflexive considerations of utility are already contained in the defined interests that form their basis; and the practices prescribed in the structure of constitutional monarchy (e.g., safeguarding of the community and the mutual protection of rights) represent the highest level of objective freedom because the desires and intentions it contains – on their way to objectivation – have completely detached themselves from all natural roots and are the expression of rationally determined characteristics of the pure Spirit. I do not contend here that the characterizations of these individual "levels" even back then – in Hegel's time – were without their faults: his depiction of romantic love and of familial relations based on it, for instance, is starkly influenced – as is generally known – by the patriarchal prejudices of his time; furthermore, in his presentation of the organs of the state he seems no longer aware that his original intention pertained to symmetrical relations between citizens who can recognize reciprocally, in the principled actions of others, an objectivation of their own striving. These issues aside, however, the fundamental idea of this three-part conception of ethical life was back then, and remains today, an enormous challenge for the modern understanding of freedom. It forces upon us the serious question of whether it would be better for our overall understanding of freedom to construe social institutions and practices as that which neither limits nor enables merely subjective freedom, but rather as the embodiment of a communicative freedom. Hegel took great care to include all means necessary for such an expansion of our understanding of freedom in the structure and central concepts of his ethical system: he singled out and distinguished between needs, interests, and individual self-worth as the three types of individual intentions that can only be realized through institutional reciprocity and can thus confer a consciousness of increased freedom. He strove to demonstrate that such an intersubjective reciprocity was in principle only possible among equals; and ultimately he even outlined the institutional complexes within which these forms of ethical, social, or communicative freedom could manifest themselves. At no point in his *Philosophy of Right*, however, can we read whether – or if at all – the institutions under consideration could in future develop in a way that would accord more readily with Hegel's underlying ambition of "reciprocity among equals." Rather, his benevolent analysis of the institutions of his time preserved instead the sacrosanctity of the dominant familial, market, and state relations, insofar as it failed to consider their intrinsic dynamism, their immanent, conflict-driven development, as even a possibility. It is this conservatism of Hegel's social analysis to which I would like to turn briefly in my conclusion, for it reflects a severe structural problem in his ethical system.

Conclusion: A New Idea of Justice

As suggested above, in no way did Hegel want to exclude the "deficient" forms of individual freedom from his ethical system; on the contrary, he was too much of a staunch liberal not to see the extent to which purely private prospects of self-delineation and of moral self-reassurance were constitutive of modern societies. After demonstrating the deficiencies of the merely negative conception of freedom and of the idea of individual self-determination in the introduction to his *Philosophy of Right*, these two concepts re-emerge – albeit under different names – in the work's main section as part of Hegel's attempt to identify two long-established institutional structures in social reality. Under the title of "Abstract Right" he recapitulates the liberal rights of freedom rudimentarily anchored in the society of his day that were to guarantee all mature individuals the inviolable right to life, ownership, and contractual freedom; under the title of "Morality" he conceives the institutionally warranted prospect of being able to assert one's own subjective idea of "right" based on moral grounds. Although Hegel does present these two institutions as precursors to the objective, ethical forms of freedom, we must not conclude from this that he comprehends them as mere prior qualifications for participation in social institutions such as the family, market, and state – as if individuals were to quasi-forfeit their subjective rights and moral autonomy as soon as, upon self-contemplation and in light of their personal beliefs, they decided to involve themselves in those institutions of intersubjective reciprocity. On the contrary, Hegel is much more convinced that the right to subjective freedom and the prospect of moral representation electively form the basis of all interactions within the three ethical spheres considered above, insofar as they provide subjects with the possibility of withdrawing themselves if need be from obligations to which they have already committed themselves or even of raising moral objection to them. Thus, in the words of the economic sociologist Albert Hirschman, it remains constitutive for the entire sphere of ethical life that all members of society have permanent access to the options of "exit" and "voice," i.e., voluntary withdrawal or morally justified protest.[11]

This inclusion of "subjective" freedom in institutionalized ethical life of course also sets off an element of dynamism, openness, and transgressivity into Hegel's theory that he is no longer able to control; for nowhere in his presentation does he exclude the possibility that the individual right to objection could add up to a collective protest aimed at challenging the constitution of the respective social institutions themselves. Although Hegel does briefly mention, above all in his analysis of capitalist market economy, the possibility of such "collective outcry" (*kollektive Empörung*), he does not at all take into account the dynamism thereby brought about in his concept of ethical life. This would imply, namely, that Hegel would have to leave his philosophical system open to conflictual, revolutionary changes that could in future arise from frictions that he himself allowed into his system of institutional freedoms. As we know, Hegel did not take that step; he did not see his *Philosophy of Right* as a kind of stepping stone to modern society's self-understanding of its own possibilities of freedom. Rather, he took it as a book, complete in itself, that tells of how, from the perspective of Spirit – self-comprehending in its institutional embodiments – objective freedom could manifest itself once and for all in the institutions of the family, market economy, and the state. From our contemporary perspective, almost two hundred years after the inception of Hegel's ethical system, we of course know better: the powers of individualization and of autonomy – the potential of negative and reflexive freedom – have unharnessed a dynamic that infiltrated his own system and that fundamentally altered each of the institutions from the normative condition in which they were originally presented. Thus Hegel's *Philosophy of Right* can no longer serve as a theoretical model for establishing social freedom in any concrete way, but it can provide an outline or structural plan for such an undertaking. It can teach us with lasting effect how impoverished our understanding of freedom really is if we attempt to grasp its essence merely with the concepts of subjective rights, moral autonomy, or a combination of both; with Hegel we have to argue that, on the contrary, individual freedom must first and foremost be understood in the social context as a personal uncoerced expansion of the self that results when the universally applicable desires of each subject are endorsed by the likewise universal desires of others.

If we understand this form of "objective" – or what we perhaps now may call social freedom – as the core of all of our conceptions of freedom, as opposed to the merely derivative conceptions considered before, then we must also – like Hegel did – draw the accompanying consequence of revising our conception of justice: that which is referred to as "just" in highly developed societies can no longer be assessed with exclusive regard to whether, and to what extent, all members of society possess negative and reflexive freedom, but rather to whether these subjects are also granted the equal chance to participate in the institutional spheres of reciprocity, i.e., in familial and personal relations, in the labor market, and in the democratic forming of the political will. Thus the core of Hegel's idea of social justice implies that normatively substantial – i.e., "ethical" – institutions require the support and protection of legal, government, and civil structures in order to realize the claim to social freedom that forms their basis. Only in the labor-divided interplay of law, politics, and public solidarity can we ultimately sustain the institutional structures to which we owe the various facets of our interlocking forms of autonomy and thus our entire culture of freedom.

Translated by Gabriel Borrud

3

The Normativity of Ethical Life

Recent years have seen a widespread tendency to pay renewed attention to Hegel's critique of the moral standpoint. In contemporary practical philosophy it is no longer an uncontested truth that norms or laws can be called "moral" only when they can be shown through an impartial testing procedure – conducted alone or in common – to be universally obligatory or binding. There are various different reasons for the departure from this model of moral normativity, ranging from a focus on the question of moral motivation to a critique of the merely prescriptive character of the obligations derived in this way. What has emerged as the decisive objection is the paradox faced by Kant and his successors that moral self-determination or self-binding presupposes a kind of freedom that can in turn be explained only by recourse to already existing moral norms.[1] Suppose, the argument goes, that we wish to reserve the predicate "moral" for those norms that we can conceive of as "freely" generated through an act of autonomous self-subjection or through an uncoerced consensus. In order to do so, we will sooner or later, but inevitably, have to bring moral norms into play so that we may first establish the agential freedom or the communicative accord that we have been presupposing. This commitment to prior norms is in effect conceded by Kant under the guise of the "fact of reason," whereas discourse ethics tends to obscure it through its seemingly innocuous reference to the need for "complementary forms of life."[2] Both of these forms taken by the commitment point to the same predicament: the general validity of certain moral norms must already be presupposed in order for the procedure of individual or communicative self-determination to be intelligible in the first place. This critique of the groundlessness of a purely constructivist moral theory has led to a resurgence of approaches that set out from an antecedently given horizon of moral norms and rules. The pendulum of historical retrieval whose operation seems to pervade all philosophical research has swung back to theories of morality that seek reconstructively to extract principles and obligations from norms already in existence.

This new orientation brings with it a danger complementary to that of Kantianism, which some have been quick to label "neo-Aristotelianism." To derive all moral norms from a historical context consisting of already accepted practical rules and forms of life, since it is they to which we owe our deliberative freedom, seems inevitably to amount to legitimizing a given moral order. The contrast between social acceptance and moral validity, which is a familiar feature of our everyday life, threatens to completely disappear, since we now lack independent criteria for distinguishing between norms that are merely socially practiced and ones that are morally justified. It is not hard to predict that until this charge of conventionalism has been answered, the voices of Kant and his disciples will continue to be a powerful influence in moral philosophy. Despite all the worries about abstract formalism, historically conscious philosophers will continue to return to approaches that set out from the idea that moral norms must be thought of as the results of some test of impartiality, be it individual or communicative, real or merely hypothetical. To find a way of escaping from this unresolved tension, I will attempt to exonerate the contextualist Hegelian account of morality from the charge of mere conventionalism. I will try to show that his concept of ethical life furnishes the author of the *Philosophy of Right* with a set of historically immanent criteria that allow him to distinguish, within the horizon of a given form of life, between valid norms and merely accepted ones. It will be important to present Hegel's method in a way that avoids, as far as possible, holding it hostage to his philosophy of spirit, which can hardly serve as an acceptable premise today. Hegel's doctrine of ethical life will be a viable option for moral philosophy only if it can be translated into an idiom that does not rely on the ontological presupposition of a universally self-realizing spirit. In a first step, I will in this way – post-metaphysically, so to speak – identify the general criteria that Hegel sets out as immanent givens of any ethical form of life (I). In a second step, I am going to examine whether this provides us with clues for discerning a certain directionality of moral development (II).

I

The demands that Hegel places on what he refers to by the umbrella term "ethical life" are the positive results of the various objections he levels against Kant's moral philosophy. The standpoint of morality, after all, is not simply to be abandoned. Instead, it should be rid of its abstractness in such a way as to render intelligible why many past and present kinds of social practice already contain, to varying degrees, some form of the principle of universalization that Kant saw fit to juxtapose to reality as we encounter it. Existing or past social practices therefore qualify as "ethical" by Hegel's lights only if they enjoin us in an inconspicuous way – in the manner of customs rather than through external imperatives – to respect other persons and accordingly to "infringe upon" our self-love.[3] Thus a neo-Aristotelian view on which each social form of life is normatively endorsed simply for its motivational and ethical power was alien to Hegel from the outset. Throughout his work he was far too entangled in the Kantian conception of moral autonomy, and far too invested in sublating it into the "objective spirit" of institutional reality, to so much as consider reasoning from the mere social acceptance of arbitrary systems of norms to their normative validity. The abstractness, formality, and motivational ineffectiveness for which he reproaches Kant's idea of morality must have been correctively absorbed by his own concept of "ethical life" in a way that of itself yields the criteria by which merely given normative practices can be distinguished from justified ones.

A first requirement that practices must meet if they are to qualify as ethical, and thus to achieve a social sublation or embedding of morality, results from the paradox of moral freedom that I briefly explained at the beginning of my talk. If it is true that insofar as we exercise moral self-determination, we must presuppose the validity of those norms to which we owe the freedom thus exercised, then practices can be candidates for "ethical life" only if their normative structure gives rise to this sort of freedom. Human activity counts as a socially realized form of morality not in virtue of being guided by any rules whatsoever but only in virtue of being guided by normative principles that allow the participants to mutually view each other both as their authors and as their addressees. Hegel is thus faced with the task of articulating a conception of human practices that exhibits this structure of reciprocal empowerment and authorization, and even at quite an early stage of his work he addresses this task by developing his concept of recognition, following Fichte.[4] This concept refers to a special set of social actions that have the following property: those who perform such actions know themselves to be subject to a certain normative obligation, which arises from the right of others to judge their actions by reference to an underlying norm. When we take ourselves to love another person according to a determinate, socially acquired norm, we feel that we are subject to the resulting duties insofar as we accord to the loved one a status that allows him or her to hold our actions to the standards we are presupposing. In the case of formal right, we know ourselves to be subject to the relevant norms because we accord all other legal persons the power and the ability to assess our practical interpretation of the obligations mutually accepted by all. Each act of recognition consists in according to one or several other persons the authority to judge the normative aptness of one's own actions. In offering recognition, the recognizing agent "infringes on" his "self-love" insofar as he now knows himself to be bound by the norm with respect to whose application he has granted the other agent or agents a say. Thus on Hegel's account a practice deserves the label "ethical" only if a group of persons, which may vary in size, follows a norm to which each among them may in principle appeal to evaluate the actions of one of the other participants. This condition excludes both unilaterally enforced interactions and action from mere routine, and only when the condition is met does social reality exhibit the interplay of self-determination and normative obligation that Kant thought could be understood only as an isolated act of reflection removed from everyday practice. I will here set aside the question whether and to what extent such practices of shared norm following, based on reciprocal recognition, presuppose the existence of collective intentionality. In his doctoral dissertation written in our department, Titus Stahl has gone a long way toward answering this question.[5]

I also need to mention here a further component of this initial characterization of ethical practice, which belongs to it no less than the possible presupposition of collective intentionality, and without which Hegel's whole approach would remain unintelligible. The *kind* of norm that a given group of agents follows by mutually granting each other the authority to judge their respective individual interpretations and applications of it also determines, at least in outline, in which role or in which aspect of their personality they can come to encounter each other in the first place. To return to Hegel's paradigmatic example:[6] when participants in a collective practice are guided by the romantic norm of love, they are able in their reciprocal evaluations to offer arguments that are more directly expressive of their emotional states than when they assess each other as members of a legal community. In this latter case, the only admissible considerations are ones in which emotions have already been to some extent neutralized, whereas in the former case agents may object to some proposed application of a norm by citing reasons that simply articulate their emotional attitudes. This dependency of the admissibility of types of reasons on the collectively acknowledged norm leads Hegel to conclude that the act of reciprocal recognition underlying the shared obligations cannot be understood simply as an ascription of deliberative autonomy, but must be thought of as according others this or that particular kind of freedom.[7] He can therefore say, putting things briefly, that in the context of the norm of love participants in a practice recognize each other as beings who have needs, whereas within the horizon of formal rights they respect each other as "legal personalities." What these qualitative distinctions mean in detail emerges only once we understand how they are respectively associated with different admissible reasons guiding the evaluation of actions. To recognize somebody as a creature with needs, or more briefly, as a lover, is then simply to accord him or her the authority to evaluate one's own actions in light of the jointly accepted norm by appealing to reasons that are purely personal and emotionally tinged. As a context of agency founded on mutual recognition, each ethical practice generates its own specific forms of deliberative autonomy and along with this its own specific type of personality, which is relative to the reasons that can be appealed to according to the jointly accepted norm.[8]

Hegel was not content, however, merely to demonstrate against Kant's moral theory that the principle of universalization abstractly emphasized by the latter is always already practiced in specific contexts of ethical activity. He also held that the standpoint of morality illicitly opposes duty to inclination and reason to sensibility. A further task for him was therefore to show how it is that within an ethical practice these aspects are not separated to begin with. To this end Hegel tries to outline a second immanent account of all forms of ethical life, which he takes to be no less important than the first one. In his view we can speak of a social embedding or sublation of morality only when the norms validated through our reciprocal recognition provide for an interdependency between our duties and our inclinations.

In opposition to Kant, Hegel insists that whenever the members of a social group have subjected themselves to some moral norm by reciprocally according each other the relevant kind of authority, the norm itself must be reflective of some ethical value that expresses the inclinations and intentions of each of the agents. Only thus is it possible for the collectively accepted obligations not to be experienced as confines or obstacles that stand opposed to an agent's own purposes, but as "determinations towards freedom," as one student transcript of Hegel's lectures on the philosophy of right has it.[9] In Hegel's view, as long as the norms endorsed through reciprocal self-subjection within a socially practiced morality are expressive of ethical purposes that each participant can view as a condition of his or her own self-realization, there is no gulf separating duty and inclination and no opposition between reason and sensibility. In fact, one should probably go so far as to say that on Hegel's view, moral norms are conceptually inseparable from values if only because in the absence of substantive ethical content, those norms would hardly be capable of setting in motion a collective process of reciprocal self-constraint. Therefore, Hegel identifies a second immanent criterion of "ethical life" or ethical action: namely that the collectively accepted norms must be such as to display a certain ethical purpose.[10] When normative rules cease to be amalgamated with values, the participants in a practice can no longer conceive of their mutually ascribed obligations as conditions of their respective self-realization, and their shared practice is then no longer an ethical one. It is already through this quite basic conceptual maneuver that Hegel makes the normative validity of any system of norms depend on a historical process that is not under the control of the agents involved in it. Even though their mutual ascriptions of authority qualify them as the authors as well as the addressees of any given norm, it is not within their power to ensure that the norm continues to have ethical resonance as individual inclinations change over time. This raises the question what role history plays for Hegel's concept of ethical life. Before I turn to that question, I will first summarize how he pictures the re-embedding or sublation of morality into the reality of social action.

As we have seen, Hegel wants to retain Kant's view that moral actions are exercises of a certain sort of voluntary self-constraint or self-subjection. Yet for reasons having to do with his diagnosis of the paradox of moral autonomy, he does not accept that such actions could take place in a noumenal realm independent of any prior normative practice, as though moral norms were first to be generated or created through them. Instead, he assumes that human individuals always find themselves already inhabiting a world of socially practiced norms, which they can subsequently make their own by according the other participants in the practice the authority to assess their contributions to it. When this sort of recognition is reciprocally granted by all the members of a group governed by a certain norm, this gives rise to the kind of obligations Hegel calls "ethical,"[11] which henceforth serve as the foundation of an ethical practice or form of life. But Hegel is enough of a realist to hold that practiced norms stand a chance of being vindicated through collective appropriation only if the demands made by them are such that participants can view them as conditions of their own self-realization. Therefore he believes that ethical obligations and ethical spheres of action exist only where the relevant intersubjective norms point to choiceworthy ends or where they reflect generally accepted values.

The two criteria just alluded to lie at the foundation of Hegel's concept of ethical life. Social norms that are objectively valid, in contrast to ones that merely enjoy de facto acceptance, are distinguished both by the fact that they are appealed to as principles for the reciprocal evaluation of actions within a group and by the fact that they express values affirmed by the members of the group. In Hegel's view this conception of ethical practice imports back into social reality almost everything that Kant's idea of "morality" had presented as a separate principle opposed to that reality. Whenever a sphere of ethical life is established – which Hegel holds to be indispensable for the reproduction of society – the curtailing of "self-love" demanded by Kant is integral to everyday reality itself and does not require a search for special motivational sources. Thus for Hegel, the standard model of the social efficacy of morality is the collective appropriation of ethical norms, whose validity is owed to the fact that the members of a group mutually grant each other the authority to evaluate their respective applications of those norms. Yet Hegel is aware that the solution he suggests does not capture all of the implications that Kant intended his idea of moral autonomy to have. For applying the Categorical Imperative is meant to curtail our self-love not just in relation to the members of our particular group but rather in relation to all human beings, and thereby to ensure that we respect them in the way morality requires. It is well known that Hegel's answer to this challenge is a philosophy of history whose task it is to demonstrate that the historical process as a whole can be understood as a progressive self-realization of spirit, which in its final stages brings forth ethical equivalents of Kantian moral universalism. My main concern in the second part of my talk, to which I will now turn, is not whether Hegel succeeded in presenting the universalist content of Kantian morality as the result of a progress in the consciousness of freedom. That will no longer strike us as plausible today. Instead, I will ask whether his standard model of ethical life contains theoretical elements that could allow us to conceive of this sort of progress even without presupposing an objectivist philosophy of history.[12]

II

In reconstructing the immanent criteria contained in Hegel's concept of ethical life, we have encountered two kinds of considerations that require us to take into account historical processes and historical trends. First, we saw that Hegel conceives of morality as socially embedded insofar as it is the result of the collective institution of norms whose individual application and exercise are subject to reciprocal evaluation by the members of a group. Insofar as the participants in any particular form of ethical life grant each other a say in what counts as the adequate realization of a norm, their shared practice becomes subject to a certain historical dynamic, since each member of the collectivity may criticize the actions of the other or others and may call on them to act in a more adequate way. Even if Hegel did not always face up to the implications of this idea, it follows that morality, understood as the totality of the norms accepted in the relevant way, is characterized by an ineradicable element of historical revisability and openness. A second respect in which ethical life turns out to be dependent on historical processes emerges from the observation, made earlier, that Hegel considers the ethical resonance or expressiveness of norms to be a precondition of their successful adoption into ethical practice. In his view, a given socially practiced norm will be appropriated by a group in the required way only if the members of the practice can jointly conceive of that norm as desirable for the sake of their self-realization. But individual inclinations and dispositions change over time, and therefore socially habituated "ethical" norms may suddenly lose the motivational power that they owe to the values they embody. Thus in this respect, too, there is an ineliminable element of historical openness in all ethical life. At any given time, practical rules that until then used to enjoy intersubjective acceptance may cease to be followed and may consequently lose their "objective" validity because they no longer sufficiently reflect the currently prevalent desires, intentions, and ends.

Even though Hegel acknowledges and explicitly mentions these two respects in which history enters into the ethical world, he does not make much of them in his presentation of progress in human history. He does at times mention the struggle for recognition as an engine of historical transformations and ameliorations, but generally speaking he relies on the ontological conception of a progressive self-realization of spirit advancing independently of any deliberate efforts on the part of human agents. Given the failure of this sort of objectivist historical teleology, the question today is whether the elements of historical change inherent in Hegel's concept of ethical life may perhaps be sufficient, or at least provide us with some clues, for making the idea of moral progress in history intelligible without presupposing the existence of an anonymous self-realizing spirit. Such a project would amount to an attempt to reverse the trajectory from Kant to Hegel in the philosophy of history while availing oneself of explanatory resources drawn from Hegel's theory of ethical life rather than from Kant's anthropology in order to outline a plausible, hypothetically intended conception of progress.[13] In closing, I will limit myself to a few remarks in this respect, which more than anything will reveal how many gaps remain to be filled in explaining such a possible progress in the realm of moral norms.

We saw that on Hegel's view, merely given, habitually practiced norms are transformed into ethical obligations when the participants in the relevant practice mutually accord each other the authority to hold their respective actions to certain fundamental standards. Thus there can be no ethical sphere, no institutionalized domain of moral action, that is not anchored in relations of reciprocal recognition. This individual empowerment gives each participant the right to cite reasons that in light of a collectively shared norm speak against one person's or several other persons' particular way of putting that norm into practice. Generally speaking, it is therefore part of the everyday exercise of an ethical practice that despite the emergence of shared habits, the application of the standards inherent in the practice remains subject to contestation since there is a continual stream of novel objections and reservations. As in other areas of habitual action, such as "writing" and "reading," the "ethos" of ethical life [*die "Sitten" der Sittlichkeit*] is not rigid and fixed once and for all but exhibits a certain flexibility and reflective corrigibility that leaves room for revisions in the light of new insights. Within any given ethical sphere, the reasons that may be brought against accustomed ways of following its standards are – on the one hand – relative to the fundamental norm of that sphere; but, on the other hand, these reasons may also emerge from new discoveries enabled by that fundamental norm. In general, all norms that are capable of being collectively adopted and thus of being elevated to the status of ethical principles – such as the principle of ancientry, the principle of care, or the principle of equality – are not only open enough to permit very different kinds of application, but also serve a cognitive function that makes them comparable to spotlights capable of illuminating ever new circumstances and states of affairs. Now suppose that participants appeal to such reasons in support of objections that over time lead to revisions in the way norms are applied, and thus to revisions in the ethical practice itself. The historical accumulation of these objections will have the effect of creating increasingly narrow constraints that each further critique must meet before it is taken into account. The various innovations in the practice of a given ethical norm, which in essence amount either to an increasing generalization or an increasing differentiation of that norm, are not lost from one generation to the next but gradually add up to yield thresholds that all future arguments offered by the members of the group must be able to cross. So conceived, the history of an ethical sphere is an unplanned learning process kept in motion by a struggle for recognition, since the participants contend for specific ways of applying an institutionalized norm according to their own respective situations and sensibilities. The further this struggle advances – that is to say, the more revisions have already been made to the practice of a given norm – the more restricted is the dialectical space that remains available for novel objections and grievances.[14] In this way the history of an ethical sphere can be thought of as a conflictual process whereby a certain validity surplus initially inherent in every ethical norm is gradually stripped away.

If we wish to remain within the space of normatively mediated conflicts and to maintain that human history is a history of struggles for recognition, we need to offer an explanation of why over time certain ethical norms lose their collective acceptability and are gradually replaced by others that are more open and more universalizable. This brings me to the second point in Hegel where history plays a role in the formation of ethical life. In his theory of ethical life, rather than in his teleological philosophy of history, Hegel argues that each conflict over the application of a norm brings about changes in the very desires and inclinations that first gave rise to that conflict. The struggle itself, we could say, has a socializing effect on those who take part in it, insofar as it forces them to better understand their own motives and thereby enhances the force of individualization. This, for example, is how Hegel views the modern institution of the family, where the adolescent in struggling for the love of others gradually develops motives that finally lead him or her to leave the familiar normative sphere altogether. When this idea of a socializing feedback effect of the struggle for recognition is transposed to larger historical contexts, the implication could be that, in the course of a protracted conflict over the adequate realization of a given ethical principle, the motives of the parties to this conflict are transformed to a point where they no longer consider the relevant norm to be desirable at all. Due to the pressures of individuation released by the struggle, their aims and inclinations and their conceptions of the good would then have changed to such an extent that they no longer regard the accustomed norm as having any intelligible value.[15] Such an ethically faded or withered norm, over whose correct application the struggles of the past were fought, would then come to be replaced by a norm whose ethical purpose is sufficiently broad to present a foothold for newly emerging goals and ends. In this way the history of ethical life could be thought of as a series of institutionalized norms such that each successive norm exceeds the previous ones with regard to its ethical capacity and its accommodation of the good. It is of course true that on this view, too, agents are not in control of the historical coming and passing of their various inclinations and aspirations. But at least the history of these changing motivations would be mediated by the same struggle for recognition that also propels the moral progress found in the spheres of ethical life.

Translated by Felix Koch

4

Hegel and Marx
A reassessment after one century

Opinions about the relationship between Hegel and Marx have been subject to significant variation from the very beginning. Since the end of the nineteenth century, every era seems to have had its own idea about the relation between them. Right after Marx's death, during the early development of social democracy, the prevailing judgment was that there were few points of contact between the two thinkers. What was acknowledged was the important influence of Feuerbach on Marx's thinking, as well as the relevance of Kant. But the significance of Hegel's philosophy went unnoticed.[1] This changed significantly when the discovery of the "Paris manuscripts" shed new light on the young Marx, leading scholars to pursue the traces of Hegel's thought in Marx's work all the way to his mature critique of political economy. It was soon recognized that the structure of the latter was deeply informed by Hegel's dialectical method.[2] After World War II, when interest in Marx's work was initially centered on themes such as alienation and reification, other connections between their respective theories began to be drawn. Now, a central issue was the influence on Marx of Hegel's idea of a necessary self-alienation of spirit into its other.[3] These Hegelian-Marxist interpretations were decisively opposed by Althusser, who launched the thesis that there was an "episte-mological break" between Marx's early writings and his later ones, marking a complete emancipation of his mature economic works from the influence of Hegel.[4] Today, the prevailing view is again the opposite. One might even say that the two thinkers are now more closely associated and read in a more cross-fertilizing way than ever before. Not only is Hegel's work regarded as a source of philosophical inspiration for Marx, as it was in Lukács's time, but it is also recognized as a treasure trove of insights in social theory that can be used to supplement and improve on Marx's doctrines.

This new evaluation of the relationship between Hegel and Marx was prompted by a number of barely noticeable interpretive shifts over the course of the past several decades. For instance, Charles Taylor's path-breaking studies have made it seem much more natural to us to view Hegel not simply as a system builder seeking to comprehend the world in its totality, but also as an empirically informed social theorist.[5] His *Philosophy of Right* is viewed today as an attempt to diagnose the dynamics and crises of modern societies, containing the seeds of a sociological analysis that anticipated central insights of this not-yet existing discipline. Further scholarship has made it much clearer to us how Hegel's notion of "objective spirit" conceptualizes the integration of societies as the result of acts of mutual recognition.[6] This, too, has brought the sociological dimension of his theory into much sharper relief compared with past readings.

At the same time, interpretation of Marx's theory has been subject to similar shifts. Max Weber and Josef Schumpeter had already taken the sober approach of viewing Marx's work simply as a competitor to their own efforts to explain capitalist societies. This trend has continued since and has even increased as actual circumstances have presented increasingly less of a reason to think of Marx's theory as a revolutionary replacement of philosophy as such and an alternative to merely explanatory approaches to understanding modernity. By now, we have become accustomed to detaching Marx's diagnosis of capitalism from its political and practical context and to treating it as what it has always been, at least in part: a determined attempt to theorize the dynamics and crises of modern societies. As a consequence of these various interpretive shifts, we no longer assume that the relationship between the two authors is marked by any sharp break or discontinuity. Instead, we tend to view them as offering competing analyses of modern society, so that it makes sense to ask what one might have learned from the other.

My goal is to compare the theories of these two authors from this still somewhat unaccustomed perspective. My starting point will be the assumptions about the philosophy of history that served as a frame of reference for both Hegel's and Marx's diagnoses of modern society. In a second step, I then turn to the advantages of Hegel's social theory vis-à-vis that of Marx. My third step consists in reversing the perspective and considering the merits of Marx's analysis of capitalism. This will finally bring me to question under what conditions and in what way the two approaches might be brought to fruitfully complement each other.

A Shared Vision of History

Looking back to the works of Hegel and Marx from a contemporary perspective, one soon notices that their social analyses rely to a surprising degree on shared premises concerning the philosophy of history. Today, these theoretical commonalities allow us to treat the two thinkers from a comparative perspective. To be sure, many other nineteenth-century social theorists shared Hegel's and Marx's aim of uncovering the moving forces and dynamic laws of modern society. Henri Saint-Simon and Alexis de Tocqueville in France and John Stuart Mill in England can stand in for an entire spectrum of views. But even abstracting from the significant differences among these three authors, Hegel and Marx are further set apart from them by the fact that both relied on a philosophy of history to grasp the social challenges of their time. Despite the differences between them, they share the peculiar assumption that modern society is the most recent stage of a developmental process in which reason manifests itself in the external world.

It is a familiar fact that Hegel's interpretation of modern society rests on a philosophy of history that postulates a process in which spirit realizes itself. He faults both Kant and Fichte for failing to properly understand the nature of reason. Although both acknowledge that reason is the basis of all reality, they fail to see that reason is not simply a human faculty, but rather an all-comprehending entity that gradually unfolds over time until it has fully realized its own potential.[7] This ontological assumption allows Hegel to interpret the whole of human history as one particular stage in the process of spirit's self-realization. After first realizing itself in nature through its own spontaneous activity, spirit then returns back into itself and gradually lets the social world be shaped by its determinations, amounting to a "progress in the consciousness of freedom."[8] Today, this framework, which appears to postulate an objective teleology of increasing freedom underlying all human history, appears quite alien to us.[9] Yet without it, Hegel's interpretation of modern society is not properly intelligible. To him, modern institutions and practices are above all embodiments of the most advanced stage within the world-historical process of an increasing consciousness of liberty, a stage marked by the realization of all the preconditions for a truly self-determined life on the part of each individual. Modern society, which Hegel views as the outcome of a drawn-out and conflict-ridden developmental process, is for him an institutional realization of freedom.[10]

Even though Marx does not subscribe to this result of Hegel's philosophy of history, he derives from it an essential element of his own interpretation of the specific structure of modern society. Born almost half a century after Hegel, Marx is no longer a philosophical idealist willing to countenance the thought that all reality is the realization of a self-determining spirit. Right at the beginning of his intellectual development, he was profoundly influenced by Feuerbach's naturalism, and the idea that all that exists is a product of the process of reason's unfolding was entirely remote to him.[11] For Marx, we as human beings are first of all surrounded by nature, and we must relate to nature in productive ways to maintain ourselves. We are capable of doing this because we have the ability to use tools, which sets us apart from all other living beings. Where Marx is at his best, he conceives of the special status of human beings as consisting in a capacity to cooperate with each other by mutually relating to one another's intentions and thus establishing an entirely new, irreducibly social class of mental operations.[12] Supplemented by recent empirical findings, this basic idea points the way to theories such as that of Tomasello, who claims the establishment of cooperative labor enabled us humans to develop basic forms of morality and multi-perspectival thinking.[13]

Despite this distance between Marx and Hegel, Marx's account of the process by which humans modify nature through their labor, based on their capacity for cooperation, closely mirrors Hegel's account of the self-development of spirit. Marx argues that once we have learned to use tools cooperatively by mutually taking up each other's perspectives, nature comes to be gradually shaped by us and comes to reflect our own rational determinations, resulting in a cumulative expansion of the realm of our freedom.[14] What Marx says here about the essential spiritual powers of man, meaning our species' capacity for cooperation, is structurally similar to the features of spirit as characterized by Hegel. Although "reason" means two different things to them – a human capacity for Marx, a property of an all-encompassing spirit for Hegel – both think of reason as something that comes to be fully developed only by realizing itself in something external to it. The difference between the two thinkers is that Marx's naturalistic assumptions lead him to date the beginning of the process of reason's self-unfolding to a point that in Hegel's view is already the result of reason's realization in nature itself. But like Marx, Hegel views the history of human society as a process in which natural constraints are gradually diminished through the work of spiritual energy, with a corresponding increase of freedom in our social practices. These parallels show that Marx always remained Hegel's disciple regarding the central assumption that the development of society over time constitutes a "progress in the consciousness of freedom." Enabled by practices of cooperation, we give objective reality to our own spirit by laboring on the natural world surrounding us, and in so doing, we come to be at home in that world in a way that opens up ever-increasing opportunities for shaping social norms and institutions.

Marx's adoption of Hegel's central assumptions regarding the philosophy of history explains why he, too, is forced to describe modern society as the most advanced stage in the historical evolution of social structures. Numerous passages in Marx's work show that he conceives of human history up to the present as a process of overcoming natural constraints and fetters, which comes to a preliminary conclusion in the comparatively free practices of contemporary bourgeois society.[15]

Yet, there are some differences between Marx's and Hegel's respective assessments of the balance of gains and losses as far as the freedom of modern societies is concerned. These differences are an indication that they do, after all, have somewhat different conceptions of the history of civilization, understood as a process of the self-alienation of spirit. Whereas Marx thinks of this process as consisting first and foremost in mankind's increasing domination over nature, as its emancipation from the constraints of both external and internal nature, Hegel's conception gives greater weight to the progressive transformation of the ways in which human beings relate to each other. For Hegel, the overcoming of natural limitations always has an impact on socially practiced moral norms, whereas Marx identifies such an overcoming more narrowly with an expansion of human productive forces – conceived broadly as encompassing the means to control both our environment and our own motivational potential. This fundamental difference shows that, despite their shared commitment to the self-alienation model of spirit, Hegel and Marx take quite divergent views regarding the substance and character of the process of alienation. Both with regard to the content of reason and with regard to the mechanism through which reason is realized in history, there is so little consensus between them that they inevitably arrive at rather different assessments of the accomplishments of modern societies. Attending more closely to these differences between Hegel and Marx regarding the character of historical progress will make it easier to appreciate the advantages of Hegel's social theory vis-à-vis that of Marx.

Both Hegel and Marx seem to proceed on the assumption that human history is a process in which our freedom is gradually realized. In Hegel's view, this is so because spirit, having realized itself in nature and then returned into itself, seeks to embody in the world of social institutions its own determinations, which consist in its self-realization free from external constraints. Spirit must therefore manifest itself in human history and society in such a way that it gradually produces the institutional preconditions required for a free communal life of all the members of a society. As we have seen, what remains of this idealist conception in Marx is the thought that spirit or reason can realize itself only by alienating itself into something external to it. But in line with his naturalist assumptions, Marx's version of this thought focuses on the process of man's engagement with nature. This gives rise to his lifelong commitment to the idea that we as human beings are capable of making freedom a historical reality just to the extent to which we rely on our cooperative potential to turn nature into a reflection of our rational aims and thereby into a place that will accommodate those aims.

Whatever differences we may discover between Hegel and Marx will be, in my view, a consequence of the fact that they locate the social realization of reason in different spheres. Hegel locates this process in the relationship between spirit and our social institutions, because spirit has antecedently exerted itself on the natural world. Marx, by contrast, locates this process in the relationship between human reason and our natural surroundings, because he is unable to countenance a prior spiritualization of nature unmediated by social practices. This divergence can also be expressed as follows: Marx describes social progress in terms of a developmental pattern that Hegel introduced to capture the prior process of spirit's realization in nature. The result of this skewed adaptation of the Hegelian schema is perhaps best described as a neglect of the ways in which the activity of reason shapes the normative order of our institutionally regulated social life. Even though his theoretical starting point – that is, the fact of human cooperation – would have allowed Marx to attend to the phylogenetic sources of social norms, his reconstruction of our species history remains limited to the ways in which our rational capacities lead to an expansion of our dominance over nature. The realization of reason thus comes to be wholly identified by him with our increased freedom vis-à-vis the natural world. The corresponding neglect of the ways in which freedom is increased in what Habermas called the "internal framework of our social interactions" (*Binnenverhältnis unserer sozialen Interaktionen*)[16] entails a number of disadvantages of Marx's theory compared with the implications that Hegel's philosophy has for social theory.

The Advantages of Hegel's Social Theory

The first advantage of Hegel's social theory is that his concept of "society" allows him to consider a much broader spectrum of institutional forms than can Marx, given the latter's more limited focus on the manipulation of nature. It is clear that when Hegel seeks to comprehend society as "objective spirit," this must include for him all those social forms in which human beings learn to satisfy their merely "natural" needs. Spirit can attain objectivity and come to be at home within a social formation only to the extent that it gives rise to the institutions that allow human beings to reproduce across generations. When Hegel speaks of what we now call "societies,"[17] he therefore has in mind a totality of social practices that are calibrated with each other by way of cultural and normative commonalities but that also, and importantly, must be capable of satisfying our most basic needs. Setting aside Hegel's idealist assumptions, the concept of "objective spirit" anticipates in a surprising way the basic insight of classical sociology: that is, the observation that societies are normatively integrated units in which a variety of stable, institutionalized, and interconnected practices serve a range of functions essential to social reproduction. By contrast, Marx's narrower focus on humanity's relation to nature leads him to adopt a more restricted conception of society. The unfortunate term "relations of production," often used by him synonymously with "society," creates the impression that all of a society's institutions are ultimately aimed at the productive appropriation of nature. But neither political rule nor familial reproduction, to name just these two arenas of social activity, can be adequately understood in their normative structure by reference to economic purposes alone.

The drawbacks of Marx's terminological choices compared with Hegel's become more fully apparent when we consider the studies of Karl Polanyi, which show that only few pre-capitalist societies knew anything like a distinctive and separate sphere of economic reproduction.[18] If we are to believe Polanyi and other economic historians,[19] economic relations of labor and exchange used to be so thoroughly embedded into other social functions that they were neither experienced as self-standing activities nor normatively regulated as such. It is then quite misleading to follow Marx in conceiving of all societies as "relations of production," as institutional manifestations of various particular forms of mastery over nature. Hegel's approach is much more persuasive here: The concept of "objective spirit" merely captures the fact that the various spheres of social activity, including those devoted to the performance of vital functions, are in the first place manifestations of general norms and thus of something "spiritual," whereas the specific content of those norms and the relations between the various functional spheres depend on the progression of human history. The idealist surplus of this conception, which consists in the idea that such norms are the products of a self-determining entity called "spirit," can be removed without too much difficulty given more recent philosophical developments. We can follow John Searle and other social theorists in thinking of the "spiritual" generation of norms as a cognitive activity performed by mutually cooperating subjects. What is then left of "idealism" is just the claim that societies depend on a certain intersubjective consensus among their members concerning the normative regulation of each of the various functional spheres.[20]

Things are no different regarding a further point of comparison between Hegel and Marx: namely, the question of how to think about the social mechanism by which the progressive realization of freedom is brought about over the course of human history. Here, too, the German idealist seems to be better positioned than his materialist successor. As we have seen, both thinkers proceed from the assumption that this process should be regarded as a consequence of the gradual externalization or alienation of spiritual processes, that is, the interaction of spirit with something other than itself. In Hegel's theory, for systematic reasons, this "other" encompasses all the institutions that are required for the reproduction of a society. For Marx, on the other hand, spirit's "other"

is external and internal nature, both of which we can gradually
master thanks to our cooperative abilities, and in which we can, in
this way, come to be at home.

  If we now ask how each of the two philosophers proposes
to explain the dynamic driving this process of reason's self-
realization, we can see that Hegel's explanatory strategy has some
distinct advantages. Even though he thinks of the realization of
reason as a process effected by reason itself, and in that sense
as an automatic development, he also needs to offer at least a
broadly plausible account of how this kind of progress in human
history can be understood as a worldly, social occurrence. Here
he relies on the instructive idea that a historical form of life comes
to an end when it no longer offers sufficient normative space
for the realization of those claims on the part of individuals that
have been able to arise on the basis of the ethical structure of this
form of life.[21] Thus, for Hegel, each social formation contains the
seeds of its own transformation, because it inevitably leads some
groups of people to develop moral hopes and expectations that
cannot be properly realized within the established institutional
framework. It is true that this "moral" explanation is sociologically
unsatisfactory, as it leaves us largely in the dark about the way in
which these structurally unsatisfiable claims are supposed to arise
in the context of social conflicts. Only in a few places does Hegel
let on that he conceives of this kind of conflict as a struggle for
recognition, in which desires for the social realization of new and
previously unknown freedoms clash with an established social
order that immanently gives rise to these very desires. But this
brief sketch suffices to show how fertile Hegel's endeavor is to find
an everyday social complement to the self-propelled process of
spirit's self-realization in objective institutions. Enriched by sociological hypotheses, Hegel's basic approach can be developed into
the fruitful idea that what drives the historical process of freedom's
realization is the occurrence of struggles for the social inclusion of
previously excluded groups.[22]

  By comparison, Marx's account of the social mechanism said
to be responsible for the gradual extension of our freedom looks
much less convincing. As many have observed,[23] his explanatory
proposals generally rely on a technological determinism that tends
to obscure rather than illuminate the connection he asserts between
an increased mastery over nature and an increase in freedom. The
point of departure for this explanatory model is again the thesis that
our capacity for cooperation enables us increasingly to appropriate

both external and internal nature. But when it comes to explaining the driving force of progress in the realization of freedom, Marx attends only to the latter dimension, our relation to the natural world around us. Marx's term for the extent of our dominion over this aspect of nature at any given time is "productive force," which refers to the totality of technological means and methods that a society has at its disposal to exploit existing natural resources for its own purposes. In a second step, Marx thinks that our ability to constantly improve and increase our capacity for cooperation entails a historical process whereby a society's productive forces are constantly increased. He believes that the further history progresses, the greater becomes societies' technical capacity for the productive appropriation of the natural world. The decisive step in · Marx's explanation is the third one. He asserts that the institutional structures of all societies – all that he attempts to subsume under the term "relations of production" – are characterized by a certain inertia and rigidity, so that any boost in productive forces brings with it a lagging adjustment of those institutional structures to the new technologies and modes of production. The essence of Marx's explanation is thus that endogenous progress in the technological capacities for manipulating the natural world regularly and neces-sarily brings in its wake a normative improvement in the modes of social interaction.[24]

What remains especially unclear about this model is why we should believe that the development of productive forces will at each stage lead institutionalized social orders to realize a greater degree of freedom. Although it may be true in some trivial sense that technological advances increase our elbowroom vis-à-vis natural constraints, it is quite dubious to infer from this an automatic increase in social freedom. Often the contrary will be the case, and improved technologies will endanger the continued existence of previously attained liberties. Marx's proposed expla-nation of the gradual realization of freedom is far too optimistic regarding the normative potential inherent in the development of productive forces. Unlike Hegel, he believes that technological progress as such is capable of liberating institutionalized social orders from social domination and inherited dependencies.

As though he had a sense of this weakness, Marx supplemented his first explanatory approach by a second one, developed at least in broad outline.[25] On this second proposal, the moving force behind the social realization of freedom is not simply the endog-enous growth of our technological abilities, but rather the struggles of oppressed social classes for the realization of their needs and interests. It becomes apparent in the *Communist Manifesto* in particular that this alternative model is not entirely independent of the first one because Marx ties the interests of the various classes struggling for predominance to the opportunities for influence afforded by a given stage in the development of productive forces.[26] Just as the bourgeoisie is said to have begun fighting for social domination at the very moment in history when its increased control over the means of production allowed it to do so, the proletariat will also be in a position to come to power once the new factory system has created the necessary economic preconditions. It is easily seen that this second explanation of social progress, which focuses on the transformative power of class struggle, still fails to accord an independent role to the historically changing ensemble of social practices. Instead, Marx claims that progress in the realization of freedom ultimately results from a series of struggles of oppressed groups fighting for the social predominance of their respective economic interests – as though we were entitled to assume that all premodern societies had already established and been centered around something like a distinctive sphere of economic production. Thus, Marx's second explanatory proposal, too, does not measure up to Hegel's approach of postulating a social equivalent to the self-realization of spirit in social institutions. Instead of leaving open exactly what kind of social inclusion and recognition are at issue in any given social group's struggle, Marx simply assumes the primacy of economic interests in a way unsupported by historical evidence. This reinforces the earlier observation that Marx was unwise to reduce the large range of forms of social organization to the unitary category of "relations of production."

A third drawback of Marx's economic reductionism comes into focus when we compare his analysis of the achievements of modern societies with Hegel's. As we saw above, both thinkers proceed on the assumption that the modern social order is the most advanced stage of the world-historical process of reason's self-realization, because the modern set of social institutions has considerably extended the space of individual liberties. Like Hegel, Marx holds that the overcoming of feudal and aristocratic social orders amounted to a liberation from the fetters of inherited dependencies and forms of subjection, so that persons now enjoy much more extensive opportunities for individual self-determination.[27] But when it comes to the further theoretical task of offering a more detailed account of those newly created liberties, we find substantial differences between the two thinkers, which I already briefly mentioned at the outset. Hegel's view was that the "rationality" of the modern social order consists in the fact that it offers its members a whole spectrum of social roles that will allow them to realize their individuality under the conditions of mutual recognition, and in that sense freely. For Hegel, this includes all the central institutions of the new social order: the family, founded on mutual sympathy, the market, and the state. Taken together, these three spheres of activity were regarded by Hegel as amounting to a modern form of "ethical life," a term he employed to indicate that individual freedom is realized in the shared exercise of established practices rather than in private acts of choice.[28] Yet despite asserting the primacy of communicative freedom over personal or private freedom, Hegel never went so far as to doubt the normative significance of modern structures of right. On the contrary, throughout his work he continued to regard the then only recently established principle of free and equal liberties as a central achievement of modern societies, because these liberties require the state to protect each individual's opportunity to check and consolidate his or her ethical decisions without the intervention of others.

This is an issue on which Marx is quite unsure how to position himself. For one, Marx harbors substantial doubts concerning Hegel's entire doctrine of ethical life, since he suspects it of glossing over the defects of actually existing social structures. I say more on this below. But in addition to this, Marx doubts that modern liberal rights should really be accorded the normative significance that his predecessor attributed to them. If we recall how Marx pictures the historical process whereby freedom is realized in the world, we are led to a quite different assessment of the achievements of modern societies. What is distinctive of this new social structure is an extension of freedom not in the interpersonal domain, but rather with respect to the relation between the human species and its natural environment. Marx believes that the liberties gained in this way, which are embodied in vastly increased productive capacities, are not yet adequately reflected in the capitalist relations of production. Our increased ability to control natural processes and to harness them for our own purposes calls for a different type of social freedom than the one established within the present institutional order. As Marx sees it, owing to social inertia, these present arrangements reflect a purely private and egoistical conception of freedom. The massively improved technologies and methods of production create the possibility – and indeed the historical need – to replace this narrow, market-based conception of freedom by a broader, cooperative conception. In the present day, the only social relations of production adequate to the state of modern productive forces would be ones that subject the organization of labor and the distribution of goods to the shared will of freely cooperating producers. But however engaging and forward-looking this socialist vision may be, it leads Marx to completely overlook the democratic potential of modern liberal rights. The protection of individual self-determination afforded by such rights appeared to him to be too focused on private interests and therefore to be of a piece with the competitive economic system of capitalism. Hence, he regarded them not as normative achievements of a new social order but as remnants of a declining one.[29]

On this point too, then, Hegel's strengths outweigh those of Marx. It is true that Hegel, like Marx, has deep reservations about the liberal tendency to equate individual freedom with the liberty to pursue one's own private interests without restraint. Like his materialist successor, Hegel does not yet recognize the enormous contribution these liberal rights were to make in advancing democratic political decision making on the part of equal citizens. Nevertheless, Hegel viewed the novel principle of according all members of a society an equal right to individual self-determination as an irreversible achievement of modern societies. Unlike Marx, he was convinced that any other, more communicative or ethical form of freedom would continue to require as its normative basis a protected right on the part of individuals to develop and pursue their own particular aims.[30]

Marx's Insights and Their Possible Place in Hegel's Social Theory

What I have been saying so far might make it appear as though Hegel's social theory was in every respect superior to Marx's historical materialism. With regard to an adequately complex conception of society, to the identification of the moving force behind the realization of freedom, and to the diagnosis of the normative achievements of modernity, Hegel offers explanations that are better or at any rate more fruitful for our purposes today. Yet, this initial comparison is misleading to the extent that it is exclusively focused on the conceptual resources for a social theory supplemented by a philosophy of history. Once we direct our attention away from these foundational issues and toward the empirical content of the two rival theories, things begin to look somewhat different and the advantages of Marx's social analysis come to light. In this final section, I present this other side of the balance sheet in broad outline. In doing so, it is important to bear in mind that Marx had the benefit of an additional fifty years' time to observe the actual development of modern societies. Whereas Hegel devised his social theory at the outset of capitalist industrialization, Marx was writing at the apex of that development, placing him in an advantageous epistemic position regarding the destructive potential of the modern economic order. It is likely that the advantages of his social theory vis-à-vis Hegel's are partly owed to this surplus of historical experience, but also in part to the greater depth of his analysis of power and domination.

As we have seen, Hegel assumed that the world-historical process of a "progress in the consciousness of freedom" had reached at least a preliminary conclusion in the social structure of modern ethical life. He took himself to be entitled to this judgment because in his view the three spheres of modern society – the family based on reciprocal affection, the capitalist market, and the modern constitutional state – provided the institutional preconditions that would allow the members of this society to realize their particularity through free cooperation with others, based on the legal protection of their individual freedom of choice.[31] It is just this image of modern society that Marx is unwilling and unable to accept. Based on his research on political economy, he assumes against Hegel that the second element of this tripartite structure, the capitalist market, contains destructive forces that undermine both the freedom of the individual and the normative autonomy of the other two spheres. To be sure, Hegel also had been skeptical of the market system (i.e., of what he called "civil society"). In his *Philosophy of Right*, he therefore recommended that the threat of market excesses be held in check by regulative and cooperative institutions.[32] But the Marxian notion that the existence of a sphere that allows for the free exchange of economic goods and services might undermine the entire web of ethical practice remained alien to Hegel. Yet, this was just what Marx's critique of political economy was intended to demonstrate and to illustrate, and his efforts yielded a number of insights with which we can substantially enrich Hegel's social theory.

In developing this critical project, all the comparative disadvantages of Marx's theory discussed so far paradoxically work in his favor. The conceptual reduction of society to a set of "relations of production" allows him to focus exclusively on the economic sphere and to study its development in abstraction from political or institutional influences. Here, Marx attends to several important phenomena that had been only dimly foreseen in Hegel's *Philosophy of Right*, if at all. Thus he argues that the employment contract, one of the normative foundations of the new economic order, does not fulfill its promise of realizing individual freedom of choice because those who depend on wage payments are forced to agree to the contract's terms given their lack of alternative options for making a living.[33] Moreover, according to Marx, their productive labor generates a surplus value for which they are not compensated, so that they are subject to structural and unjustifiable exploitation.[34] The entrepreneur reaping the resulting profits is for his part continually forced to reinvest his gains with the aim of generating further profit, requiring him to tap ever-new markets for his products. This gives the capitalist market an expansionary dynamic, leading to a gradual subjection of all areas of life under the principle of marketability, which Marx calls "real subsumption,"[35] and resulting also in a further expansion of the capitalist's power, to the point where government turns into class domination and the rule of law yields to "class justice." These four elements of Marx's analysis of capitalism are complemented by an explanation of why it is so difficult for those involved in this economic system to understand its harmful mechanisms. The explanation, in his view, lies in the existence of legitimizing, concealing, and obfuscating interpretations that he calls "ideologies." One of his aims is to show that practices of economic exchange necessarily give rise to such ideologies.[36]

Not all of these basic assumptions of Marx's analysis of capitalism have survived the critical scrutiny to which his theory was soon subjected. Some claims have needed refinement in the light of objections from economists and other social scientists and some claims have had to be abandoned altogether. For instance, there is probably hardly anyone today who still subscribes to Marx's labor theory of economic value, which forms the background of his thesis about the structural exploitation of wage laborers. Similarly contested are his assumptions concerning the cognitive effects of ideologies said to emerge in some way from the economic practices themselves. But the two central elements of Marx's analysis of capitalism – his thesis about the unfreedom of wage laborers and his thesis about the expansionary dynamic inherent in the competitive market – have turned out to be resilient in the face of later developments and hardly open to doubt. Especially after witnessing the so-called neoliberal breakdown of economic barriers over the past several decades, we can safely assume today that there is a pressure inherent in our economic system that tends to undermine individual freedom of choice both for wage laborers and in other areas of life. But this sober observation should prompt us to turn to Hegel's social theory once again.

We have seen that, despite its philosophical merits, the engagement of Hegel's social theory with contemporary society did not take sufficient account of the perilous dynamic of capitalist economic systems. Therefore, the question now is how the aspects of capitalism identified by Marx might be incorporated into the framework of Hegel's social theory without completely destroying its inner architectonic. In conclusion, I would like to offer some conjectures about how this problem might be addressed.

Every attempt to reconcile the two theories in the way just hinted at – that is, by retaining a mitigated version of the German idealist's social theory and supplementing it with the results of his materialist disciple's analysis of capitalism – faces a number of serious obstacles. The greatest challenge is certainly the fact that Marx presented his analysis of capitalism in a way that seems to shield it from any attempt at adapting it for other purposes. The internal structure and the expansive dynamic of the modern economic system are depicted, under the influence of Hegel yet in an idiosyncratic fashion, as though they were being caused by the automatic activity of "capital," forming a closed cycle immune to external influences. Whichever interpretation of this methodology one chooses, whether one regards it as modeled on Hegel's *Logic* or rather on his *Phenomenology*,[37] it is not straightforwardly compatible with Hegel's sketch of a social theory. For Hegel, after all, social structures are shaped most basically not by "capital," but rather by an "objective spirit" consisting of shared social norms.

To integrate the results of Marx's analysis of capitalism into the framework of Hegel's social theory, we need first and foremost to break through Marx's apocryphal mode of presentation. We must abandon the idea that "capital," like Hegel's "spirit," proceeds autonomously and pervades all areas of society with its inner dynamic. Instead, we should adopt a much more open conception of the capitalist economic sphere that gives due place to the

influence of changing social norms.[38] Only through such a reorientation of political economy can we do justice to the historical
fact that the opportunity to pursue the profit principle varies with
institutional and cultural circumstances, being much greater today,
for instance, than forty or fifty years ago.[39]

A consequence of this first modification is that the capitalist
economy comes to be seen as partly dependent on the content of
the institutional rules that Hegel designated by the term "objective
spirit." A second modification that is needed to fuse Marx's analysis
of capitalism with a social theory inspired by Hegel concerns not its
explanatory content but its sociological framing. We have already
seen that Marx's notion of "relations of production" depicts all
social spheres as directly or indirectly concerned with the goal of
mastery over nature. In the context of his analysis of capitalism,
this gives rise to the problem that he lacks the conceptual resources
to identify just what norms are being violated when the dynamic
capitalist principle of marketization comes to permeate other
spheres of social life.[40] Another way of describing this deficit would
be by saying that Marx lacks an understanding of the functional
complexity of societies, which requires that different spheres of
activity be subject to different sets of norms that allow those
activities to fulfill their various specific functions. He is therefore
unable to explain why we should find it in any way dangerous
or problematic when the capitalist principles of profitability and
marketization come to inform and eventually to dominate other
areas of social reproduction not previously governed by economic
concerns. Thus on this point, too, Marx's analysis of capitalism
needs certain revisions if it is to become a fruitful element of
a Hegelian social theory. What is needed is an awareness that,
within modern societies, the capitalist market is only one sphere of
social activity among others and that each of these spheres serves
particular functions requiring that its activities be governed by
their own specific set of norms.

What I have just said indicates that Hegel's social theory,
for its part, does not meet all the requirements that it would
need to fulfill to fruitfully incorporate the important insights of
Marx's analysis of capitalism. If Marx lacks an understanding
of the functional complexity of modern societies, Hegel fails to
recognize that there can be deep normative tensions between the
various functionally specialized social spheres.[41] Hegel's doctrine
of ethical life admits the possibility that failures on the part of
the state or deficits of rationality on the part of its members may

cause the norms governing any particular sphere to dry up, as it were. But he does not allow for the possibility that one of these different sets of norms might intrude into other social spheres and undermine or incapacitate the norms proper to them. We could say that Hegel took the process of social differentiation to be an irreversible given, something that could not possibly be changed by future developments. Whatever other internal threats a modern, rationally ordered society might face, the functional separation among the family, the market, and the state is taken for granted as a permanent feature of the new social order of modern societies. Yet this assumption deprives Hegel's theory of the conceptual means to analyze the kinds of processes that Marx sought to describe under the aspect of a "subsumption" of all spheres of life under relations of capital. Hegel never allowed for the possibility that the capitalist mindset might come to intrude into the non-economic spheres of life. In this respect, then, his theory stands in need of fundamental revision. The functional differentiation of modern societies should not be regarded as a permanent empirical given but merely as a normative goal that may be more or less fully realized in a society's institutions at any given time, depending on the social struggles present at that moment.

This is not the only element of Hegel's social theory that needs to be systematically revised if his theory is to serve today as a conceptual framework for Marx's analysis of capitalism. A further revision concerns Hegel's reliance on the idea that the notion of contract supplies the economic system of the market with a legal foundation that ensures its general rationality and legitimacy, since the obligations of contracting parties are voluntarily undertaken. What is wrong with this picture is not the idea that contract is a legitimate basis of the new economic order in that it grants to each individual the freedom to determine how to employ his or her economic resources and services, in contrast with previous economic systems resting on personal ties and dependencies. This normative virtue of contract-based economic orders is one that Adam Smith articulated quite clearly in *The Wealth of Nations*, so that Hegel was able simply to follow him on this point.[42] The problematic aspect of Hegel's view lies rather in the fact that he simply transposes the features of contracts between commercial parties onto the relationship between entrepreneurs and wage laborers. His naïve disregard for the influence of duress and coercion testifies to his more general tendency to neglect the phenomena of power and domination. Hegel's doctrine of ethical life seems to be completely unaware of the possibility that individuals' consent to existing, "ethical" obligations may be owed, not to rational considerations, but instead to a lack of alternatives, to threats of force, or to subtle persuasion. Yet these are just the kinds of factors that Marx aimed to place at the center of his account of capitalism when he depicted the apparent voluntariness of the employment contract as a mere illusion, given that those dependent on wages had no choice but to consent or face indigence. Hegel's faith that the ethical structure of modern societies had given institutional reality to the idea of freedom led him to completely overlook the kinds of social mechanisms that continue even today to contribute to the coercion and oppression of particular groups of people. He went astray in dating the conclusion of the historical struggle for inclusion and recognition to the beginning of modernity and in depicting social relations after this point only in the optimistic terms of voluntary and uncoerced cooperation.

Correcting this serious deficit of Hegel's social theory would require more than simply supplementing his model of modern ethical life with the notions of force and coercion. Rather, it would require that we use Hegel's own categories to demonstrate for each of the social spheres which mechanisms inherent to it enable some subset of its participants to dominate others: for instance, how the norms of love and mutual affection may be used by men to oppress women, or the norms of loyalty to country be used to mobilize consent, by way of a "naturalization" and rigidification of the associated duties. Only when this has been accomplished – that is, only once it has been shown that the different institutional forms of mutual recognition can give rise to specific kinds of exclusion and coercion[43] – can the results of Marx's analysis of capitalism be properly incorporated into Hegel's social theory. For only then can the deprivations of freedom generated by the market and targeted by Marx's critique of political economy be integrated into a more comprehensive picture of modern societies, one that extends its focus to other forms of oppression as well.

The various revisions I have outlined still take us only halfway toward the goal of establishing a cross-fertilizing relationship between Hegel's and Marx's approaches to social theory. So far, I have not mentioned what is surely the greatest challenge facing such a conciliation of views: namely, to revise Hegel's concept of spirit in such a way that it would come to be at least somewhat closer to Marx's theoretical starting point, that is to say, the cooperation among socially embedded individuals. My call for revisions on both sides notwithstanding, the question remains how one might go about reconciling materialism and idealism, the image of man placed in nature and the appeal to a self-determining spirit. But for the purposes of this contribution, I hope to have shown that Marx's analysis of capitalism could only benefit from being embedded within a social theory derived from Hegel. The valuable insights contained in the younger philosopher's theory could be better and more accurately articulated if they were transposed into the framework developed by his older predecessor.[44]

Translated by Felix Koch

5

Economy or Society?
The greatness and limits of Marx's theory of capitalism

It would certainly be impossible to pass an overall judgment on the "greatness and limits" of Marx's social theory, as my subtitle has it, within the short space of an essay. The effects Marx had on subsequent thought are too complex; the philosophical sources he brought to bear on his work are too wide-ranging; and, finally, the aims he pursued in his analysis of capitalism are too varied to be covered in a relatively short study. In what follows, I shall therefore focus on a single line of thought in his writings in order to examine how his theory fares from the perspective of our present knowledge. My discussion will center exclusively on his contribution to our understanding of modern, capitalist societies, while as far as possible leaving aside all he had to say about the general course of history, the role played by humans within the historical process, and the importance of thinkers before him. The discussion will thus be limited to the greatest possible extent to his analyses of the fundamental structure and dynamic of the capitalist world. But this is no easy task, for everything depends on whether, when he embarked on the design of his mature analysis of capitalism, Marx abandoned the premises of his early philosophical work, or whether he continued to be guided by those fundamental assumptions. I shall begin my reflections with a discussion of this question, which has remained an important topic ever since Louis Althusser published his interpretation of Marx in the early 1960s.[1] Only once we have established whether Marx's analysis of capitalism still draws on his early anthropological intuitions shall I approach the question of the greatness and limits of his fully developed social theory.

I

It would surely be wrong to claim that the young Marx – politically very active, but philosophically still very undecided – had something akin to a systematic social theory. In his attempt to get to the bottom of his feeling that something was not quite right about the slowly emerging bourgeois-capitalist world, he was inspired by a very diverse range of contemporary thinkers.[2] Marx was not only irritated by the isolated political, social, and economic facts of this social order but, as one might put it, suspicious and critically alert toward the whole manner of communal life in bourgeois society. Throughout his attempts to identify the causes of these "miserable" social conditions, the young Marx, up to his time in exile in Brussels (1845), was constantly looking for convincing answers. As an unhappy student in Berlin, struggling with his law degree, he had come under the influence of the Young Hegelians, who took their cue from the critical philosophy of Ludwig Feuerbach. For a time, Marx shared the group's belief that the root of all contemporary social evil, the cause of man's self-estrangement, was religion. On this view, religious images of the world project all of the human being's natural faculties and capabilities onto an omnipotent, transcendent being, with the result that human beings lead an impoverished existence, no longer able to enjoy these positive characteristics in their earthly lives.[3] But Marx was not convinced by this isolated critique of religion for long; soon, the very existence of religious belief came to appear to him not as the cause of the current crisis but as emblematic or symptomatic of it. Still, he would never altogether shed the idea of the presence in social life of structures with god-like, transcendent powers onto which human beings project their real powers in an act of reversal and misjudgment that deprives humans of these powers in worldly life. But detaching himself from the isolated critique of religion allowed the young student to focus increasingly on the social-economic conditions that, with the emergence of industrial capitalism, slowly began to establish themselves in Germany, as elsewhere. The first pieces of evidence for this turn toward social analysis can already be found in Marx's contributions to the 1844 volume of the "Franco-German Yearbooks" – the only volume ever published – of which he was co-editor.[4]

It is interesting that these tentative approaches were guided theoretically by Hegel's *Philosophy of Right*, which at the time

Marx's Young Hegelian companions saw as the clearest expression of the German idealist's conservatism. Marx shared their political reservations, but believed that the basic distinctions drawn in Hegel's text were correct and fruitful, and that it could thus be interpreted, against the intentions of its author, as an outline of a critique of current conditions. Hegel's distinction between a sphere of "civil society," or the economic market, and the sphere of the "state" Marx considered to be empirically correct: in the former, subjects act exclusively as egoistic "private individuals," and in the latter, they are citizens pursuing the common good.[5] Altogether wrong in his eyes, however, was Hegel's belief that this factually existing split within society was sacrosanct, and even an embodiment of reason. In truth, it was an irrational separation of the "empirical" human being and his needs from his universal nature as a communal being – as a "zoon politikon," as the "Introduction" to the *Outline of Political Economy* would later put it.[6]

In "On the Jewish Question," Marx pursued this theme of the unhappy divided existence of human beings who – because of the differentiation between market and state – can live only as either "bourgeois" or "citoyen," but never as both at the same time, that is, never as citizens working for the social community. In this text, the problem takes the form of a critique of law. At this point, Marx's engagement with the "droits de l'homme" proclaimed by the French Revolution – which he distinguishes sharply from the "droits du citoyen," that is, the rights of the citizen[7] – becomes so decisive and comprehensive that the reader may be forgiven for thinking that Marx intends to carry out his analysis of capitalism through a critique of legal form.[8] According to Marx, all "so-called *rights of man*" protect only the characteristics or capabilities that the individual possesses qua *"member of civil society."*[9] Whether these rights are meant to guarantee individual freedom, private property, security, or even "equality," their sole purpose is to enable the social "separation of man from man"; each of these rights is a "right of the *restricted* individual, restricted to himself."[10] Human rights, as Marx succinctly puts it in the same passage, know only the human being as "an isolated monad who is withdrawn into himself."[11]

Here the law itself, at least when it takes the abstract form of fundamental liberal rights, appears as a decisive social force that advances social separation. At this point, Marx does not take the law to be merely "superstructural," a legitimizing veil covering economic exploitation. Rather, he sees it as an independent factor in the fundamental process of transformation to which the human being is subjected in the course of the emergence of the new market society. This independent role is emphasized further by the fact that, elsewhere in the text, Marx has very positive things to say about "political rights," that is, "civil rights," which, as we saw, he clearly distinguishes from human rights. From Marx's perspective, such civil rights, which pertain to the "citoyen" and *not* to the "bourgeois," do not separate human beings from each other, do not transform them into isolated and egoistic private individuals, but, on the contrary, enable *"participation* in the *community,"* because they are rights that can "only be exercised in community with others."[12] In this early text, the law is thus thematically treated as partly positive and partly negative; it is presented as having significant powers to bring about social transformation. In Marx's later works, this ambivalence toward the law never entirely disappears. As we shall see, even in his mature analysis of capitalism he is not entirely clear about the role of law in economic processes that are determined by the compulsion of capitalist accumulation.

In "On the Jewish Question," however, Marx had still not yet recognized accumulation as a fundamental aspect of the capitalist economy. Nor does this text talk about "commodities" as the central organizing principle of the new social order, or refer to the conflict of interest between "capital" and "labor." Instead, Marx provides an account of the historical emergence of the "free" market that is in many respects surprisingly similar to Karl Polanyi's later analyses.[13] This fascinating excursus takes as its point of departure the thesis that in the "old society," based on feudalism, the "civil life" in which "the mode and manner of work" was grounded was still "elevated in the form of seignory, estate and guild to the level of elements of political life." Civil life remained a matter of "public affairs." The price – thus the gist of Marx's further argument – a "people" had to pay for this integration of their economic activity into the "universal" was very high: exclusion from any involvement in the activities of the state. But at least long-term communal cohesion and the usefulness of the work people did was guaranteed.[14] For Marx, this social integration of the economy, which he obviously saw as a central feature of the feudal social order, is lost the very moment that, in a "political revolution," a people is given the right to shape the exercise of governmental power. At that point, the destruction of "all the estates, corporations, guilds and privileges" begins, and thus "the *political character of civil society"* is suddenly abolished.

Civil society is increasingly seen as a sphere ruled exclusively by the egoistic economic activities of private individuals.[15] For the Marx of "On the Jewish Question," the transition from feudalism to the "new society" saw a dramatic reversal in what the members of society took to be the realm of "public affairs." Where before the economy – or "civil society," as the text calls it – was understood to be a matter of communal activity, now the activity of the state is the sole locus of public interest. With this change, the economic activities of individuals lose their communal dimension, a process accompanied and supported by the institutionalization of liberal civil rights. In this severing of the ties between individual economic activity and the community Marx saw the malaise of the social formation that was about to emerge.[16]

As mentioned above, Marx carried out this analysis of economic history without even once drawing on categories such as the market, commodity exchange, or capital. At this point, he was still moving wholly within the conceptual orbit of Hegel's *Philosophy of Right* and its distinction between "civil society" and "state," only that he accused Hegel of approving with his work the split between a private, egoistic persona and a public persona that the distinction entails, and of completely missing the anthropological problems that are thus created.[17] It is highly likely that Marx came to recognize the need to base his reflections on the separation of the economy from communal matters more firmly in economic theory only after some of his friends, among them Friedrich Engels, made clear to him the importance of political economy for an understanding of the contemporary situation.[18] It was only then, first in Paris, then in Brussels, that he began to engage intensely with the writings of Jean-Baptiste Say, Adam Smith, and David Ricardo, and in this way to examine in more detail the mechanisms of the economic sphere that he had hitherto, following Hegel, called "civil society." The initial result of these studies was the so-called "Economic and Philosophical Manuscripts," a collection of notes and synopses in which Marx tried to bring the fruits of his readings into a systematic order.[19] These manuscripts see the return, in a different guise, of the critique of religion, which Marx had briefly dropped, and a laudatory reference to Feuerbach.[20] Marx describes how the workers who produce commodities for the market create a "world" in which they necessarily feel estranged and inferior because the things they produce are not their property and they cannot even control what happens with them: "the more the worker exerts himself in his work, the more powerful the alien, objective world becomes which he brings into being over against himself, the poorer he and his inner world become, and the less they belong to him. It is the same in religion. The more man puts into God, the less he retains within himself. The worker places his life in the object; but now it no longer belongs to him, but to the object."[21] This is not the place to go into the detail of how Marx establishes the fact of alienation, but we may say that Marx's critique of the "misery" of the new economic system is now based on an intellectual approach that is different from that of his earlier writings, which were firmly grounded in Hegel.

In the earlier writings, the *dividedness* of human beings was the blight of modern society; now, it is the fact of human *self-estrangement* that is the fatal consequence not of the social order as a whole but of the capitalist market. Marx thus – without making it explicit – narrows the perspective of his theory considerably. He no longer looks at the overall structure of society – the separation between the public state, the private and egoistic economy, and the law that somehow mediates between the two – but instead exclusively at relations of production. This shift in perspective must have been brought about by his new thesis that the fate of modern man is determined solely by economic relations – more precisely, by the private ownership of capital and the "degradation" of the worker. From here on, Marx will therefore analyze the "new" society almost exclusively from the perspective of its economic relations, and the way in which they change the relationship of subjects to their fellow human beings, their social environment, and themselves in a way that is incompatible with their original nature. At this point, however, Marx does not yet claim to have any explanations in the strict sense; he is not offering a social theory that demonstrates why the relations are the way they are or how they will develop in the future. For the time being, he is mainly interested in political economy and the economic system as it is – the former being a theoretical reflection of the latter – because both invert real human relations by treating living labor purely as an "object" and the things produced, by contrast, as real subjects. In that way, we are presented with, as Marx puts it, the "complete domination of dead matter over men."[22]

Over the next ten years, Marx will shed his reticence about providing explanations regarding the new relations of production and their further development. If we leapfrog over important writings such as *The German Ideology* and *The Communist Manifesto*, and go straight to the so-called *Grundrisse* of 1857–8, the rough draft for what will eventually be *Capital*, we can see that Marx's theoretical intentions have by this point been transformed.[23] He now wants to achieve both things at the same time: provide an economic explanation of the development and future of capitalism, and expose this "bourgeois" economy as a relation of social reversal. In the next step, I hope to demonstrate that this double project leads to a number of uncertainties about what exactly is the object of Marx's critique of political economy. Is it simply the emergence and development of a specific economic system, namely capitalism? Is it the overall social system that is molded by this economic system? Or is it a social culture or form of life – something that must be understood as altogether novel and unique in the way in which it forms and conditions the human being?

II

It is immediately clear from the *Grundrisse* that Marx has no plans to cast aside the "social inversion" motif derived from the critique of religion. No other mature text shows more clearly that talk of an "epistemological break" or "caesura" in Marx's development – the alleged shift from his original anthropologically based critique to a strictly scientific project in the second half of the 1840s – is unfounded.[24] Yes, it is true that these preparatory drafts for *Capital* reveal that the author has considerably raised the stakes when it comes to his claims about the explanatory power of his critique of political economy. He now seeks not only to examine the ideological substance of the dominant political economy, but to determine the social forces that have brought about the new bourgeois economic system and that will continue to transform it. However, as part of this explanation, Marx, in these rough drafts, also intends to demonstrate that the "modern" form of economic activity as such represents a relation of social estrangement. He is convinced that the subjects involved in this activity must necessarily experience the existing conditions of production as processes with a life of their own over which they have no power. When confronted with these conditions, Marx believes, the subjects therefore experience themselves as merely passive; they feel deprived of their own vitality and thus as lacking any human subjectivity. In what follows, I briefly sketch the two levels of argument in the *Grundrisse*, the explanatory and the diagnostic.

In so doing, I illustrate the extent to which Marx begins to blur the boundaries of the subject of his analyses.

The political-economic explanation of capitalism that Marx provides in the *Grundrisse* differs in several respects from his later analyses in *Capital*. It makes freer use of empirical material, draws more extensively on history, and also seeks to include non-economic factors. The impression is of an author who is still seeking the key to a comprehensive presentation of capitalist relations of production. There is a tenacious attempt to follow the model of Hegel's *Logic*: capital is conceived of as a concept whose internal articulation must be presented.[25] But this systematic undertaking is still not pursued with any of the rigor that characterizes Marx's later publications – and that presents such a challenge to interpreters to this day. In the *Grundrisse*, Marx traces the emergence of the new, modern, and – as he calls it – "bourgeois" economic system, and takes as his guiding thread the slow historical process through which the worker was gradually separated from the "natural" and social condition of his own activities. Initially, in the predominantly agricultural modes of production that characterized Asian, ancient classical, and Germanic communities, every producer was a member of the political association and, as a rule, owned a small part of the commonly held land, on which he could cultivate what was needed for the preservation of his family and the reproduction of the whole group. At this stage, economic activity does not yet aim at the "*creation of value* ... rather, its aim is sustenance of the individual proprietor and of his family, as well as of the total community."[26] Under such conditions, in Marx's neat formulation, "the individual can never appear ... in the dot-like isolation [*Punktualität*] in which he appears as mere free worker."[27] The active subject can still take everything that is necessary for his work – that is, the land and the tools required to work it – as "part" of his own subjectivity, and this makes the surrounding world a "laboratory" in which he may test his natural "forces."[28] But the development in the forces of production and the growth of the population quickly put an end to this stage of property relations and relations of production. Economic exchange and trade become indispensable, first at the margins but then within the expanding community itself. According to Marx, this is the beginning of the second stage in the development of the worker's relation to the conditions of his labor. The expansion of the exchange of equivalents, which will eventually lead to the institutionalization of money, dissolves traditional forms of land ownership. The first forms of private property appear, and labor gradually takes on an "artisan-like and urban" form, intensifying the shift from agricultural production to manufacturing.[29] However, as Marx points out, the individual laborer still retains control over the "conditions of production." He may no longer claim part of the communally owned land, as he did in the previous stage, but in the emerging "guild-corporation system" he remains the "owner" of the tools required for his activities. At this point, then, his existence has not yet been decoupled from the necessary conditions of his activity.[30]

How sketchy and provisional the model outlined in the *Grundrisse* still is shows in Marx's struggles to find a place for "slavery and serfdom" within it. He does not want to present these feudal forms of production, slavery, and serfdom as belonging to a stage at which the workers are already fully severed from the conditions of their labor, for Marx believes that this ultimate decoupling takes place only with the advent of the "bourgeois" economic form (to which his presentation, accordingly, quickly progresses). That said, he recognizes that neither slave nor serf has control over the conditions of his labor, because these conditions are dictated by the lord or landowner. This problem is internal to Marx's developmental model, and the conceptual maneuver Marx uses to solve it consists in treating slavery and serfdom as "modified" versions and "negative developments" of the first stage of communal property.[31] The assumption is that, at this stage, it was always possible to violently appropriate an "alien will," and to consider the forced labor thus appropriated in the same way as the fruit of the soil – namely as "inorganic" or "objective" conditions of production.[32] We must assume that Marx at this point takes slavery and serfdom to be phenomena resulting from the dissolution of older economic relations, rather than specific relations of production in their own right. They therefore do not upset his model of the gradual separation of the worker from the means of production.

However, Marx carries out these maneuvers to be able to claim that it is only with the new economic form of "bourgeois society" that the workers are finally and completely separated from the conditions of their activity, and thus reduced to "*plucked*, objectless" individuals.[33] A number of internal developments have to take place in the second social formation, the one based on the crafts and economic trade, for this novel mode of production to emerge. Marx tries to list these developments at various points in the *Grundrisse*. There had to be an expansion in commodity exchange, via the medium of money, sufficient to create a central role for the pure exchange value of goods, and thereby for "greed" and profit-seeking as independent motives.[34] It was also necessary that, as agricultural labor was concentrated and intensified in the pursuit of profit, a large mass of individuals were set free – free not only in the sense of no longer living in bondage or serfdom, but in the sense of *"free of all property*; dependent on the sale of its labour capacity or on begging, vagabondage and robbery as its only source of income."[35] According to Marx, these two processes were, however, not sufficient to create the economic preconditions for the emergence of the new production and property regime of "bourgeois society." There also had to be a "stockpiling" of "monetary wealth" in the hands of merchants, who then used this wealth to buy the "objective conditions" of production and the newly freed labor, and set both to work in the interest of increasing profit. The birth of the new economic form of capitalism thus coincided with the historic moment when working subjects were, for the first time in human history, completely deprived of any control over the objective preconditions of their activity. Driven into urban areas as "non-guild day-labourers, unskilled labourers" or beggars, and driven on to "the narrow path to the labour market" by "gallows, stocks and whippings,"[36] they had no choice but to sell their labor power in an (unequal) exchange with "merchant's and usurer's wealth."[37] With this act, they finally lost all control over the conditions of their own activity, and, in the hands of those who appropriate "alien labour" without genuine "exchange," there emerged the "productive wealth" that Marx will from now on call "capital."[38] In much of the *Grundrisse*, he analyzes how this "capital" becomes the "active middle ... of modern society,"[39] gains "general power" over society, and subjects "the whole world of gratifications, labours, etc." to its rule.[40] Marx's use here of the concept of the "active middle" betrays the extent to which he is already attempting to attribute the properties of Hegel's "spirit" to "capital." The negative consequences of this problematic aspect of the *Grundrisse* would become clear only several years later, in the finished book. Nevertheless, the draft text firmly establishes what will remain perhaps the greatest achievement of Marx's mature theory of capitalism: his insight into what distinguishes the new, capitalist mode of production from all previous forms. His analysis of economic history demonstrates, with impressive lucidity, that what distinguishes the capitalist mode of production is that its purpose is no longer to secure the subsistence of all members of society, but rather to constantly increase value-creation and thus maximize economic yield. For Marx, the specificity of this novel economic form, its historical uniqueness, lies in the compulsion to look for ever new opportunities for the productive realization of monetary wealth as part of the competitive struggle with other economic enterprises, a compulsion that arises out of the emergence of private "capital." The inclination toward "greed," about which Marx talks a great deal in the *Grundrisse*,[41] is not a fundamental psychological-cultural trait of the new mode of production. It does not owe its existence primarily to a change of attitude or mentality; rather, its necessity is dictated by the need to maximize economic yield, which is a structural aspect of capitalism.

Before I briefly sketch how Marx, in the *Grundrisse*, tried to combine the conclusions of his analysis of economic history with his diagnosis of alienation, I note some further characteristics that already point toward the main aspects of his mature social theory. First, the theme of the "dividedness" of the human being, with which we are already familiar from "On the Jewish Question," is taken up again, but is given a dramatically different meaning. In modern society, the individual is not "divided," or split, between being a "bourgeois" and "citoyen"; rather, the working subject, as a point-like, object-less individual, is separated from all of the conditions of production with which he used to be associated. The split that so appalls Marx is no longer a matter of two separate social roles that the human being must inhabit simultaneously without being able to unite them; rather, it is a divide that runs right through the worker. This transformation in the diagnosis of separation results from another new feature of the social analysis developed in the *Grundrisse*: Marx no longer follows Hegel in understanding modern society as a functionally differentiated structure in which the market and the state co-exist in tense relation. Rather, society completely coincides with the market, so that there seems to be no place left for other social spheres or functional areas. Nothing expresses this development in Marx's social analysis better than his use of the term "bourgeois society." Marx retains this Hegelian category, and even uses it with the meaning given to it by Hegel (that is, as denoting the world of market-mediated inter-course between isolated private individuals), but he now takes it to signify the totality of all social processes and interactions in modern society. There is no longer any space for a public sphere that stands in opposition to it. For this reason, the *Grundrisse* does not so much as mention the "citoyen," the political citizen, who in "On the Jewish Question" at least still led a diminished life in the shadows. In the place of the old opposition between political citizen and economic citizen, "citoyen" and "bourgeois," there is now the antagonism between capitalist and worker. This is a clear indication of Marx's view, which by this point had become a firm conviction, that the analysis of capital as social relation is the key to his comprehensive social theory.

The problem with these shifts in Marx's basic theoretical outlook is that they rest on a questionable premise, or at least on a premise that requires further justification: namely, that the theoretical point of departure should be the natural or essential unity of the working subject and the conditions of work – the land to be tilled, the tools to be used, or other instruments essential to specific activities. It may well seem intuitive that work processes will go more smoothly if their necessary conditions are freely available to the worker. But to turn this intuition into the essence of work surely requires more argumentative effort than Marx is willing to invest.[42] Nor will I reiterate here the much-discussed fact that Marx's historical sketch of the emergence of capitalism focuses in a very one-sided fashion on the development of the productive forces and population growth, and the transformation of property and economic forms that those entail. The *Grundrisse* repeatedly mentions "wars" as intervening events – much more frequently than *Capital* does.[43] It highlights the importance of colonization,[44] and even places an unusually strong emphasis on the transformations in everyday attitudes and moral orientations that were necessary before the original accumulation of capital could take place.[45] At the same time, however, Marx fails to give the formation of states, changes in legal relations, changes in family relations, or the revolutions in forms of communication the attention they clearly deserve. Rather, all these innovations and transformations are understood solely as functional adaptations to the development of the relations of production, so that the ultimate impression is of an explanatory model with an overly narrow economic perspective.[46]

Those questions have been the subjects of extensive discussion, and I want to focus on an altogether different problem, which seems to me of particular importance for contemporary engagements with Marx. We have seen that from his early writing onwards Marx consistently uses the Hegelian term "bourgeois society." But crucially, in the *Grundrisse* he uses it with a much broader meaning that encompasses not just the sphere of the market-mediated interactions between private individuals, but the totality of all institutions and processes that are structurally relevant in the dawning social formation. In employing this expanded term, Marx can still point to the fact that Hegel too spoke of market relations as bourgeois "society" – albeit without explicitly admitting that Hegel's term refers not to the entire institutional system that makes up a nationally bounded society, but only to that "social" part of it that involves mediation between subjects exclusively in terms of legal-private relations.[47] In taking Hegel's term for this sub-sphere and using it to characterize the entirety of the new society, Marx – whether wittingly or not – blurs the boundaries between economic processes and the rest of social life. By not making this expansion of the term's conceptual scope explicit, he suggests that capital has flowed into all corners of modern society and now determines all areas of life. For instance, at one point in the *Grundrisse*, he says bluntly that "capital" now represents the "inner construction of modern society."[48] Marx's conceptual strategy invited his successors to make free use of the category of "capitalism," which he himself never used. In some usages it referred to a specific economic form that is characterized by the compulsive accumulation of capital, in others to the totality of modern society. But in these latter cases, the question of whether all spheres of society really are determined by capital was never truly addressed.

A brief look at Marx's analysis of alienation in the *Grundrisse* reveals, unfortunately, an even more serious dilution of conceptual clarity. The claim that workers are divided, that is, separated from control over the conditions of production to which they should be entitled, is only part of the social pathology of modern society. The more important aspect is a kind of "alienation" that, according to Marx, affects not only workers but all members of the new social order. For Marx, a capitalist economy necessarily involves "alienation" because it creates the impression that the objective products of "living labour" exist independently of the laborer; subjects therefore experience themselves as deprived of all power to act, as passive and helplessly exposed to objective conditions.[49] Marx seems to have in mind something like the fact that, in their everyday opinions, members of society are inclined to view commodities and modern production plants as autonomous active beings that bring about effects by themselves, and to see themselves as powerless and unable to exert an influence on the production process and its results. The allusion to Feuerbach's critique of religion quickly becomes clear if we substitute "God" for what Marx here calls "personified conditions of production."[50]

In any case, the *Grundrisse's* many passages on "alienation" are not attempts to say something about the specificities of the new economic form or the specificity of the new society. Rather, they aim to say something about the everyday consciousness of contemporary citizens. When Marx speaks of contemporary "alienation," the object of his analysis is the culture or form of life of the new society, which he claims is formed by the economic compulsion to accumulate capital. In providing this analysis, however, Marx – again, whether wittingly or unwittingly – set in train a process in the course of which "capitalism" would come to denote a cultural totality, a form of life and thought that differs strikingly from all previous forms of human existence. With the young Lukács's investigations into "alienation" and Adorno's claim about a "universal delusive context," this manner of speaking soon became a theoretical commonplace.[51] And with that, the conceptual confusion is complete. Now, the meaning of the term "capitalism" depends on context, personal preference, and political intention; it may be invoked to refer to an economic formation that is driven by the profit motive, an entire social system that is dominated by that motive, or a culture that is characterized by tendencies toward "reification." When we turn to *Capital*, we will see that this removal of conceptual boundaries allows Marx to present capitalism as a closed system that develops in a "spiraling" fashion.

III

At first glance, one of the greatest achievements of the three volumes of *Capital* is that they transcend the boundaries of pure economic analysis and examine the condition of the new society in its entirety, including its specific culture, or form of life. Marx is extraordinarily skillful, especially in the first volume, published in 1867, at integrating his presentation of the production process of capital with reflections on the fate of other spheres and on typical modes of thought, and in this way he creates an impression of a complete portrait of a social formation.[52] This totalizing perspective was made possible by a methodological decision that Marx probably finally made only in the late 1850s, when he was struggling to give a coherent form to the vast amount of material collected in the *Grundrisse*. In the end, his solution was to adopt the presentational form from Hegel's system.[53] This meant that Marx had to find a subject-like force in the contemporary economic system that could take on the all-pervading role played by spirit in Hegel's system. The obvious candidate for the role was "capital," which the *Grundrisse* had already talked about in terms of an "active middle" and an active subject.[54] In what follows I leave aside questions about the detail of the transposition of Hegel's concept of "spirit" to Marx's of "capital." (For instance, did Marx aim to juxtapose the linear process of "capital" with depictions of the damage it does to the lifeworld?[55] Did he even draw on literary models for representational purposes?[56]) For our purposes, the interesting fact is that using Hegel's system as his point of orientation allows Marx to suggest that a purely economically defined entity, for which he invents the technical formula M-C-M',[57] possesses the power to shape all of society's essential institutions and intellectual patterns. I aim to demonstrate that this methodological strategy, the fulcrum of Marx's theory of society, creates persistent problems for his theory because the material cannot be fully subsumed under the guiding interpretative framework. My thesis is that, because of their idiosyncratic structures or content, the phenomena refuse, in some cases, to be conceived of as the results solely of the process of capital becoming independent. If that is correct, we must conclude that what appears to be *Capital*'s greatest achievement is in fact also its greatest flaw: it aims to show that the modern economy, society, and culture are spheres that conform to one principle, but at many points the material does not bear this out.

There may be reason to suppose that a comparison of *Capital*'s material and its representational method should start with the beginning of the first volume, where Marx discusses the forms of consciousness that allegedly typify members of modern society: the everyday mentality of the contemporary individual. Here, in the famous and stylistically masterful section on "The Fetishism of the Commodity and Its Secret," he picks up his old theme of "inversion," but now tries to give it a precise form.[58] As Marx famously puts it, anyone involved in the exchange of commodities – in principle every member of modern "bourgeois" society – is forced to misunderstand the "social characteristics" of his "own labour" and instead to perceive the relation between the commodities, dressed in monetary form, as a "social relation."[59] According to Marx, this category mistake – taking thing-like objects to be living beings that enter into social relations – necessarily arises under present conditions because individuals can no longer recognize the socially coordinated labor invested in the commodities that are exchanged on the market. The commodities themselves are therefore taken to be the real actors in the social process. Put another way, Marx claims that the members of capitalist societies possess an almost reflex-like inclination to attribute creative powers to the world of commodities, while experiencing themselves as relating to each other as unfree, lifeless things. There is surely something plausible about this stark thesis. It is certainly possible that the amount of labor actually expended in the production of commodities is forgotten in their consumption, whether because of a lack of knowledge or indifference, and that the commodities therefore appear utterly alien to us.[60] The far-reaching conclusion Marx draws from this is nevertheless untenable. The fact that when consuming commodities we no longer perceive the whole network of activities that went into their production does not imply that we have granted the world of commodities a vitality and subjectivity that truly belongs only to us as human beings.[61] My objection here, however, does not amount to the kind of immanent criticism to which I referred earlier, the awkward tension between *Capital*'s material and method of presentation: because the passages in question do not refer to any contemporary historical phenomena, there can be no talk of a tension between historical material and systematic account. "The Fetishism of the Commodity and Its Secret" presents conclusions drawn from a number of premises regarding the phantasmagorical independent life of commodities; it is not the result of a friction between his theory and the actual intellectual habits of the existing population.

The equally important sub-chapters that appear 200 pages after the "fetishism" discussion are another matter altogether. These later sections conclude chapter 10, "The Working Day," and follow just after the secret of the creation of surplus value, that is, of the M-C-M' formula,[62] has been revealed. In these two sub-chapters, Marx discusses "The Struggle for a Normal Working Day" through British factory legislation, a topic that requires reference to historical detail.[63] In this context, the compatibility of the historical material with the interpretative framework – "capital" as the all-pervasive formative power – can therefore be examined.

Marx's presentation of the struggles over the length of the working day in Britain during the first half of the nineteenth century begins with a short summary of the miserable situation of wage laborers at the beginning of the century. Since the "birth of large-scale industry," there had been no legal regulations on "capital," limiting what counted as a normal working day. As a result, capital celebrated its "orgies," and extended the working day for men, women, and children "to the limit of the natural day of 12 hours" so as to draw the maximum profit from their labor power.[64] It is already clear from these introductory passages that the author is about to make full use of the talent he deployed in his earlier writings – namely his ability to present historical events, with unconcealed irony, as complex conflicts between the interests of diverse groups.[65] Over the next 25 pages we hear the voices not only of different factions of capital and the emerging self-organizing workforce, but also the voice of the legislative body, the British parliament, and the "factory inspectors" it commissioned. The last two actors deserve our particular attention. They do not seem to fit into the framework of a progressively independent capital, for they represent the interest of the "law" in regulating the working hours of wage laborers, and thus in protecting them. Only three pages into Marx's report – completely out of the blue – parliament's voice can be heard when it expresses its intention to regulate and set a temporal limit to child labor.[66] According to Marx, the various perfidious countermeasures taken by capital had little effect. Only two pages later – we are up to 1844 by now – we read about a new "Factory Act" that "placed under protection a new category of workers, namely women over 18," whose working hours were limited to 12.[67] The factory inspectors, Marx reports, played an essential role in the implementation of these regula-tions. Despite intimidation and attempts at bribery, they diligently carried out their duties, and strictly enforced the factory owners' obedience to the new restrictions. At this point, one wonders: where did this group of state administrators find the normative resources to pursue their legal brief so diligently, given that the social system is supposed to have been exclusively constituted by capital? Indeed, only a page later Marx admits that in the same year, 1844, the Factory Act was amended so that the legally binding 12-hour working day applied in a "universal and uniform" way to all wage laborers.[68] As if anticipating the above question, the text introduces the amendment with two sentences that contradict one another: one claiming that the new laws were "natural laws of the modern mode of production," the other that they were "the result of a long class struggle."[69]

This strange contradiction reveals Marx's quandary: how to explain the fact that the law was able to intervene under condi-tions of the rule of capital. It is a clear indication of how difficult he found it to make all his material fit with his theory. The historical facts he presents suggest that the state intervened in the labor market to defend civil rights and liberties. This is precisely what Marx cannot acknowledge, so he quickly formulates alternative – but contradictory – explanations as a stopgap. The first of these alternative explanations is that it is part of the nature of capitalism not to let the profitable commodity of labor-power go to waste. The second, by contrast, is that the working class successfully waged a struggle that forced the state to intervene. The separate historical account that Marx gives of the "struggle for a normal working day" does not alter his peculiar strategy of denying the legal enactments of the state any autonomous effect. In the pages that follow, Marx seeks to avoid, at any cost, admitting that liberal rights, once enacted, may themselves oblige state actors to protect the physical well-being of citizens. His account repeatedly mentions empirical evidence that points exactly in that direction – for instance the fact that "factory legislation" was "compelled gradually to strip itself of its exceptional character" and to bring all workplaces under the same legal regulations, as if there were a compulsion at work that is internal to the law.[70] But even in the light of such evidence, Marx never concedes that modern law possesses a normativity of its own.[71] This refusal, at this early point in his study, means that Marx is unable to present the development of modern society as the gradual working-out of the antagonism between the capitalist economy and democracy based on the rule of law.

Marx's attempt, in the same section, to explain the emergence of worker resistance to the new relations of production fares no better. In this case, too, the historical evidence on which he draws ultimately speaks a different language from that of his presentational framework. As Marx frequently makes clear, his framework implies that the revolutionary resistance of the proletariat should be understood as a purely immanent counter-movement that is produced by capital itself. If modern society is constituted and held together solely by the activity of capital, then any resistance must necessarily be grounded in this activity. As Marx puts it, "the working-class movement … had grown instinctively out of the relations of production themselves."[72] Indeed, in many places in the text he tries to prove that the emergence of proletarian resistance is an example of such an automatic, reflexive reaction.[73] But a lot of what Marx has to say about the budding workers' movement in England fails to correspond to this methodological intention. For instance, he states, surprisingly, that the "working class's power of attack grew with the number of its allies in those social layers not directly interested in the question."[74] This statement alludes to the general moral atmosphere of society, which here is granted a surprising plasticity and a flexibility that extends beyond class antagonisms. Marx says that, because of the continued existence of slavery in the United States, an "independent workers' movement" is unable to set down roots there,[75] which implies that certain historical conditions either promote or hinder the movement, and therefore that the emergence of proletarian resistance cannot be the result of a purely automatic process. Moreover, elsewhere he even suggests that the awakening of the English workers' movement went "hand-in-hand" with the "physical and moral regeneration of the factory workers."[76] This introduces a factor for which Marx's investigation should have no space whatsoever. For what does "morality" refer to here, given that, we are supposing, only the class interests created by the movement of capital have roles to play? According to Marx's own view, neither "morality" nor "law" can have any independent power to shape the situation in the capitalist system. But here, located inconspicuously within Marx's historical excursus, there is a reference to morality as a driving force in the historical development of the new social formation.[77]

Perhaps all we may conclude from this is that Marx faced significant problems in adhering throughout to the presentational framework of capital as the only socially formative power. As soon as he makes even the smallest digression into concrete historical reality, difficulties arise. At these points, modern society, with its legal constitution and moral resources, raises its idiosyncratic voice, so to speak, and objects to the interpretative framework applied to it. But what if the forms of social life were normatively and culturally more complex than the theory permits – and not only at those places where Marx tries to flesh out some of his basic categories with facts from social life? We have so far considered only the "struggle for a normal working day" as an example. We saw that, as soon as the theoretical veil of his presentational framework is lifted, there appear a number of social phenomena that Marx cannot have anticipated in this form: the state legislating in the interests of the workers, "allies in those social layers not directly interested in the question," "factory inspectors" who act in strict accordance with the law, and – last but not least – a proletariat that pursues not its own interests but its moral convictions. The question with which I conclude is therefore this: what would follow from the claim that all *Capital*'s key concepts possess a hidden, undiscussed side, a layer that is kept from view by the method Marx employs and that anchors these concepts in modern society? We would probably need to retrace Marx's intellectual development in reverse: to conceive of society not as the product of the capitalist economy but as the foundation and institutional framework of that economy.

IV.

We might summarize the various stages of my reconstruction by saying that the trajectory of Marx's thought involved a gradual unbounding of the concept of "bourgeois society." In his early writings, he followed Hegel in using the term to refer only to that part of contemporary society that is home to the economic market, and juxtaposing it with the sphere of public affairs. As Marx began to engage with political economy, he increasingly came to use the term to refer not just to the market – or, in his own words, generalized commodity production and the associated capitalist exploitation of labor power – but to the new social relations as a whole. From this point on, the term came to denote the emerging social formation as a totality, including its legal institutions, culture, and forms of social interaction. An initial conclusion of my reconstruction was that, with this step, we lose the boundary between the economy and other spheres of modern society. Everything that seems to have an independent existence outside the economy must now be understood as a social structure that is formed, or deformed, by capital. In the *Grundrisse*, to which I turned in the second step of my reconstruction, Marx was still testing possible answers to the question of how – given the vast amount of economic material he had to cover – he could present these capitalist social relations, which are now understood as a single system, in a uniform way. He was uncertain as to how this could be achieved, and at this point still afforded more space to social reality than he later would, but the *Grundrisse* already reveals Marx's tendency to understand culture and the basic institutions of the new society as mere emanations of the economic relations of production. It is only in *Capital*, the last stop in my reconstruction, that Marx provides the ultimate answer to his longstanding question of where to find a uniform representational framework. With admirable consistency, he tries to understand the surplus-demanding movement of capital on the model of the activity of Hegel's "spirit": that is, as a process in which capital, like a creative subject, gradually appropriates all spheres of social life and molds them in accordance with its own coldly calculating mentality. However, as I tried to demonstrate, the empirical material of social life resists incorporation into Marx's presentational framework. Whenever he seeks to use empirical or phenomenological evidence from social reality to illustrate the extent to which conditions are already determined by capital, the evidence clearly speaks a different language from that of his presentational framework. The question we are driven to ask, and with which I concluded, is whether this tension between material and method may reach even beyond the historical passages – whether it may affect all of *Capital*'s concepts.

Interestingly, Marx himself claims that one key category in his magnum opus possesses a "double character"[78] because of its very "nature": because, that is, it denotes an economic function whose efficacy cannot be appropriately described without falling back on the social lifeworld. Early on in the first chapter of the first volume, we are told that the "exchange value" of a "commodity" can be realized in economic trade only if the commodity also has a "use value," which refers to its "usefulness" for a community whose needs and customs constantly change.[79] If use value is the hidden, material side of exchange value, that is, that aspect that remains rooted in social life, then the purely economic aspect of the category is clearly too vague to be really helpful in the explanation of economic processes. For the ways in which social needs develop, and which forms they take at particular points in time, cannot be deduced from the exchange value of commodities, but only from their variable use values, which change in accordance with historical circumstances, moral climate, and cultural custom. Of course, Marx could not have foreseen that, not long after he wrote, there would emerge an advertising industry that would seek to influence the needs of consumers in such a way that commodities would realize the exchange value sought by capitalists. But even this development – which the internet may well have taken to a new level[80] – does not invalidate the point that there can be no straight application of purely economic categories to social reality. Such an application must always take into account a social lifeworld in which needs and desires develop according to a cultural logic to which Marx's presentational method has no access. It was Thorstein Veblen's great achievement to have clarified, with his concept of "conspicuous consumption," the extent to which the usefulness of goods, that is, their "use value," can be a function of the interpretation of social participants.[81]

What applies to exchange value may equally apply to most other concepts that appear in *Capital*. Almost all of them possess – albeit to varying degrees – a hidden material side through which they are tied to the overall social structure, and without taking the latter into account, we cannot establish anything about the actual effects of the factors the concepts denote. Take, for instance, the central category of Marx's book: capital. Its material foundation – through which it relates back to the changing society – consists in the historically specific legal and civil spaces that make it possible to achieve returns and form monopolies. It is much the same with its opposite, "labor." This concept possesses a plethora of such material ties, for both its productivity, that is, its use value for society,[82] and the mode in which it is performed or provided depend to a great extent on society's institutions and normative rules. In addition, the distribution of wage labor is usually based on mechanisms of segregation between hierarchically differentiated groups. These groups are deeply rooted in the social structure of modern societies through the practices of "white" or "male" domination, which are effective at micro as well as macro levels.[83] Marx is unable to acknowledge the rootedness of social labor in institutional social structures because he decouples the concept of labor from its material roots. Finally, take the category of "exploitation," which Marx also seeks to explain in purely economic terms[84] but which also possesses a hidden material side that reaches deep into the social lifeworld. Whether the appropriation of surplus labor uses coercive means, say threats of physical punishment, rests on the pretense of patriarchal magnanimity, or takes an at least partially cooperative form by granting a degree of participation, makes a significant difference to the laborers concerned, and also to the productivity of the business. All the recent discussions in the critical sociology of labor about "manufacturing consent" or "labor process" concern aspects of this hidden material side of surplus value creation that is rooted in the lifeworld.[85] These brief remarks provide some support for the thesis that the double character that Marx attributes only to the category of the "commodity" is, in truth, possessed by all the concepts that guide his enquiry. All the economic phenomena he mentions are characterized by the fact that, like commodities, albeit to varying degrees, they have an economic, often even quantifiable, outside, and yet on the inside they possess a number of "symbiotic mechanisms," to use Luhmann's expression,[86] by which they remain closely entangled with the cultural and normative processes of their social environment.[87]

On this account, Marx's grave mistake was his gradual shift from using the concept of "bourgeois society" to refer to the capitalist market to using it to refer to modern society as a whole. Regardless of how daring or subversive it may have been, this shift made it impossible for Marx to study the capitalist economic process in the context of the full sweep of institutional forms that capitalism can take given the influence of changes in culture, institutionalized morality, and the law.[88] For Marx, within the new social formation the capitalist market no longer possesses the sort of social outside that Karl Polanyi tried to capture in terms of lifeworld concepts and the moral motivations contained within them, and which allowed Polanyi to explain the always existing possibility of resistance to unfettered market forces.[89] The decision Marx took toward the end of the 1850s to apply the method of Hegel's system to the systematic presentation of capitalism, which by that point he understood as a "system" and equated with society, only deepened his earlier mistake. For now he was forced to describe capital as a subject that works its way, step by step, through all social phenomena, with the result that his theory leaves no space for idiosyncratically formed social structures that are not economically determined – no space, even, for society as such. Marx's mistake was not that he tried to describe the movement of capital and the generalized exchange of equivalents as a process that threatens to take hold of all social interactions and make them conform to its own laws. On the contrary, the major achievement of his analysis of nineteenth-century capitalism was that, early on, it demonstrated the dynamic and power through which the imperative of capitalist accumulation would come to demand ever new niches for profitable exploitation, and in this way would endanger the civil conditions of democracy based on the rule of law. Under current social conditions – though these should not be seen as unchangeable – this process of capitalist accumulation has even led to the paradoxical result that, through privatization and the erosion of their legal core, welfare benefits, introduced as a countermeasure, are gradually becoming a new source of profit. Rather, Marx's mistake was that he did not see that the very same process remains tied throughout, as if by invisible threads, to the institutional relations of society. The moral climate, legal organization, and political constellations around these relations can influence the course of the capitalist process. The character of capitalist accumulation is determined at every point by the political, legal, and moral constitution of society – not, as Marx seems to have believed, the other way around.

Translated by Daniel Steuer

6

Three, Not Two, Concepts of Liberty
A proposal to enlarge our moral self-understanding

Even among those of us who are not altogether convinced by Isaiah Berlin's famous essay "Two Concepts of Liberty,"[1] it has become commonplace to adopt a distinction which largely coincides with the one he offered. On the one hand, we think that the culture of modernity adheres to a "negative" concept of freedom, which grants to the individual the widest possible sphere of protection from external intervention in the pursuit of purely personal interests. On the other hand, however, we are just as strongly convinced that individual freedom only truly exists when one orients one's actions according to reasons that one personally holds to be appropriate, and in this sense determines oneself. We sometimes adopt a distinction within this second, "positive" model of freedom between an "autonomous" and an "authentic" form of self-determination. This distinction serves to contrast individual action oriented according to moral norms, and individual action oriented toward the realization of one's own nature and the most individually experienced needs.[2] But such a differentiation nonetheless largely conforms to the more fundamental classification of our freedom into negative and positive variants. In the following, I would like to argue that this bifurcation of the concept of freedom, which has developed under Berlin's influence, is incomplete in a significant respect. The two models foreclose the possibility that the intentions of an agent can only be formed in reciprocal interaction between multiple subjects, and thus can be realized without coercion only by acting together. This idea cannot be captured by the now commonplace notion that individual freedom consists in the realization of one's own already existing or reflexively achieved intentions. Rather the realization of freedom should itself be thought of as a cooperative process; and only in the course of this process does it become clear which intentions should be realized.

I want to proceed first by illustrating with some well-known examples how we must understand such a form of cooperatively realized freedom. This first step should demonstrate that we have experience with this third category of "freedom" in our everyday lives, but that we lack the language to identify such experiences as a form of "freedom" (I). In the second part I want to recall briefly the philosophical tradition in which this idea of "social freedom," as I would like to call it, has always had a central place. Thus I hope to reveal that the aforementioned examples from our everyday lives have already been associated by some political philosophers with a third, separate category of freedom (II). Only in the last part do I want to delve into the systematic question of whether the model of freedom which I have suggested by example in fact designates a third concept, which does not conform to the traditional bifurcated understanding. Here my purpose is not only to describe the respects in which social freedom is distinct from the other two models of freedom, but also to explain why we cannot abandon this third concept in our self-understanding (III).[3]

I

I begin with an example from our political everyday lives in which the exercise of freedom should be easily recognizable. Consider our regular or only occasional participation in processes of democratic will-formation, when we join political discussions, call for protests, sign petitions, or merely distribute leaflets at demonstrations. What is immediately obvious about such actions is how difficult or even impossible it is to describe them with the traditional category of negative freedom, although we quite obviously perceive such cases as exercises of individual freedom. To be sure, in making political statements of this kind, we make use of a space that is legally protected from governmental interference, which allows us to proclaim our beliefs freely and without fear of coercion. But it is fairly misleading to think of the author of such opinions only as an isolated "I," separated from all others, in the way the negative model of freedom suggests. So too is it misguided to think that the action is already completed with the proclamation, and thus that the expression of an opinion is the final step in the exercise of freedom. The political belief that is expressed in public statements would be in some sense falsely understood if it were ascribed to the private resolution of the will of a solitary acting subject. The determination of the individual will would then be undertaken purely monologically, and directed toward a merely private realization of its content. This understanding of political expression fails to capture its true dynamics. When the subject contributes to political discourse, she refers in her expression to a chain of earlier statements, which she attempts to correct or improve, such that she can only appropriately be understood as a member of a previously constituted, self-reflexively given, and already present "We." This means that the exercise of the "free" action cannot be regarded as complete with the mere proclamation of her belief. For what the individual proposal aims at, and where it finds completion, is in the reaction of the addressed "We," or of its individual representatives, who once again attempt to correct or improve upon the beliefs of other participants with their own. This description suggests that the participants in democratic will-formation must be able to understand their respective statements of opinion as intertwining with one another in such a way that they cannot avoid assuming a "We" which they together sustain through their contributions.

Although we obviously have the tendency to interpret participation in democratic will-formation as an exercise of individual freedom, such freedom cannot readily be described as an exercise of merely negative freedom.[4] This is because the three distinguishing elements of negative freedom have little plausible application to such cases. The actor cannot be represented as a private subject who formulates the intentions of his actions by himself; nor is he "free" in carrying out his action only when other actors do not "arbitrarily" interfere; and, finally, his action is not complete as an exercise of freedom with the expression of his own opinion, but rather only temporally concludes if the other participants have reacted to it in a rationally comprehensible fashion. The actions of my fellow citizens therefore do not place an obstacle to my own free political act; nor do they merely constitute the conditions of its possibility. Rather their actions are so intrinsically interwoven with mine that it is difficult to speak of an individual act at all. It therefore seems that we can only realize this democratic freedom through a collaborative process, in which we understand our individual expressions of opinion as complementary contributions to a common project of identifying a common will.[5]

One reason why this "intersubjective" or "cooperative" structure of political freedom so easily falls out of view may be that we usually think of voting as the standard case of democratic participation. Thus it can seem as though freedom consists in the singular and secluded act of forming a private opinion about one's own preferences, and of secretly recording it without the influence of arbitrary intervention. This picture of democratic action falsely takes the part for the whole. John Dewey famously railed against this view because he saw that it masked the essential participatory element of democracy.[6] A myopic focus on voting fails to recognize that the casting of the ballot is preceded by public discussion, including open media coverage and thus the process of reciprocal influence. Such deliberative discussions are a constitutive rather than merely an incidental feature of democracy.[7] Taken in isolation, the casting of the ballot itself can perhaps be thought of according to the model of negative liberty. But this act is only a snapshot of a much more comprehensive process, which is meant to ensure that through appropriate instruments for the exchange of experience and opinion individual beliefs are not only aggregated, but are as far as possible bound together into a rational "general will." Even when such an agreement concerning the common good cannot be reached, because starkly divergent views predominate, the resulting conflict over the better interpretation of the general welfare must be described as a cooperative process. Whoever participates in these consensual or conflictual processes of identifying the public will can no longer imagine the related experiences of freedom and the absence of coercion according to the standard of implementing private interests with the least possible interference. To be able to formulate one's own intentions, one must be able to take up the perspective of others, and accept their potential corrective power. In this way democratic will-formation can be understood as a cooperative undertaking which serves the search for the common good.

So as not to create the misleading impression that only democratic will-formation resists description as an exercise of purely negative freedom, I want to give another well-known example from our everyday lives, which, despite its many distinguishing features, shares several common elements with political participation. Personal relationships of friendship and love may also be interpreted as exercises of freedom on the basis of their non-coercive quality and the attendant loosening of the boundaries of the self; but they resist description by the standard of the undisturbed realization of privately determined intentions. Even the first premise of a negative conception of freedom does not plausibly apply to this case: someone who is maintaining a sincere friendship or romantic relationship will understand his actions within this relationship as "free," but generally will form his intentions only in relation to the wishes and needs of his companion. The free action obviously emerges here not from interests or purposes anchored in the will of a solitary actor. But even if the negative concept of freedom were not so strongly associated with the presupposition of an isolated "I," it would still not adequately capture the structure of freedom within love or friendship. For not only are the interventions of other persons into one's own sphere of action not felt as limitations, which would conform to the principle that only "arbitrary" or "uncontrolled" interferences impair the exercise of negative freedom,[8] but also the wills of the participating persons are so attuned to and enmeshed with one another that talk of "intervention" loses its meaning. The limitation of one's own will with respect to the concrete other frequently rises to such a level that it becomes impossible to distinguish clearly and definitively one's own interests or intentions from those of the other. The aspirations of both persons overlap not only in certain respects, but permanently interpenetrate each other, so that their fulfillment can only be understood as a common concern.[9] Where, however, individual interests are melded with those of others, where "mine" and "yours" can no longer sufficiently be distinguished, the freedom of a person should no longer be measured according to whether her "own" intentions can be realized without arbitrary interference.

It should already be clear that the examples of democratic will-formation and personal relationships have more in common than it would appear at first glance. The point at which the negative model of freedom fails is nearly identical in each case. In both democratic participation and personal relationships, it is unclear what constitutes one's "own" will, in respect to which the unrestricted realization of the free act of the individual could be assessed. In the case of democratic will-formation, a subject only understands her political actions correctly if she thinks from the concurrent perspective of a "We," the permanent renewal of which she contributes to with her own beliefs. But because of the necessity of remaining open to other perspectives, the aspect of these beliefs which is truly proper to the individual subject is only something preliminary and tentative. The beliefs therefore cannot accurately be taken as a stable output variable that is used to measure the unhindered realization of freedom. Something similar is true in the case of friendship and romantic relationships, in which the boundary between one's "own" intention and that of the other fall away to an even greater extent. Because of the shared perspective of a "We," the plans and the aims of the other are implicated in the determination of one's own will, such that the aspirations of both participants become intertwined. Both in such personal relationships and in democratic political life, the negative model of freedom is inappropriate to describe the kind of freedom individuals practice. In these social contexts, freedom consists in an unforced cooperation, which assumes a higher degree of consensus concerning the aims of action than the negative model of freedom is capable of accommodating.

One might object to the argument up to this point that these examples, even if they do not represent instances of negative freedom, can nonetheless be understood in terms of positive freedom. Since we draw upon this second category to clarify certain aspects of our normative culture, by speaking, for example, of moral autonomy, it would make sense to attempt to understand democratic participation and love and friendship in terms of the other model of freedom Berlin put forward. But this attempt, too, quickly reveals itself to be inappropriate for articulating the kind of freedom we realize in these cases. With concepts of positive freedom, we no longer describe an individual action as "free" insofar as there are no arbitrary, external obstacles to its exercise. Rather the freedom of an action is understood in terms of its realization of higher ends or values – whether this should mean agreement with moral norms, as for Kant, or the actualization of one's own natural needs, as in the romantic tradition.[10] As long as we understand freedom, however, only as an activity performed by an individual subject, in which it practices a given capability (such as norm orientation or the articulation of needs), then the free character of the activities described in the examples above has not been adequately disclosed. For their distinctiveness consists in the fact that multiple subjects must act for one another in order for each to experience her activity from her own individual perspective as a common practice of freedom. There is indeed some overlap here with the idea of positive freedom, insofar as citizens or lovers or friends must orient themselves to certain ideals – such as the good of egalitarian popular sovereignty or the good of trusting intimacy – in order to act for one another in the appropriate sense. But it is this "for-one-another" which constitutes the entire difference between these forms of freedom and the traditional idea of positive freedom. For in democratic will-formation and intimate relationships, the good that is striven for can only be realized when multiple subjects carry out uncoerced actions, which reciprocally complement one another and thus enable free collaboration.

To be sure, this suggestion could also mean that the difference between positive freedom and the third form of freedom we have been searching for only consists in the kind of good pursued, rather than in the mode of exercise itself. Whereas in the case of positive freedom goods and values are searched for which are "individual," in the sense that they are only realizable on account of individual capabilities, these distinctive cases of freedom could be said to concern the pursuit of goods or values that have a "collective" character, because their realization is only possible through the united efforts of several subjects. Then we would take democratic will-formation or friendship or love as representing collective versions of positive freedom – a possibility that Berlin occasionally touches upon in his famous essay, if only in order to discard it because of the inherent danger of its despotic misuse.[11] The reasons for his rejection certainly make it plain that he conceives the collective exercise of positive freedom by precisely the same measure as its individual enactment: namely, that the members of a homogeneous group must all perform the same action, in order to realize in consonance those values and goods the achievement of which is the goal of freedom. But such a picture does not in any way correspond to the kind of freedom we have discerned in democratic will-formation or romance and friendship. The participants in these cases do not behave like the members of a group who have been forced into line. To the contrary, they must always renegotiate amongst themselves how they would like to apportion the responsibilities resulting from the shared value orientation, and thus assign reciprocally complementary contributions to the common project. The "We" that must be assumed between citizens or lovers or friends is therefore something totally different from the collective subject Isaiah Berlin had in mind with his idea of positive freedom. In the collective positive freedom Berlin described, one is committed to an ethical end which guides the action contributions of all individuals uniformly.

In the cases we have considered, participants are indeed oriented toward certain values, but must continually renegotiate the form in which common tasks are to be distributed in light of their ongoing reinterpretation of common aims. Alongside the limitation of his will with respect to those of others, the individual nonetheless retains a right to have a say in how the relevant activities should intertwine with and reciprocally complement one another. In democratic participation it thus becomes clear that the participants in the cooperative production of a common will can always choose whether they want the role of speaker or listener, of demonstrator or spectator. Likewise, in the case of love or friendship, the participants recognize the possibility of motivating one another to take on a new distribution of tasks and obligations. The participants in these examples are involved in the commonly assumed "We" in a different way than the members of the collective which Berlin imagined as the bearer of a supra-individual process of realizing positive freedom. They retain a right to have a say in how they want their intentions intertwined with one another in the pursuit of a goal that is constantly redefined collaboratively, and thus to behold in the freedom of others a condition of their own freedom. We can therefore provisionally conclude that the collective version of the concept of positive freedom is inapposite to capture the form of cooperative freedom which is evidently performed in the social practices of democratic participation or love and friendship. In these cases, my freedom is grounded upon the unforced intermeshing of our activities. On this basis, I can envisage the other not as a limitation but rather as a requirement for the realization of my strivings, without thereby giving up the possibility of co-determining the goal to be achieved, and the form of this intermeshing. Before I pursue this train of thought further, I first want to examine whether one can find suggestions of such a third, social or intersubjective model of freedom in the philosophical tradition.

II

The thesis that the form of social praxis exemplified by democratic will-formation and personal relationships constitutes an independent category of freedom has been an undercurrent in political-philosophic thinking since Hegel. Hegel himself believed that the two forms of freedom, which Berlin would later label as positive and negative, did not reach the highest level of freedom which ought to be available to members of modern society. Instead, he conceived of a third stage of freedom, which he called "objective freedom," the meaning of which remains contested by scholars.[12] The basic thought Hegel proceeded from is woven into the terminology of his philosophical thinking, but can be rendered independent of this framework in a much simpler form: If a person's individual action is conceived of as free only in the negative sense that there can be no impediments to the exercise of the will in the external world, such a conception fails to consider that the intentions underlying the action can only truly be freely formed when they too are independent from causal force and thus anchored in self-posited reasons. Kant, following Rousseau, had similarly concluded that the will can be free only when its content is determined by rational considerations. Hegel argues that this Kantian view, however, leads to the equally peculiar consequence that there is no guarantee that self-determined intentions can actually be realized in the objective world. From the defects of these two concepts of freedom, Hegel developed a synthetic view, according to which the complete idea of individual freedom would only be achieved if the self-posited resolutions of the will can be thought of as furthered or "willed" in, or even by, reality. For Hegel this was possible in those "ethical" spheres of modern society in which the freely chosen intentions of participants intertwine with one another, complement one another, and thus find "willed" fulfillment within social reality.

It is not yet altogether clear from this rather formal, broad-brushed presentation what Hegel meant to convey with his idea of a third, "objective" freedom. Here the different interpretations of Hegel depend upon how strongly Hegel is thought to remain influenced by Kant's conception of freedom. According to Robert Brandom, Hegel only "socializes" the Kantian idea of "positive" freedom, in that he makes the ability of individuals to bind themselves to norms dependent upon the recognition of a community of others whose recognitive authority is also freely recognized by the individual herself. The resulting reciprocal recognition constitutes the normative horizon in which a subject makes use of his positive freedom to renew the shared cultural potential through her own "expressive" initiatives.[13] This interpretation converges with the idea of social freedom I have hinted at so far, insofar as the core of the Hegelian idea is understood as connecting individual freedom to the assumption of the perspective of a "We." But the freedom which is realized through this participation in a community of subjects reciprocally recognizing one another's autonomy is, in Brandom's interpretation of

Hegel, understood only as an individual exercise, as the expressive act of the individual who lends a new accent to the shared culture. In contrast I believe that Hegel understood the freedom made possible by reciprocal recognition as itself a common or cooperative practice. According to Hegel, it is only by complementing each other that the intentions of the individuals can achieve the individually (subjectively) desired conclusion. Thus freedom in its "objective" sense is not something an individual subject can perform on his own, but rather is something he is only able to achieve in regulated collective action with others.

I have similar reservations with regard to the profound interpretation which Frederick Neuhouser has given to the Hegelian idea of "objective" freedom, the subjective dimension of which he attempts to reconstruct as "social freedom." According to his interpretation, Hegel sets out in his *Philosophy of Right* from the idea that a complete concept of individual freedom must comprise all the institutional requirements which allow the members of society to articulate their particular identities without coercion in the external form of social roles, and thus to accept institutionally established paths of self-realization.[14] Here too individual freedom is linked with the assumption of the perspective of a "We," which makes it possible to understand specific, freedom-enabling institutions as rooted in common interests. But, as for Brandom, Neuhouser understands the practice of "socially" conditioned freedom as an individual act which every participant should be able to perform for herself without requiring the reciprocal action of another subject.

In a similar vein, Robert Pippin interprets Hegel's concept of freedom as referring primarily to the rational agency of the individual subject, though he acknowledges that such freedom is for Hegel only possible in the context of social institutions that provide individual agents with the appropriate recognitive status.[15] According to my interpretation, however, Hegel is driving at a much stronger intersubjective idea with his conception of freedom: the individual can only realize the freedom which is available through certain institutions when he acts in cooperation with others whose intentions make up an element of his own. Not only is it necessary for Hegel that the exercise of individual freedom proceeds from the taking-up of the perspective of the "We," which either makes possible the constitution of a community of recognition or a common commitment to freedom guaranteeing institutions; in addition, such an exercise of freedom must be undertaken with the expectation that the other members of the community will carry out actions which correspond to my intentions or needs. Only this doubled intersubjectivity, as both a condition and as an end to be produced from my free action, makes it possible to understand why Hegel again and again thought of love as the paradigm for his own idea of freedom. Here, according to the famous formula, one is "at home with oneself in the other," in the sense that one can understand the actions of the other as requirements for the realization of one's own, self-determined intentions.[16]

As the famous formulation "to be at home with oneself in the other" already suggests, Hegel intended far more with his idea of "objective" freedom than to identify for therapeutic purposes certain possibilities of unforced and thus free collaboration in modern society.[17] Ultimately he wanted to construe our entire relationship to the world in terms of the recognition of our own posited ends in the Other of objective reality, and thus also to underscore idealistically our freedom in relation with the natural environment. For our purposes, however, it suffices to limit ourselves to the accomplishment of freedom in the social world, since this is the context which would be elaborated by later authors, who would furnish it with new aims. Already in early French socialism's critique of market relationships, which were expanding at that time, there was an idea of freedom which can only be appropriately understood with reference to its roots in Hegel's *Philosophy of Right*. Unlike the understanding of freedom in classical liberal law, which is charged with the legitimation of purely private interests in the capitalist market, freedom is understood in the writings of Fourier and Proudhon as a solidary activity of being-for-another, which both thought was manifest in the unforced cooperation between craftsmen. Just like Hegel, Proudhon suggests that individual freedom must be thought of not merely "as a barrier" but rather as a "help" to the freedom of all others.[18]

Hegel's concept of freedom appears even more starkly in the early writings of Marx.[19] The young Marx sketches the image of a social community where the members no longer work "against each other" but rather "for one another." Here we find the guiding idea of socialism, namely, that one can speak of members of society having real freedom only when the actions of individuals complement one another in such a way that the freedom of the one is the precondition for the freedom of every other.[20] As for his French predecessors, the playful interweaving of action in the cooperation of craftsmen serves as Marx's historical model. According to Marx's conception, the subjects in such interactions are "free" in a particular way, because each can learn from the other participants that his contributions to the coordinated plans for action are acknowledged and seen as necessary and welcome complements to the others' intentions. The idea of "reciprocally complementing" one another makes it clear how much Marx's cooperative model owes to the Hegelian idea of freedom. The attempt to imagine the social integration of a future society entirely according to the measure of such unforced economic cooperation, namely as a community of subjects working for one another, constitutes in my view the core ethical impulse of socialism. Here the social form of the exercise of freedom, which Hegel only saw at work in individual spheres of modern societies, is carried over without differentiation into the entire society, in which the members are thought of as cooperative partners who reciprocally strive to satisfy the needs of one another. I do not want to go further into the difficulties that attended this original vision of socialism, as it ignored the requirements of the functional differentiation of modern society. For my purposes it is necessary only to recall an undercurrent of political-philosophical thought in which the idea of a distinctively social freedom was already thought of as valid in the nineteenth century.

In the following century, a similar thought was taken up by Hannah Arendt, who understood democratic action to express the original intersubjectivity of human freedom. Whereas for Marx labor itself was seen as a potential context for social freedom, for Arendt only in the political sphere, understood as a realm of public contestation over the common good, are we free, because there the individual sheds his private concerns and must widen his previously egocentric perspective in collaborative activity.[21]

While it is certainly not the case that Arendt's concept of social freedom was inspired by Hegel, his influence is clearly apparent in the last of the representatives of the philosophical tradition of freedom I will mention: John Dewey, under the direct influence of Hegel,[22] argued throughout his life that individual freedom is falsely understood if it is exclusively understood as a capacity or possession of a solitary subject. Rather, the degree of our freedom increases when we participate in socially cooperative activity, because we are better able to realize our intentions and wishes the more various the interactions in which we reckon with the responses and contributions of others. For Dewey as for Hegel, the true form for the exercise of individual freedom is represented in contributions to the distributed labor of realizing a common aim, because in such projects the realization of my "will" is also intended by others. I thus want to conclude my short reminiscence of the largely forgotten tradition of social freedom with a citation from Dewey, in which the underlying idea of social freedom is beautifully expressed: "Liberty," according to the American pragmatist, "is that secure release and fulfillment of personal potentialities which takes place only in rich and manifold association with others: the power to be an individualized self making a distinctive contribution and enjoying in its own way the fruits of association."[23]

III

Adherents of Berlin's conception would surely object to this plea for a third, social concept of freedom that it has the fatal propensity to confuse the value of freedom with other ideals shared by humanity. Just as little as we should surreptitiously smuggle the goal of social justice into the concept of individual freedom, we may not underhandedly furnish it with the aim of coexistence in solidarity, for both efforts would ignore the irreducible pluralism of our values and deny the possible conflicts between them.[24] In this last part of my essay, I want to forestall this objection by once more working out the aspect of freedom in the aforementioned patterns of interaction, in order to prove, first, that these do in fact concern a separate kind of freedom. Next, I want to show that the exercise of this freedom in or through cooperative actions need not be bound to the common pursuit of the same aim, but rather is compatible with the achievement of completely divergent values. For this reason, the constant factor in such practices is the particular form of social freedom, whereas the values that are pursued thereby can vary and thus ought not be confused with the underlying shape of freedom itself.

If we look back again at the previously presented examples of social freedom – democratic will-formation, love and friendship, and finally, for socialists, economic production – the first remarkable element is that the participating subjects must understand themselves as members of a "We" without, however, losing their individual independence. To be sure, the successful performance of actions is bound up with the assumption of complementary actions on the part of others, so that the participants reciprocally take up the perspective of the "We." But this in no way suggests that they together constitute a collective which acts like a univocal, merely enlarged "I." With Philip Pettit, we can label the social ontological position in which this intersubjective exercise of freedom can best be grasped as "holistic individualism." This concept assumes that the realization of certain human capacities requires social groupings and thus entities that can only be described holistically.[25] But this does not in any way preclude the existence of independent individuals. Why, nonetheless, should individual actions that presuppose a community of cooperative subjects be understood as a particular class of freedom? What is so distinctive about such unforced intertwining of actions that makes it justifiable to introduce a new category of freedom alongside the existing models of negative and positive freedom?

Here, in my view, Hegel and Dewey point in the direction of an answer, because they each point to different aspects of the same phenomenon. Both are of the opinion that the distinctiveness of the reciprocal process of unforced intertwining of ends lies in the fact that the contribution of each is experience as willed by the other. In contrast to all other actions, which can be understood as either "negatively" or "positively" free, this class of cooperative actions shows that we can each assume the consent of the other and thus can carry out our own action with a consciousness of unforced responsiveness. Not only is there no expectation of arbitrary interference from partners to the interaction; more than this, one can trust that what one freely does will also be freely wished by the other or all other participants. In more systematic terms, the uncoerced nature of a communicative action is here increased because both sides know of each other not only that they perform a freely chosen action, but also, that the carrying out of this action fulfills an autonomously generated intention of the other. Hegel emphasizes above all the cognitive side of the exercise of social freedom as it should exist in the reflexive structure of commonly shared knowledge. Dewey much more starkly stresses the affective side, in the enjoyment of experiencing how one's own actions are seen by others as preparing the way for completing their own ongoing actions.

The exercise of such a form of freedom certainly requires, as already indicated by the accompanying consciousness of a "We," that the participants pursue common aims or values, because these common aims and values require them, in forming their own intentions, to take the intentions of the others into consideration. Each participant limits herself to carrying out such actions which she knows will contribute to furthering their shared aims. Whereas positive freedom is related to the assumption of a reflexive act of self-determination or self-articulation, social freedom is bound to the assumption of the development of a common will. Where such a common will is not present and the perspective of a "We" cannot be taken up by the subjects, it is not possible to form in their consciousness an agreed-upon scheme of cooperation which would allow them to act "for one another" through their complementary contributions. To this extent the idea of social freedom, unlike the concept of negative freedom, but like the positive concept, is a selective category of human freedom. It does not designate a general, unconditional capacity of subjects, but rather one which is bound to the existence of certain social conditions, namely, belonging to a community of ethically concordant members.

This assumption of membership in an ethical community cannot, however, be misunderstood to mean that the participants have completely lost their capacity for personal initiative and independence. Why this cannot be so can now be more precisely formulated, because we have learned that in the case of social freedom one's own contributory actions must fulfill the autonomously generated wishes or intentions of one's fellow participants. This assumption can remain valid only so long as I concede to the other the opportunity to place the negotiated scheme of cooperative action into question when her individual needs, interests, or positions have changed. Because such a claim must be reciprocally acknowledged, so that all participants can understand their contributions as fulfilling the autonomous wishes of others, the exercise of social freedom must be bound to the assumption of the recognition of the claim of every other to co-determine the commonly practiced schema of cooperation. Though social freedom can be exercised only in the pursuit of common aims, the determinate content of these aims always remains open for revision and contestation by the members of the "We."

This "right to have a say" – or better, this recognized claim – cannot itself be understood according to the standard of "negative" or "positive" freedom, as though another form of individual freedom protruded from outside into the exercise of social freedom. What the participants invoke when they place the previously agreed-upon scheme of cooperation into question is the result neither of a purely private consideration of interest nor of purely individual self-determination, as Kant had in mind. Rather, they discover the content of their will against the normative background of jointly entered responsibilities, in order to check whether their wills remain in agreement with the negotiated scheme of cooperation. The difference here is that the participants in this process of discovery do not proceed from an ethical null point, as suggested by the models of negative or positive liberty, but rather from the acceptance of responsibilities they already have with regard to others in the pursuit of common aims. Thus they will bring to the table only those suggestions for adapting the scheme of cooperation, which appear necessary in light of their changed needs or interests, to the extent that these are compatible with collectively settled goals. The claim to have a say in determining the distribution of burdens and responsibilities in romantic relationships, friendships, or democratic communities is not externally imposed, but is rather an intrinsic element of the social freedom that the participants together enjoy in such relationships.

These considerations lead to the last point of my essay, in which I want to come back to the question of whether the suggestion of a third, social model of freedom commits the mistake of confusing the value of freedom with the value of solidarity. Such a reproach immediately suggests itself because the participants can allow their intentions seamlessly to intertwine with one another only insofar as they together strive for the common goal of solidarity grounded in trust, whether this takes the form of sexual intimacy in love, the reciprocal support of friendship, or the egalitarian elaboration of a common will in a democratic community. The reason why this works for all contributors – so the objection runs – is the unified realization of the good of solidarity and not, as I would have it, the value of a particular kind of freedom. However, this objection requires more information about what the value of solidary cohesion should truly consist in. And thus one confronts the true difficulty, namely, that although one can identify such positive experiences as reciprocal trust or mutual aid, this does not serve to explain the special quality such solidarity has for us. What difference would it make if the various forms of solidary relationships drew their value for participants from the fact that they constituted different variants of social freedom? Then that which makes love, friendship, and democratic collaboration worth striving for could not simply be explained by reference to the good of solidarity. Rather solidarity would draw its value for us from the fact that it allows us to exercise in different ways a form of freedom

in which others are not experienced, as in the usual case, as limitations, but rather as conditions of the possibility of forming and
realizing our own intentions. We strive for solidary relationships
not for their own sake, but rather for the particular kind of freedom
which they embody in various forms. What attracts us to solidary
experiences, and what makes these kinds of relationships worth
striving for, is an experience which is precluded in other forms of
social life: namely to see, in the reflection of our own intentions and
wishes in the complementary intentions and wishes of our counter-
parts, that we can only realize them by acting-for-one-another.

These considerations allow us to conclude that we are not able
to assess the value of solidary relationships without reference to
the positive experience of social freedom. But beyond this, the idea
of social freedom represents the overarching evaluative concept
for the special cases of solidary relationships. For what makes the
experience of solidarity valuable for us can be explained only with
reference to "finding-oneself-again-in-others," which is what is
meant by the idea of social freedom. "Social freedom" is related
to solidarity as type to token: The various forms of solidarity are
empirical manifestations of that which makes "acting-for-another"
into a human good. Then, however, the objection no longer obtains
that the idea of social freedom falsely confuses the value of freedom
with that of solidarity. Precisely the opposite is the case: We are
totally unable to comprehend the value of certain social forms of
being-together unless, alongside the concepts of "negative" and
"positive" freedom, we have at our disposal a third concept of
freedom which makes it clear to us that we strive for such forms of
being-together for the sake of experiencing the complete absence
of coercion. The distinctiveness of this third form of freedom is
the complete withering away of all hindrances which the intentions of other subjects generally pose for me. Only here do I find
in the social world a sort of "home," which Hegel already knew
could exist only where I am at home with myself in others. Let me
conclude therefore by noting that under the historical conditions
of the increasing juridification and economization of our culture,
and thus of the rise of a purely "negatively" understood freedom,
it is high time to recover the buried tradition of the idea of "social"
freedom.[26]

Translated by Blake Emerson

Part II

Deformations of Social Freedom

Part II

Determinations of Social Freedom

7

The Diseases of Society
Approaching a nearly impossible concept

For better or worse, it has long been an integral part of our practical and ethical self-understanding to talk about "diseases of society"; we seem to be convinced that one can speak of pathologies or systematic disorders not only when it comes to organisms and individual psyches but also with reference to entire collectives or even societies.[1] Eventually, the possibility of thus ascribing an internal principle of intact functioning to the collectivity itself was opened already by Plato in *Republic* (*Πολιτεία*), his famous dialogue on the ideal constitution of a free state. Plato paves the way for a mutual transferability of psychological and political vocabularies as soon as he sets about studying the body of the state in a manner analogous to the singular person in order to draw normative conclusions about the principles of the just social constitution from well-organized psychic powers (in the fourth book of his work). Thus the prospect of talking about a "diseased," "ill," or pathological society also seems to be given.[2]

Since then, the idea that a social system in its entirety can fall ill has become endemic in all discourses on the forms of ideal and deteriorating collectives. It is not only found in works of fiction – one needs only to recall the writings of such authors as Tolstoy or Chekhov, Flaubert or Thomas Mann – but also in the works of the philosophical and sociological tradition, where it has gained currency at least since Rousseau's famous *Second Discourse on the Origin and Basis of the Inequality among Men*.[3] Among the many perils of this manner of speaking, there was, from the very beginning – clinging to the idea of the diseased society – the risk of its being used arbitrarily to degrade other communities.

Precisely such a misuse of the term, as in declaring the community of the alleged enemy "degenerate" or "alien" and thus "ill," was especially perfidious in twentieth-century German history. This is, however, far from being the only nuisance that needs to worry us about the attempt to apply the concept of disease to entire societies.

Inherent to the idea itself has always been the tremendous difficulty that it is not really clear who precisely is supposed to have fallen ill in the first place: Is it only some sufficient number of singular persons? Is it the collective understood as a macro-subject? Or is it "society" itself as having been encroached upon by a particular disorganization of its social institutions in their functional efficiency to such an extent that one can confidently speak of a distinctively social "disease"? For all three alternative attributions – that is, the sporadic individuals with the sum of their illnesses, the collective with its own particular clinical syndrome, and society itself as fallen ill – sufficient instances can be found in the corresponding literature. Thus, for instance, Freud and Sartre speak explicitly of the "collective" or "social neurosis" and thereby conceive of the homogeneous group as the bearer of social diseases.[4] The sociologist Émile Durkheim, by contrast, is referring to a functional inefficiency of the societal whole when he is talking about social "anomie" or "pathology."[5] And, finally, most of those who today make use of the idea probably have hardly anything more in mind than a certain number of ill individuals infected by social conditions. The many attempts and suggestions to speak, not in a merely figurative sense but quite literally, about the "diseases" of a society, have been matched by the many conceptions of *who* is supposed to have been stricken by the disease in question.

In order to find a way out of the conceptual perplexities lying at the very heart of this way of talking, it might be helpful to take a new look at Alexander Mitscherlich's attempt to come to terms with the subject matter. Mitscherlich, who still is very well known in Germany but probably less so in the Anglo-Saxon world, was a leading psychoanalyst and social psychologist in the period after World War II; he was the first to uncover the horrendous role many physicians played within the terror regime of the Nazi government, and he later became the director of the Sigmund Freud Institute in Frankfurt am Main. Among his many studies are the influential research on the incapacity of the German population to mourn the Holocaust directly after the war and many essays on social psychological tendencies within Western culture. It is my hope that by basing my reflections on one of his most important articles, his work will become more familiar to the English-speaking world.

Alexander Mitscherlich begins his essay on the "diseases of society" by making clear why the social causes of certain symptoms demand renewed scholarly attention.[6] He begins by pointing out that an increasing number of the patients he treats as a physician or as a therapist are suffering from relatively "shapeless" symptoms, such as frequent dizziness, sweating, and sleeplessness, for which a diffuse "impairment of performance" (*"Leistungsversagen"*) seems to offer the only available diagnosis.[7] So far, all attempts to explain these dubious symptoms by reference to purely bodily events have failed, and one is obliged to conclude that the cause for these phenomena might be found in psychic constellations – namely, in "experiential disorders." However, as soon as such emotive tensions or psychic irritations make themselves visible as conditioning factors in the diagnosis, Mitscherlich argues, the physician has no choice but to also take the entire "social environment" of the patient into account. This is because disorders of individual experience – that is, in reality control and coping with anxiety – can only be traced back to some sort of deficiency in the integration processes of the individual into society: to something being wrong in the relation between individuation and social environment.

Following these introductory remarks, Mitscherlich backs up the general conclusion, to which he believes himself to be entitled, by briefly recollecting how Freud, given completely different symptoms (psychoneurosis), also found himself bound to include societal processes into the diagnosis: if a specific class of illnesses, which, lacking sufficient physiological explanation, seems to be caused by psychic disorders and to occur increasingly among the members of society, then adjustment problems between the individual and the society must be seen as a contributing factor. Otherwise, it is difficult to explain how so many members of society can be stricken by the same symptoms at the same time. Thus, it seems appropriate to say "diseases of society" are making these individuals, in fact, fall ill.[8]

Before I follow up on this Mitscherlichian line of thought and ask how to measure such social functional disorders, it might perhaps be appropriate to draw some initial conclusions with regard to our general theme. At first, Mitscherlich ties the existence of a social disease to the existence of a conspicuous number of the members of society suffering from symptoms of a psychic abnormality to such a degree that they consult in droves physicians or therapists. Without this first indicator of a suffering from psychic functional impairment, experienced en masse, there seems to be no reason, in Mitscherlich's picture, to look for deeper disturbances in the process of social integration. Similarly, for Freud, whose cultural diagnoses clearly set the example for Mitscherlich's inquiry, the neurologists first need to register a rapid increase in a specific class of only psychologically explainable illnesses before the sociologically invested analyst can go on to search for their causes in the societal apparatus. Without his initial therapeutic discovery of a modern form of nervous illness among the members of the bourgeoisie, above all among women, Freud would not have found it necessary to reflect on the harmful effects of the characteristically modern tightening of sexual morals.[9]

However, this very first premise – the claim that "diseases of society" initially must be reflected in the psychic suffering of a sufficiently large fragment of society's members – is all but self-evident. At least two considerations speak against establishing an all too intimate bond between some conspicuous tendencies of social life that might strike one as pathological and the symptoms of a widespread illness among individuals.

First, there might be cases of merely vague indications of a social discontent, or even simply a diffuse prevailing social atmosphere, giving enough reason to infer to dubious one-sidedness or friction in social life, without their having to find direct expression in personal disorders experienced as suffering and identified in terms of an "illness." Take the propensity for private consumerism, for instance, that Hannah Arendt held as pivotal for the tendencies of a modern "world alienation" because of its accompanying growing disinterest in communication about public concerns.[10] Or take the growth in egocentric attitudes due to the lapse of bonds of solidarity that Émile Durkheim held as a symptom of anomic disintegration.[11] In both cases we are confronted by examples of "diseases" in our society that seem to have no influence on individuals' perception of private health and that as such cannot have been reflected in the therapeutic findings of physicians.

Second, neither can the opposite case be ruled out. The medical indicators of the increase of certain exclusively psychologically interpretable symptoms might not allow conclusions to be drawn that some significant pathology or characteristic functional disorder is at play in the patients' social environment. This might be the case, for example, in a social context where declaring a certain level of psychic suffering means gaining social distinction, as it is taken as expressing a particular degree of ambition or some form of admirable self-sacrifice.

Furthermore, it is also possible that physicians and therapists at a certain point in time come to strongly corresponding verdicts in their diagnoses of psychic illnesses only because they let themselves be dazzled by a trendy new interpretive framework. The analysts, then, without further ado, bring quite different symptoms that are otherwise hard to grasp under one general heading. Moreover, such feedback effects of short-lived interpretive keys that initially look very promising might explain why, for some decades already, every single prophesy of a particular widespread contemporary psychic illness so quickly gets replaced by the next one (narcissism, borderline, depression, burnout).

In light of all these objections and considerations, it seems an obvious conclusion that the very first premise in Freud's and Mitscherlich's attempts to define "diseases of society" cannot withstand the criticism that we ought not to assume that the appearance of a vast number of people suffering from psychic illnesses, as the physicians might diagnose them in consultation, presents a necessary condition for determining functional disorders of social integration. The connection, then, between medical diagnoses of individual psychic illnesses and the discovery of societal "diseases" is much looser than Freud and Mitscherlich wanted to believe. The physicians and therapists might not get things right, and individuals must not necessarily suffer from the pathologies that can be hypothetically found in their social environment.

Nevertheless, the second premise, on which Mitscherlich and Freud are basing their arguments, seems much more convincing. Regarding the problem of attribution – to whom these illnesses are to be ascribed – both are arguing for the strong thesis that diseases of society are separate phenomena, to be found solely at the level of society itself, not at the level of its individual members. Neither Mitscherlich nor Freud make the mistake of transferring the illnesses they diagnose in a multitude of cases of individuals to the higher level of the societal organization simply in order then to speak of a "neurotic" or "performance-impaired" society. They never endorsed the idea that social pathologies would present nothing but the generalized or extended psychic disorders of the members of society. On the contrary, both perceive society as an entity *sui generis*, whose potential functional disorders also have to be of another categorical kind than the illnesses that might strike singular persons during their lifetime. The "diseases" of society are to be understood as the causes of individuals' illnesses, but between these two terms stands an ontological difference prohibiting the use of one and the same psychological or psychoanalytical language in both cases.

Thus, Mitscherlich and Freud (at least Freud as we know him from his studies on "modern nervous illness") feel themselves obliged to switch to a social-theoretical vocabulary in their inquiries as soon as they turn to investigating the social causes of the psychic illnesses previously diagnosed by them in consultation. On this second level – that is, the level of a theory of social integration – the sociologically invested analyst must determine the "diseases" or functional disorders typical of his times and society by means of independent categories; and once the analyst has found the key to such a diagnosis of pathologies, then he has thereby also defined the social conditions that explain why so many of his contemporaries suffer from one and the same psychic disorder.

Now that we have finally reached an overall view of Freud's and Mitscherlich's argumentative logic, it seems appropriate to return once more to the problems of attribution I mentioned at the outset. Against this background, it is much easier to consider the pros and cons of the diverse options for entities to which these "diseases" might be attributed. If the attribution will be understood such that it is merely the members of society who are stricken by the functionally disordered social "disease," then a clearly false course has been taken in the inquiry: such a "disease" of society must imply more than the mere number of individuals suffering from the same symptoms and located in the same social environment.

In order to speak of pathologies or diseases of social life, what is required is a transition to the independent organizational unit of society, which is irreducible to the sum of its individual members' behavior. This applies to the idea of "collective neurosis" as well, providing that the idea is to denote something more than the mere enumeration of individual persons' psychic disorders. It might, then, be intelligible against the background of a holistic conception of individuals developing an abnormal, neurotic, or else disturbed behavior only because and insofar as they act with each other in groups and masses and are subject to the peculiar laws of the collective. Nor in the case of such collective phenomena, however, have we entered the level on which we can in fact talk about the pathologies of society. Rather, such language requires, as we have already seen, a perspective on functional disorders damaging the society as a whole, at the subtle junction of individuation and social integration. Individuals will not be able to conceive of themselves as cooperating, associated members of a publicly tangible society if something goes wrong in these processes. Thus, we can preliminarily speak of a societal disease or pathology.

Still, what seems to be true in Freud's and Mitscherlich's first premise (the assumption of an intimate bond between such pathologies and individual symptoms) is that without noticing anything odd or irritating about social life, one would hardly come to think of looking into potential sources of such irritations in societal functional disturbances at all. There would be no reason to give thought to potential "diseases" of society if the failures of individual socialization did not generally reflect themselves in behavioral abnormalities of the members of society. Hannah Arendt and Émile Durkheim, to draw a parallel to this alternative theory tradition once again, are both motivated toward a diagnosis of pathologies because they perceive destructive and disturbing behavioral patterns in their social environment; for Arendt the observed behavior is the restless propensity to mere consumption of commodities, and for Durkheim it is the tendency toward moral isolation and disintegration of the individual. However, such abnormalities display a lower degree of visibility than those symptoms by which therapists or physicians diagnose an individual's illness. In Arendt's case, the behavioral phenomena provoking the diagnoses are residing on a clinically inconspicuous level of productive, positive action; that is, the pleasure-invoking expenditure of financial means for the acquisition of quickly consumable things.

Freud's and Mitscherlich's mistake, then, does not lie in binding the initial suspicion that something might be pathological about society itself to destructive behavioral tendencies among the society's members, but rather in restricting these tendencies to such psychic illnesses as lend themselves to be diagnosed by physicians. In contrast, one ought to hold on to the insight of the Arendtian and Durkheimian tradition that societal abnormalities, which raise suspicion about something being pathological, can also consist of behavioral patterns that cause no individual suffering and thus also do not necessarily constitute psychic disorders. That widespread excessive craving for recognition or *amour propre*, which led Rousseau to reflect on a potential pathology of bourgeois society,[12] along with the obsessive engagement with sexuality and its perversions, which gave Foucault reason to speculate about a bizarre one-sidedness of the modern relation to self[13] – these were virtually creative, performance-stimulating social phenomena that in both thinkers still succeeded in raising the initial suspicion about social pathology.

Admittedly, such initial observations can only prove themselves to be successful by actually providing a key to a convincing diagnosis of functional disorders in the social apparatus – to "diseases" of society. If the described behavioral tendencies lack any sufficient contact surface for examining whether social integration really does fail, then they must be taken as the outcomes of an overly sophisticated, idiosyncratic power of observation. Freud and Mitscherlich cannot be blamed for not having at least tried such a path to social analysis; as we can see, both struggle in their analyses to trace back their initial clinical findings to causes rooted in a functional disorder of society itself. In a second step, I want to consider the question: how far Freud and Mitscherlich reach and whether or not there might be found more attractive alternatives to their approaches.

For Freud, still very much a child of the Victorian era, the social-theoretical solution to the rapidly increasing psychoneuroses unfolding before his eyes still seemed relatively simple and clear. In his essay on "modern nervous illness," he develops the idea that the conspicuous symptoms of compulsive acts and hysteria are to be explained by reference to socially institution-alized sexual morals, which, by demanding strict monogamy, offer too little room for the satisfaction of libidinous drives. The argument is that because they are brought up to avoid premarital sex, adolescents are bound to express in some other, indirect ways the sexual needs that make themselves powerfully felt during puberty. Only a part of this surplus of drive potential in the human being can be sublimated for other psychic or bodily activities; the remaining part must be satisfied by masturbation – above all, in the case of boys – or by postponing fantasies to the future in the case of girls. And once a couple finally marries, the spouses get caught in a downward spiral of mutual frustrations, since they are unable to find mutual satisfaction: "Every man whose libido, as a result of masturbatory or perverse sexual practices, has become habituated to situations and conditions of satisfaction which are not normal, develops diminished potency in marriage. Women, too, who have been able to preserve their virginity with the help of similar measures, show themselves anesthetic to normal intercourse in marriage."[14] "[I]n these circumstances," Freud goes on laconically, "the most obvious outcome is nervous illness."[15]

The social theory that forms the background for this diagnosis of a functional disorder of society as causing the psychic suffering includes very few components. The institution of a social order based on work and the reproduction of the species is, according to Freud, only possible by channeling, through moral education, the pressing potential of the human surplus of sexual drives, such that, on the one hand, there remains enough energy for the sublimating execution of the required practices and, on the other hand, there will be left over sufficient libidinous appeal for reproductive sexual intercourse. According to this theory, in such a functional whole of social reproduction and moral drive-control, disorders and pathologies appear as the established sexual morality dries up the energetic supply either for the necessary execution of work or for the exercise of the sexual drive. The latter (the exhaustion of genital sexual interests) represents for Freud the distinctively modern social disease, since here, in the moral commandment of marital monogamy, the mark of drive-suppression has been overstepped so far that, in effect, the mutual desire of the married couple will inevitably be thwarted.[16]

Only on a couple of occasions in the few pages devoted to his social analysis does Freud make clear that his standard for measuring social pathologies does not consist merely in the maintenance of the societal faculty of reproduction; thus, it is said almost at the end of the essay that, because of the traditional hedonism passed down to us, "we are still ... to include among the aims of our cultural development a certain amount of satisfaction of individual happiness," by which the integrity of a social order should be measured;[17] correspondingly, earlier in the text it is claimed that a culture is active, intellectually energetic, and thereby healthy enough to the extent that it holds out the prospect for a sufficient sexual permissiveness.[18]

However such normative extensions of a crude Freudian functionalism might now look, as a whole his social theory still bears witness to measuring social pathology as the collapse of the societal faculty of reproduction. The specific aspect that assures the functioning of a society, and whose collapse infects it with a social disease, lies essentially in safeguarding the necessary degree of willingness to work and procreate for social reproduction. Naturally, seventy years later, Mitscherlich can no longer adhere to such a primitive conception of the demands of an intact social order. Not only has sexual morality been essentially transformed in the meantime and become much more flexible too, but also, in sociology, Durkheim, Mead, and Parsons have developed incomparably more complex descriptions of the processes of social reproduction by means of normative regulation of behavior.

Mitscherlich employs a blend of such novel approaches in his own attempt at sketching out what such "diseases of society" might consist in, and that would then, he hopes, help to explain the psychic disorders that occupy him in consultation. His empirical starting point, the widespread impairment of performance, whose symptoms are less clearly demarcated than those of psycho-neurosis, requires conceiving a much more inclusive process of moral regulation of social behavior than Freud had ever done, since, in contrast to Freud, Mitscherlich cannot identify sexual disorders as primary in effecting the symptoms of his patients, and neither may he regard sexual morals as the sole instance of normative integration of the members of society. Rather, he must cover all those values and moral norms that, at a given point in time, provide for the willingness to social cooperation by virtue of their controlling effect on behavior.[19]

Thus, to Mitscherlich was disclosed a perspective that allowed his theory of social reproduction to be modeled nearly according to Parsonian structural functionalism: as it was expressed following the biology of that time, born with open instincts, the human being must first learn, in an educational process by means of prevailing values and norms, to develop in herself through internalization the kind of environmentally compatible patterns of behavior that are already given for other animals as fixed patterns of reaction.

In order for this costly process of social adaptation of the offspring to succeed, values and norms must meet two conditions, which also determine the parameters for measuring the functional efficiency of specifically human collectives: (a) the rules of behavior to be learned must not be so rigid and restrictive as to suffocate the characteristically human need for individuation; and (b) these rules must be constantly adapted to an environment in steady flux due to being transformed by human innovative capacity in a manner that allows for motivated and competent adolescents. Openness for individual deviation and power to provide security in dealing with new technological or social challenges – flexibility as well as confidence-giving determinacy – these are the two not easily combined capacities that, according to Mitscherlich, prevailing norms and values need to have if social integration is to run smoothly. And if the normative rules of behavior – that is, all the ideals and duties that the upcoming generations are supposed to internalize – deviate too much from these requirements, then one should, going by what Mitscherlich says, count on failures of socialization and the disease of an entire community.

Correspondingly, Mitscherlich needs to distinguish between two types of social pathologies or diseases according to the set of normative rules – the set of flexibility-allowing norms or that of determinacy-enhancing norms – that has been wounded. In the first case, where values and norms are too fixed and dicta-torial, the individual spontaneity required by any given society will eventually wither; in the second case, where values and norms are too indeterminate and empty, there will be a loss of individual security in coping with life. In one longer passage of his essay, Mitscherlich summarizes these differentiations in a way that reveals what kind of diagnosis of pathology he actually is after:

> Social life apparently enters into pathological change from both ends of its spectrum. Social diseases occur if the social matrix becomes too weak to demand a binding socialization of the individual, leaving her thus without guidance in many situations in life, and thereby arousing rather unconscious than conscious anxieties. On the other end of the spectrum, social diseases occur if the claims of society are effected into the individual in such a terroristic way that deviations from laws and norms of behavior arouse permanent intensive anxiety and thus paralyze the spontaneous individual response to social conditions. Both conditions jeopardize the society in every single one of its members and effect pathological patterns of behavior. Thus, under such conditions, one can rightfully speak of social disease.[20]

Even if there is again a slight confusion in the last couple of sentences as to who actually is to be stricken by the social disease, society itself or merely the sum of its members, the outset of the quoted remarks makes still perfectly clear that Mitscherlich is thoroughly convinced of the possibility of a functional disorder at the level of societal reproduction as a whole. In his view, such a pathology of social life can occur because of either too little or too much normative binding force (*normative Verbindlichkeiten*), as the members of society are integrated into the structural order of society. If one, then, recollects the historical atmosphere in which the essay was written (the late 1950s), it quickly becomes clear what kind of disease Mitscherlich saw threatening his coeval society: in his patients' fear of impairment is reflected the menace that, due to the rapid erosion of moral idols and norms, the members of society do not feel secure enough in their behavior to cope successfully with the rapid change in technology and culture. Contrary to Freud, Mitscherlich's time diagnosis does not settle with a thesis of normative overregulation, but concludes instead with the verdict of a normatively *under*regulated mode of social interaction.

What interests me, however, is not so much the content of these two analyses (in fact, there is much reason to regard both as outdated) as their theoretical foundations and terminology. If one takes a closer look at the respective arsenal of background assumptions, one will soon reach the conclusion that not only Freud but also Mitscherlich applies a relatively simple standard for establishing if a society has to do with a functional disorder or pathology. For the founding father of psychoanalysis, it was the faculty of material and physical reproduction as a standard that led him to consider a society damaged if its members lack the motivational force for the execution of necessary work as well as for natural procreation. Mitscherlich, born half a century later, successfully avoids such a purely biological criterion of social survival and includes in his diagnosis the subjects' quest for identity. This additional dimension, however, he takes into consideration only to the extent allowed by neutral propositions independent of societal development.

For Mitscherlich, societies become pathological if the values and norms responsible for their social integration either give no room for creative individuation or, conversely, offer individuals too little security in their coping with a changing environment. However, what is to be the correct measure – what is to count as sufficient for the personal development of individuals or necessary for the mastery of novel challenges – shall in his view be established independently of any information about the normative self-understanding of the society in question.

Like Freud, though not by the same naturalist means, Mitscherlich wants to determine the societal conditions of survival objectively, without historical qualification, in order thereby to obtain general conclusions about the functional disorders or diseases of societies. This is highly implausible, since, in contrast to pre-human collectives, determining what makes a human society capable of survival always involves regarding the normative beliefs of its members, and these beliefs are subject to change and cultural variation. From this point of view, then, determining functional disorders of social life on the human developmental stage is not possible without considering such historical conditions. This can easily be demonstrated with regard to the very first criterion of Mitscherlich's diagnosis – the required openness of specific institutional values and norms for individual deviation – since conceptions of the subjective need of individualization, of the subjective claim to personal particularity, have been significantly intensified with the transition to modern societies, and, later on, expanded still further.[21]

If, however, the parameters for what counts as worth preserving in a society constantly change in the course of historical epochs, then so also do the criteria for what is to be regarded as a functional disorder or social disease. To cut a long story short, determining the functional requirements of social life and, with it, getting to the bottom of what a potential systematic disorder might consist in, involves restricting oneself to the current self-understanding of a historical epoch. Paradoxically, it follows that the more distinctively specific human needs and human social interests are pointed at in determining the functional requirements of society, the more imperative the need to consider historical circumstances and self-understandings. As his diagnosis of pathologies claims to include the demands of socially mediated individuation (*Subjektwerdung*),[22] Mitscherlich makes himself much more gravely vulnerable to the accusation of historical indeterminacy than Freud's biologism ever was in restricting itself to measuring social diseases only by the damage made to natural reproduction.

Beyond this obliviousness to history, the two authors share one more weakness in the theoretical background assumptions of their attempts. This shortcoming reveals a further condition that a diagnosis of social diseases would have to fulfill if it aspires to make really convincing and coherent propositions. In their attempts to discover the social causes of the symptoms they diagnose in consultation, both Freud and Mitscherlich seem to concentrate exclusively on one single dimension of social reproduction. From all evolutionary processes, as if it were self-evident, they select as relevant for their inquiries only those that, in the form of moral socialization, contribute to the societal adjustment of the individual drive potential. In their view, it is only here, at this very junction of society, where mediation is needed between the human inner nature and the cooperative constraints of society, that disorders of social reproduction can occur at all. But this is, again, altogether unconvincing, as the maintenance of a social order, in every instance, depends on much more than merely processes of a normatively regulated drive-control or articulation of needs. Even if one were to see the conditioning of all sociality herein, as Freud clearly did, it would still be difficult to deny that human communities depend nearly to the same extent on a specific mastery of their natural environment and on a normative stabilization of their social relations of interaction.

As it happens, confrontation with external nature, social shaping of inner nature, and regulation of inter-human relations are all, according to the traditional line of inquiry from Marx to Parsons, precisely the challenges that societies have to cope with in order to preserve themselves for a certain period of time. Corresponding to each of these constraints on survival, we find, in a given social order, a function that must be fulfilled by means of institutional arrangements and with an eye to the reproduction of the social order itself. It remains somewhat mysterious why Freud and Mitscherlich choose just one of these functions of societal self-preservation and concentrate only on its unique disorder or nonfulfillment as paradigmatic for any disease of society. Certainly, in his social analysis, Freud does consider the imperative of societal work, but he does not take note of the particular relation to external nature. Mitscherlich, however, seems to be concerned solely with the process of normatively mediated socialization of the individual when he sets out to formulate his own diagnosis of pathologies.

As an interim result, it should be concluded that functional or systematic disorders of social reproduction can be detected in all three functions mentioned above. If the term "social pathology" is to denote a disease of society itself, social pathologies can take place not only in the context of socialization but also in the contexts of working on external nature and of intersubjective relations of recognition. On top of this neglect of the cultural predicament of diverse social functions comes then the mistake of overly narrowing the diagnostic gaze. The way things are looking at the moment is that there must be many more possible diseases of society than either of these theorists was ready to accept.

Without further ado, the question must be addressed as to whether the path we have walked with Freud and Mitscherlich so far is even likely to lead us to a plausible and coherent concept of social diseases or pathologies. Have we possibly been lured down the wrong track? If we look back, we can see how both our theorists passed the idea on to us that such diseases must always consist in the failure or disorder of a function whose fulfillment is required for the sake of the social order's preservation. Correspondingly,

in a turn against Freud and Mitscherlich, we concluded that there
need not be only one, but that there are more likely to be as many
diseases of society as there are self-preserving social functions,
since every collective can fail at coping with any of these different
tasks. At this point, however, we had to introduce a considerable
restriction as we realized that, with regard to human forms of
socialization (*Vergesellschaftung*),[23] one cannot simply speak of bare,
invariant functional constraints. Rather, these imperatives of self-
preservation are always already cultural; they are understood as
representing particular demands that can only be introduced by
taking the normative self-understanding of a society into account.
On the whole, we seem to be drawn to the conclusion that one can
speak of a societal disease or pathology if a society in its institutional arrangement fails, according to its prevailing values, at one
of the tasks it takes up within the functional cycles of socialization,
processing of nature, and regulation of relations of recognition.

Yet, is such a failure according to self-defined ends of self-
preservation really what we intuitively mean, when we speak of
the disease of an entire society? Does this not imply a restriction to
such phenomena that we normally describe with concepts such as
"malformation" (*Fehlentwicklung*), "crisis," or "failed state"? Has
not all that is characteristic about diseases or illnesses now been
completely pushed aside? In fact, as I said earlier in this discussion,
we would take a wrong course if we tied the idea of a "disease" of
society too intimately to the condition that at the same time a sufficient number of individual members of society must be stricken
with the disease. Such a restriction too easily blinds us to the fact
that diseases of society take place on a level set principally above
that of the subjects and, thus, do not necessarily find expression in
the suffered and experienced functional disorders of individuals.

On the other hand, when talking about diseases of society, one
ought also not abandon the analogy to the concept of "illness"
such that its underlying intuition wholly vanishes. This intuition
says that we are somehow dealing with an interference that we
experience as a restriction of freedom. A characteristic feature of
any disease, as Mitscherlich stresses time and again, the experience
of a restriction of the personal creative freedom (*Verengung von
Freiheitsspielräumen*), must be preserved as a reference point in
the conception of a disease of society if the resort to such strong
concepts is to be intelligible at all.

For this reason, I want to conclude with a suggestion as to how
to breach the gap between the reflections developed here so far and

the traditional concept of "disease," without leaving behind the higher ontological level of "societies" as in contrast to the number of their members. To this end, we should not speak of diseases of society, as was done so far, simply with reference to disorders or failures in coping with culturally defined ends of self-preservation. As long as we stick to such a way of speaking, applied with certain restrictions by Freud and Mitscherlich, it will not be quite clear why we are dealing with the case of a disease and not merely with a malformation (*Fehlentwicklung*) or an institutional maladjustment.

It would be something quite different, indeed, if we were to turn our attention not to singular, separate functional cycles but to their interplay – that is, their mutual adjustments. Here, on this higher level of the entanglement of diverse functional spheres, there might also occur disorders and frictions, namely, in cases where the respective institutional regulations contradict or even mutually disable each other: the socially established patterns of socialization as well as their decisive values and norms can clash on a deeper level with the institutionalized material production, which, again, can be under strain with the normative regulations that direct the relations of recognition among the members of society and make them binding. What such frictions and tensions have in common with individual illnesses is that they display a troubled relationship of a subject to itself, whether this subject is a person or a society. And in the case of societies, the restriction of freedom, which belongs to our concept of "disease," consists in these functional spheres' mutually preventing each other from successfully developing, as their specific institutional solutions get in each other's way.

The parallel to the living organism that comes to the surface in such formulations is not arbitrary and cannot be avoided. One can only eventually speak of "diseases of society" coherently and substantially enough if one represents the society as an organism in which the individual spheres or subsystems, thought of as organs, are cooperating so harmoniously that we can work out an idea of its unhindered, "free" development. This idea loses its disconcerting, old-fashioned character if one recalls that, following Hegel – who, in his "Philosophy of Right" made it almost self-evidently essential to his exposition by the assumption of a goal-directed interplay of all social spheres – it was utilized by Marx and Parsons in their respective social analyses. The founding father of historical materialism employs it in his analysis of a conflict between productive forces and relations of production as he tacitly presupposes an ideal of an organic interplay between both social organs. The theorist of structural functionalism uses it in order to understand the undisturbed reproduction of society as a process of interconnected systems serving the end of realizing ultimate values. Without rehabilitating this organic conception that has long since been declared dead, I fear, the thesis that societies also can be stricken by diseases cannot be justified.

Translated by Arvi Särkelä

8

Education and the Democratic Public Sphere

A neglected chapter of political philosophy

Ever since its beginnings in the nineteenth century, the history of the public education system in democratic constitutional states has been a history of conflicts over the structure, form, and content of the instruction provided in schools. Neither the stratification of the school system nor the teaching methods or the curricula remained unaffected by the acrimonious disputes between state agencies on the one side and representatives of social groups and parents' associations on the other. The state's recognition of a right on the part of each citizen to receive an education had an explosive potential which Immanuel Kant may have anticipated in the following sentence from his lectures on pedagogy: "Two human inventions can probably be regarded as the most difficult, namely the arts of government and education; and yet there is still controversy about their very idea."[1]

For Kant, the parallel between the art of government and the art of education was suggested by the fact that both are socially created practices fulfilling the same function, albeit in the distinct dimensions of species history and individual history, phylogeny and ontogeny. Through the prudent choice of means and methods, which is to say, in an "artful" way, both are meant to instruct us on how to effect a transition from a state of "minority" to a state of freedom: be it with regard to a whole people, consisting of individual subjects, or be it with regard to a child still subjected to the rule of nature within himself. What initially looks like a mere analogy is developed far beyond that in the course of Kant's lectures, where he points out that education and a republican political order mutually presuppose each other. The young human being, governed by nature, has to undergo an educational process aimed at freedom before he can become a member of a self-governing political community; conversely, only autonomous citizens are able to institutionalize a system of public education that enables their children to attain political maturity. Good upbringing and a republican political order require each other because the former, in the form of public education, first produces the cultural and moral capacities that make it possible for the latter to exist and thrive in such a way that the active citizens even take an interest in the political emancipation of the lower orders of society. As in Jean-Jacques Rousseau's *Émile*, Kant's *Pedagogy* draws on the idea of the "good citizen" as a link between pedagogic theory and the theory of government, between a conception of education and political philosophy.[2] Neither could exist without the other, since both spell out inseparable preconditions of a democratic political community.

It is this very close, internal interrelation that explains why within the political and philosophical discourse of modernity virtually no notable theorist of democracy has failed to offer a systematic contribution to educational theory. Beginning with Rousseau and Kant, through Friedrich Schleiermacher, and up to Émile Durkheim and John Dewey, numerous important thinkers found it natural to devote entire books to the subject of public education.[3] They thought of pedagogy, conceived as the theory of the standards and methods of the adequate teaching of children, as the twin sister of democratic theory. Without proper reflection on how to render a child both capable of cooperation and morally independent, it seemed to them impossible to explain what it could mean to speak of the project of democratic self-determination. The idea of the "good citizen" was not an empty phrase or an ornament for political speeches but a practical challenge calling for the theoretical elaboration and even the experimental testing of suitable school types and teaching methods. Thus, when it came to the challenge of re-habituating an entire population – the German one – to the practices of democratic politics that had been systematically eradicated under National Socialism, the American occupying forces found it natural to draw on the pedagogical writings of Dewey.[4]

The ties between democratic theory and pedagogical practice were still so close, and the internal relation between them still appeared so obvious, that the project of teaching democratic habits to the demoralized citizens of a thoroughly destroyed unjust state was not perceived as objectionably paternalistic. Since then, however, the conceptual link between democracy and education, and between political philosophy and pedagogy, has been severed. To be sure, efforts are still made to reinvigorate theoretical reflection on democratic education, but nowadays these efforts tend to come from a pedagogical discourse abandoned by philosophers; they are no longer at the center of political philosophy itself. Democratic theory in all its manifold guises and voices tends to be silent on the pedagogical aspect of its subject matter. It has nothing to offer with regard to either the methods or the contents of primary and secondary education. Political philosophy today seems to have lost the insight that a thriving democracy must continually reproduce the cultural and moral preconditions of its own existence by way of general educational processes. These remarks on the intimate relation between education on the one hand and political freedom and democracy on the other are merely preliminary, and I will elaborate them in more detail in the second part of my chapter. Before I do that, I will in the first part venture an explanation for the decoupling of pedagogy from political philosophy. It will turn out that the reasons for this development are found in the confluence of two causes that have, as it were, an elective affinity with each other: first, a certain problematic conception of the cultural presuppositions of democracy; second, a misunderstanding of the idea of the neutrality of the state. Once I have my case for a rapprochement between the two areas in both negative and positive terms, I will proceed in a third step to outline the challenges faced by a reinvigorated program of democratic education. Since an extended treatment of this last point would require much more space than I have available here, I will limit myself to some brief remarks with regard to it.

1. The Decoupling of Pedagogy from Political Philosophy

Whereas Kant, Durkheim, and Dewey considered the topic of democratic education an intrinsic part of their respective projects in political philosophy, its role in contemporary normative democratic theory has become a marginal one. It is still occasionally mentioned, and introductory texts sometimes identify it as a part of the general subject matter of political philosophy, but its proper delimitation and development is left to educational theory.[5]

Democratic theory has uncoupled itself from its twin sister, the study of the adequate organization and methods of democratic education, and it has thereby deprived itself of the chance to make a proper contribution regarding the normative functions of pre-school, primary and secondary education, and adult education. Some might rest content with observing that this development simply reflects a more general differentiation of scientific disciplines over the course of the past two hundred years. Just as philosophy in the second half of the nineteenth century parted ways with social theory, which then established itself as the discipline of sociology, so, too, the increasing specialization of philosophy required it to withdraw from the project of determining the educational processes required for the development of mature democratic politics. But it is quite apparent that things are not so simple when one considers that political philosophy constantly encounters the problem of education without having so much as the beginnings of a solution to it. With the political establishment of compulsory education, state-administered schooling has become a crucial instrument for forming the habits and abilities of each new generation, influencing future citizens for better or for worse. The type, methods, and contents of school education may affect a democracy either in positive ways – for example by fostering cooperativeness and individual self-esteem – or in negative ones, gradually undermining democracy by teaching moral conformism and unquestioning obedience to authority.[6] Thus the question regarding the proper kind of state-mandated education has been at the heart of political philosophy from its very inception – just think of Plato's *Republic*.[7]

Any serious reflection on the question how a state or a political community should be constituted given the fundamental features of human nature has had to confront the closely related question what and whom to teach, and by what methods to do so. The fact that this question has nowadays largely vanished from political philosophy and is no longer being pursued by it in either positive or negative terms cannot be due simply to the thought that the topic can be more productively and more adequately pursued by a specialized discipline. The problem of state-organized education is far too central to political agency and far too consequential with regard to the possibility of democracy and the rule of law for it to be straightforwardly separable from the theory or philosophy of politics. If we wish to explain the current separation between democratic theory and educational theory we must therefore look to causes other than the progressive differentiation of academic disciplines. I suspect that the explanation will be located at a more fundamental, conceptual level having to do with a proper demarcation of the extent to which democracy is able to affect itself. As a rule of thumb we can say that this extent will be more limited the less a democratic state is able to influence the conditions of its own existence, be it due to normative constraints or because of its operative limitations. When this space for self-generating activity on the part of the democratic state is thought of as being quite confined, the political significance accorded to school education will be correspondingly reduced, since it is then no longer regarded as a powerful instrument of change. It seems to me that theoretical shifts of this sort – that is to say, a certain disillusionment about the self-generative powers of democratic communities – are primarily responsible for the fact that school education and its administration by the state receive only scant attention from political philosophers today. Let me mention two of the theoretical sources that may account for the fact that over the past few decades, democratic theory has unwittingly and through almost imperceptible changes lost its faith in the value that state-run education has for democracy. To be sure, one could cite other causes besides these, such as the observation that children's characters are formed through socialization in early childhood and thus during a developmental phase over which the state has little control. But I will restrict myself to the following two aspects, since they fall squarely within the domain of political philosophy properly speaking.

First, the idea that the liberal democratic state has only a very limited ability to regenerate the moral and cultural resources on which it relies may owe its currency in part to the view defended by the German constitutional lawyer Ernst-Wolfgang Böckenförde (and therefore often referred to as the Böckenförde theorem) that a democratic state depends for its reproduction on a supply of cultural traditions that themselves precede democracy. Although Böckenförde seems originally to have intended this view in a rather narrow sense, as pertaining to the ethical preconditions for the functioning of modern legal systems, his thesis is nowadays given a much broader interpretation, and is taken to refer to the cultural dependency of democratic constitutional states quite generally.[8]

On this more general reading, democratic political systems require the cultural support of ethical customs and habits whose cultivation and flourishing these systems themselves lack the means to promote. At the most general level, the so-called Böckenförde theorem is even taken to assert that democracies owe their social survival to the existence of moral attitudes that can thrive only in tradition-oriented communities governed by substantive ethical or even religious conceptions. Once this last view is adopted, it is only a short step to the conclusion that state-run educational processes, that is to say school and pre-school education, lack any value for the formation of democratic habits and attitudes. For whatever moral attitudes facilitate cooperative political decision-making – tolerance, empathy, a concern for the common good – they are acquired not as a response to school teaching, no matter how well thought out, but solely through processes of ethical socialization within pre-political communities. Whereas in Böckenförde there are at least some hints that "education and schooling" are capable of fulfilling the relevant functions, the common reception of his view reduces it to the claim that democratic societies are forced to rely on the survival of tradition-based ethical communities.[9] All efforts on the part of the state to ensure a general democratic education are thought to be in vain, since they are held to be unable to generate the ethical virtues whose existence is vital to the continued functioning of any democracy.

The increasingly widespread adoption of this view within political philosophy is likely to be one of the factors that have led recent democratic theory to avoid questions regarding public education. Such questions are bound to appear irrelevant to the extent to which it is assumed that democratic dispositions are acquired not through state-mediated educational processes but rather in the pre-political environments furnished by tradition-oriented communities. Yet the popular version of the Böckenförde theorem is not the only thing that accounts for the increasing distance taken by contemporary democratic theory from its twin sister, educational theory. The tendency just described is met from another, more normative direction by the tendency to construe the idea of state neutrality in such a demanding way that even the principles of democratically organized collective decision-making are no longer permitted to shape public school education.

Just like the culturally conservative reinterpretation of democracy, according to which the latter can survive only thanks to a supply of cultural traditions that precede it, so too the radicalization of the ideal of state neutrality has taken place as it were behind the backs of political philosophers, rather than having been consciously intended by them. It may even be that this second theoretical shift has been an unintended consequence of a well-intentioned effort to accommodate the increasing plurality of ethnic and religious cultures within contemporary society by emphasizing the strict impartiality of state-administered education. Of course, the degree of state neutrality has always been subject to changes in political attitude that reflect, albeit in complex ways, the ethical convictions of a majority and thereby a variable balance of social power. Ultimately, the only constraint that the ideal of neutrality imposes on the legitimacy of a political commitment to substantive values is simply that the universalist principles of democratic constitutions must not thereby be violated. In the longstanding debate over the inevitable partiality of the state's activity, the tradition from Kant to Durkheim and Dewey that I identified earlier took it for granted that state-administered education should embody exactly those values that led to the decision to make such education compulsory for all future citizens in the first place. The right of the parents to impart to their children their own particular values had to end at the school door, so that the pupils could then practice the reflective habits that would enable them to take part in the process of joint public decision-making. But if it once appeared completely natural for school teaching to be geared toward the democratic procedures that were operative in making school attendance obligatory in the first place, doubts are increasingly voiced today. Some appeal to the constraint of state neutrality to caution against overburdening school education with political values alien to its purpose; others, for example concerned parents, complain that placing too much emphasis on the theme of democracy might get in the way of promoting career skills. When these kinds of well-worn reservations meet with unexpected public support owing to the growth of multiculturalism, which does in fact speak in favor of removing certain ideological relics from our schools, we are faced with a vague mixture of truths and falsehoods that leads to the rejection of all forms of partiality in school education as equally harmful or objectionable. The political constraint of state neutrality is thereby extended to the point where even the very idea of a democratic education is no longer a matter of normative common sense.

To be sure, these radicalized conceptions of state neutrality have not yet become pervasive in contemporary political philosophy. There is an ongoing debate about how to properly adapt this part of the legacy of liberal political thought to the increasing heterogeneity of cultural values in present-day societies.[10] But when we take into account the culturally conservative reinterpretations of the survival conditions of democracy that I was describing earlier, we can discern a theoretical development that may well result in the view that the methods and contents of state-administered education must be purged of all democratic goals. This is the direction indicated, for example, by proposals that schools should be in charge only of an educational "civic minimum," that parents should be given vouchers allowing them to choose educational options with this or that specific ideological tendency, or that teachers should no longer be considered as state agents but rather as answerable solely to the parents.[11] However tentative such considerations may initially be, the further they are taken – and the more public schools thus come to be thought of as subject to the constraint of ethical neutrality, in juxtaposition to a plurality of ethically committed private schools – the greater becomes the threat to one of the very few instruments that a democratic society has at its disposal to regenerate its own ethical foundations. In this way conflicts over a state-run school system – regardless of whether they concern its structure, curriculum, or methods – are always at the same time conflicts over the sustainability of democracy. No philosophical tradition was more aware of this nexus than the one initiated by Kant and culminating in the work of Durkheim and Dewey.

2. Educating "Good Citizens"

The considerations I have advanced so far have been of a negative sort. The criticism of some tendencies in contemporary democratic theory has already revealed the premises on which we will have to rely, if we are looking to understand the public school system as a necessary complement of democratic decision-making, and in fact as an integral and prior part of it. We have seen that we must neither sacrifice the guiding hypothesis that it is possible for education to foster the capacity for public deliberation even outside the specific contexts of early childhood socialization and traditional ethical communities, nor must we jeopardize the authority of the constitutional state to infuse democratic goals into the educational structures it sets up. Viewed from a positive angle, we can say that foremost among the tasks of a democratic constitutional state is the task to provide educational opportunities that will equally enable each of its future citizens to participate in the public legitimation of

his or her own choices "without fear or shame." In Kant's treatise
on education, which was strongly influenced by Rousseau's *Émile*
without following it in every respect, this general idea results only
in a defense of "public" education, accessible to all, against the
champions of "domestic" education. The advantage of the former,
according to Kant, is that it can foster in each pupil the virtues and
capacities of a "future citizen" while sidestepping the danger of
perpetuating "family mistakes."[12] Everything that such educational
processes are meant to impart – first, mechanical skills; second,
pragmatic prudence; third, moral autonomy – is subordinate, in
Kant's view, to the goal of creating within the individual a corresponding number of layers of self-respect and self-esteem, which
taken together allow him to act with self-confidence as citizen of
a republic.[13] The question of how these three sets of pedagogically
imparted abilities are supposed to contribute to the exercise of a
profession in adult age does not arise here at all, since all these
abilities are considered solely for the contribution they make to an
individual's acquisition of various kinds of self-esteem. Kant anticipates a famous thought found in the work of John Rawls when he
maintains that a future citizen must first and foremost have access
to the key good of "self-respect" before he is able to participate in
republican self-legislation as an equal among equals.[14]

Professional skills, civic competence, and moral principles are
here conceived of not primarily as teachable means by which
individuals are enabled to secure an income for themselves, but
rather as generalized media of social recognition, which the young
acquire through a pedagogical process and which gradually make
them aware of possessing a certain "worth" or "value" in the eyes
of others. By learning technical skills, the young person gains
respect "with regard to himself as an individual" (as Kant puts it,
almost in the same words later used by Hegel); the acquisition of
civic knowledge affords him "public worth" as a citizen; and the
acquisition of moral principles earns him "value in view of the
entire human race."[15]

Despite all his remarkable insight regarding the interrelation
between general public education and reciprocal recognition within
a republican political community, Kant is still quite far away from
drawing conclusions with regard to the proper methods and organization of school teaching. He is thinking of the individual male pupil
who is to develop self-esteem through the pedagogically mediated
acquisition of knowledge, rather than of a cooperative community
where each individual must be able to act as a recognized member

in concert with all others for the purpose of joint decision-making. While at some points of his *Pedagogy* Kant senses that a republic has a much greater need for fostering the communicative virtues than it has for simply imparting knowledge, he still recoils from the consequence of identifying the public school first and foremost as a place where democratic capacities are formed.[16] This step is taken about one hundred years later by Durkheim and Dewey, both of whom seek in their works to elucidate the internal relation between education and democracy, between learning at school and becoming a democratic citizen.[17]

Even though the basic assumptions made by each of these two thinkers appear to be in deep conflict with those of the other – on one side, the sociologist with scientistic inclinations; on the other, the vocal exponent of pragmatism in philosophy – their reflections on democratic education share a surprising range of features. Among the three functions that a contemporary perspective would attribute to education in primary and secondary schools – to provide essential qualifications for entering a profession, to compensate educational deficits stemming from family or social background, and to offer a general preparation for the role of citizen – Durkheim and Dewey focus exclusively on the last. For them, just as for Kant, the acquisition of professional knowledge is merely a side product of the training of democratic dispositions; and the task of educational compensation is thought to lie with the individual community that is each particular school. In justifying the state's authority to put the tax-funded educational system in charge of generating civic capacities, both thinkers advance similar arguments (to the extent that they think arguments are needed here). If it is granted that the introduction of compulsory schooling by the state can be conceived as a democratically legitimate act only when it is interpreted as joint civic effort to equally enable all citizens to exercise their political rights, then it is not cogent to abrogate the state's right to use school teaching to train the requisite abilities and practices.[18]

Yet, such considerations at the level of democratic theory constitute only the general framework within which Durkheim and Dewey develop their more detailed studies regarding the content and structure of school education. Here again, we find significant parallels between their respective arguments. Their common point of departure is the thesis that to prepare for the role of citizen is less a matter of acquiring the right kind of knowledge than it is a matter of acquiring certain practical habits. What the pupils should learn in school is not primarily testable knowledge of political or historical facts, but rather modes of conduct that enable self-confident action within a cooperative community. It may not come as a particular surprise that the pragmatist Dewey was led in this direction and came to view schools above all as places where a public engages in communal inquiry.[19] But how it is that a similar line is taken by Durkheim, who likewise looks at schools for how they can train the capacity for democratic cooperation, is something that I will need to briefly elaborate on.

In contrast to Dewey, who was much more optimistic in this regard, Durkheim is initially guided by the Kantian idea that a child's innately egoistic inclinations need to be curbed by moral discipline before it can learn to autonomously conform to the social rules of a democratic community. Yet he departs from his philosophical teacher in picturing this preparatory educational process as proceeding more smoothly and with greater chances of success the more it engages the child's passions and desires, that is to say, her sensible nature, for example by drawing on practical role models and playful activity.[20] Thus for Durkheim the overcoming of infantile egoism is not in fact a process of moral discipline, even though he repeatedly describes it as such; it is rather a process of affective habituation. By participating in practices that are adequate to her in that they engage her inclinations, the child initially comes to master at a merely habitual level the rules of democratic existence that she should later, with increasing age, come to comprehend in their rational validity. With regard to schools and their methods of education, the conclusions Durkheim reaches on the basis of these revisions of Kant's view are almost the same ones at which Dewey arrives from his quite different Hegelian premises: through cooperative learning, through active participation in all the school's affairs and through communal rather than individualized kinds of criticism and encouragement, pupils should be habituated early on to acquire the spirit of democratic cooperation that will allow them in adult age to present themselves with self-confidence in the public political arena. Thus, neither of the two thinkers shares the view commonly taken today that the primary goal of school attendance is the development of individual autonomy. Instead, their models of education are shaped by the idea that the pupils should acquire a reliable sense of what it means to treat their fellow pupils as equal partners in a shared process of learning and inquiry. If a public school has the task of engendering in each successive generation the practical dispositions that are vital for the possibility of democratic decision-making, then it must aim at habituating those it seeks to educate into a culture of association,[21] rather than just at imparting to them a grasp of moral principles. The crucial contribution that school education can make to the regeneration of democracy lies not in teaching individual rules of right action but in a communicative practice that fosters moral initiative and the ability to take up the perspective of others.

We should, of course, note that not only did one hundred years pass between Kant's *Lectures on Pedagogy* and the arguments just presented; another hundred years have passed since then. In view of this long interval some may shake their heads and triumphantly point out that along with the social and economic conditions, the requirements on schooling have radically changed, too. The greatly increased number of pupils, the economic demand for flexibility and motivation, the educational deficits that despite many efforts persist in the lower segments of society – all this seems to leave highly developed capitalist countries with no other choice but to place increasing emphasis in school teaching on selectivity, individualized assessment, and the encouragement of competitive behavior.[22]

In the United States, politicians, economic experts, and managers are already calling for a thoroughgoing reform of the entire education system, proposing measures whose cumulative effect it would be to make teaching entirely subservient to the goal of transmitting marketable skills. According to these proposals, the effectiveness of all American schools should be subject to ongoing quantitative comparison, where the success of individual teachers is measured by their students' placement in nationally standardized tests.[23] Controls of this kind, which sooner or later would have the effect of marginalizing all subjects not amenable to statistical evaluation, are discussed not only in the United States but also in Europe, as though here, too, one were hoping to subject schools to the dictate of economic developments by employing measurement methods familiar from the financial sector. Given these circumstances, there might seem to be little point in recalling times when public education was regarded as the linchpin of democratic self-renewal. Not only democratic theory but politics itself seems to have lost interest in the only kind of institution that is suited to constantly regenerate, albeit tentatively and with great effort, the fragile preconditions of a people's democratic decision-making.

If these tendencies seem to point to the abandonment of the idea of a democratic education, they are at the same time contradicted by a multitude of empirical findings that have resulted from comparative education studies and from the PISA surveys over the past several years. These data marvelously illustrate what Durkheim and Dewey anticipated in their reflections a century ago, when they insisted on a close correlation between cooperative, democracy-oriented teaching methods on the one hand and pupils' performance at school on the other. The school system that consistently comes out on top in all international comparisons of scholastic achievement is the same one that comes closest to realizing the democratic ideals of the two thinkers: in Finnish schools, pupils from different educational backgrounds remain in the same schools together as long as possible; tests and examinations are reduced to a bare minimum; communicative responsibility and mutual trust are given much greater weight than individual attributability; and choices regarding teaching methods are made by the professionally trained teachers themselves, in cooperation with student representatives.[24]

It is true that descriptions of the Finnish school system do not employ the terminology used by Durkheim and Dewey. There is talk neither of habituation, nor of communal morality or cooperative methods of education. But such re-translations into a language of democratic education could easily be supplied and would then reveal an instance of the rare and fortunate situation where what is politically and normatively right coincides with what is pragmatically useful. The types of school education that are best with a view to pupils' cognitive achievements and abilities turn out to be those that are also most suited to the regeneration of democratic dispositions. In times when talk of growing political apathy is ubiquitous and when some even speak of the threat of "post-democracy," there is no reason whatsoever not to revive the tradition inaugurated by Kant, Durkheim, and Dewey and to conceive of public education as a crucial instrument for the self-reproduction of democracies.[25]

3. Challenges for Democratic Education

What I have been saying so far may have created the impression that like the proper methods of democratic education, its contents, too, are fixed once and for all, removed from all historical change. Kant in particular played a part in suggesting such a view, since he tied the acquisition of the necessary forms of civic self-respect to the successive mastery of timelessly valid portions of knowledge. But also Durkheim exhibits a tendency to prescribe a certain fixed subject matter to all processes of cooperative education.[26] Only Dewey resisted this tendency, and soberly pointed out throughout his pedagogical writings that along with the various challenges that require public problem solving, the material to be taught in schools must also change. Like Durkheim, he believes that a hierarchical ordering of subjects is indispensable (curiously, he accords the highest rank to geography), but what exactly it is that pupils should cooperatively learn in these disciplines is in his view determined by the historically changing tasks of democratic decision-making.[27] Before I end this chapter, I would like in a Deweyan spirit to at least briefly name those two historical challenges whose consequences for our democratic co-existence create a particular need for adjustments in school curricula. In both cases, more detailed considerations would likely show that the challenges cannot be properly treated within the confines of any one individual subject, and that they should rather be addressed more or less across the entire range of the curriculum.

For any observant person there can be no doubt that the digital revolution of our communicative relations will lead to profound changes not only in the ways in which private relationships are initiated and maintained, but also with respect to the processes by which political views are formed. The internet, which brings about both a de-spatialization and an acceleration of each individual's interactions with others, is creating an ever more quickly growing number of virtual public spheres whose outer boundaries are in permanent flux.[28] It is certainly a task of primary and secondary education to prepare schoolchildren both technologically and socially for the use of this new medium. But this hardly exhausts the efforts that will be required to address its historical consequences. It seems to me that it will also be necessary for children to jointly explore both the potentials and the limits and dangers of the new medium by experimentally investigating how digitally disseminated topics and bodies of information are generated.[29] This might be done, for instance, by examining the genesis and quality of specific Wikipedia entries. Selective reconstructions of this sort would require the close cooperation of different subjects, since specific knowledge of the relevant fields would be needed over and above purely technical and economic expertise. This one particular example will have to suffice to illustrate the much broader idea that what is needed in our schools today is the ability not merely to use the internet but also to understand its specific mode of production and the range of its effects. In the spirit of Dewey, the cooperative use of computers should prepare the pupils for the mature and responsible use of new instruments of political decision-making.

The digital revolution is the first of the two historical challenges facing the democratic public today. The second one is the increasing heterogeneity of the population of Western countries.[30] As with respect to the novel medium that is the internet, so also with regard to multiculturalism few will disagree that schools have to do everything within their powers to prepare their pupils for these changes in the conditions under which public opinion is formed. But here again we need to ask which pedagogical methods and contents will be best suited to this task. The idea of a democratic education that my chapter has tried to recall offers an answer to the first part of this question, regarding methods: the less a pupil is treated as an isolated subject meant to deliver a certain performance, and the more he or she is approached as a member of a cooperative learning community, the more likely is the emergence of forms of communication that allow not only for a playful acceptance of cultural differences but that positively conceive of such differences as opportunities for mutual enrichment.[31]

But to point in this way to the power of democratic education to facilitate recognitive relationships does not yet answer the second part of our question, concerning the consequences that the growth of multiculturalism should have for the content of what is taught. Let me close by suggesting that at present we cannot even adequately imagine what that content should look like fifteen or twenty years from now, if fair and equal consideration is to be given to the cultural and ethnic composition of school classes. In order for those future pupils to grow into mature participants in a highly heterogeneous and colorfully mixed public sphere, they will have to learn to approach history, literature, geography, and most other subjects from the same sort of decentralized perspective that we today are still struggling to gradually teach ourselves in the context of a number of academic disciplines.

Translated by Felix Koch

9

Democracy and the Division of Labor
A blind spot in political philosophy

To survey the contemporary world of work in Western capitalist societies is to be confronted with a series of alarming tendencies. On the one hand, the heyday of permanent employment and the welfare state seems to have come to an end several decades ago; the policies of deregulation that began to be implemented toward the start of the 1980s led to the erosion of the security afforded by work contracts, to the loosening of conditions of dismissal, and to the creation of ever more informal, precarious, and poorly remunerated employment relations.[1] Taking these phenomena as a whole, people often speak today of a dualization of the labor market, thus pointing to the division of employment relations into a protected category of highly-qualified workers and a precarious category of poorly paid, unqualified workers in the manufacturing and service sectors.[2] On the other hand, the looming prospect of automation threatens to result in a great wave of layoffs, as the increase in digitalized control processes would seem to imply the redundancy of a multiplicity of jobs based on registration, supervision, monitoring activities, etc. It is, to be sure, as yet far from clear to what extent this loss of jobs will be compensated for by the creation of new branches in the automation and robotics industries; but it seems clear enough that the coming transformations will lead to a massive increase in unemployment.[3] In light of both of these phenomena, it is surely reasonable to speak of a growing crisis of labor in the capitalist countries of the West. The most succinct encapsulation of this development is simply that, today, work is unable to sustain and assure the livelihoods of workers and their families.[4]

Given the significance of these developmental tendencies for our *Lebenswelt*, it is more than a little surprising that the topics they throw up hardly get a hearing in political philosophy. Academics within this field carry on as though one might safely ignore the changes taking place in the world of work when investigating both the conditions and dangers to contemporary democracies. To be sure, all manner of conceivable explanations for crisis phenomena continue to be subjects of discussion – the functional irrelevance of political parties, deparliamentarization, the loss of national sovereignty, the hollowing out of democratic institutions[5] – but the idea that the erosion of secure employment relations might play a causal role in this context goes practically unconsidered. I am not, it should be noted, alluding to the by now well-attested phenomenon whereby, in the face of growing migration, social groups that fear their displacement from the labor market incline to anti-immigration attitudes, and thus come to prefer so-called "populist" parties with undemocratic tendencies.[6] Rather, I mean to draw attention to a far more fundamental state of affairs; namely, that the quality of democratic participation and, thereby, the functioning of political decision-making depends essentially on the economic presupposition of a fair, transparent, and maximally inclusive division of labor within a society. It is this often opaque connection between democracy and the division of labor which I would like to investigate in what follows.

My suspicion is that political philosophy betrays a tendency to neglect the significance of work and employment because it has almost totally lost sight of how democracies are rooted in the economic relations of a given society. Yet to support the thesis that the quality of democratic decision-making depends decisively on the nature of a society's division of labor, I must first demonstrate its general significance for the integration of modern societies. I will then be better placed to substantiate the thesis that the readiness of individuals to participate actively in political decision-making depends to a considerable degree on their being in a position to grasp their role within a transparent cooperative system, and thus to understand themselves as valuable members of a society (1). Having sketched the nature of the causal dependency involved, a few remarks will be in order regarding traditional conceptions of the division of labor; for, as we shall see, these prove limited and one-sided in a number of respects and so need to be corrected before we can begin to determine what might be the normative requirements on a division of labor more conducive to democratic societies (2). Finally, on the basis of this improved conception of the division of labor, I'll develop certain normative perspectives that ought to be borne in mind if we want to strive for greater inclusiveness in the process of democratic decision-making (3).

1.

Allowing ourselves a certain over-simplification, it's fair to say that there have, in modernity, been two contrasting conceptions of the sources from which modern societies draw their solidarity and cohesion. To avoid unnecessary complications, I shall designate these two traditions simply with the names of the authors who have defended the corresponding conceptions in a particularly representative fashion. On the one hand, we have the position advocated by de Tocqueville and Hannah Arendt, according to which it is political collaboration and cooperation amongst citizens which establishes the social bond: because all adult persons in modern democratic societies are called upon to participate in political decision-making, be it on a communal, regional, or national level, de Tocqueville and Arendt expect such ongoing communication to issue in the measure of normative assent required for social integration.[7] On the other hand, we have the position exemplarily represented by Marx and Durkheim, according to which it is the division of labor which provides for the necessary cohesion amongst the members of modern societies. Even if Marx projects this integrative effect of cooperation into a future in which a society has achieved a "communist" economy, he is nevertheless in basic agreement with Durkheim on the crucial point: only when members of a society collaborate in the labor processes necessary for that society's reproduction can there be the normative accord required for social integration. Insofar as social reproduction can be achieved only collectively, each member of society knows herself to be indebted in her work to other members, with the result that all members see themselves united in the goal of increasing overall welfare.[8]

Both approaches share a range of weaknesses, which, for the most part, stem from their reliance on a high degree of abstraction. Thus, for example, with the exception of Arendt, all of the aforementioned authors neglect how their proposed sources of social cohesion frequently require the fuel of national sentiment as a precondition of their integrative efficacy.[9] Yet if one makes a direct comparison of the two approaches, it soon becomes clear that the second, represented by Durkheim and Marx, both enjoys greater persuasive power and has a more general application. I will initially sketch the weaknesses and difficulties of the first approach before outlining the advantages of the second:

a) A first objection to the idea that democratic communication between citizens can be the source of integration in modern societies goes back to Benjamin Constant. In his famous text, *The Liberty of the Ancients Compared with that of the Moderns*, Constant put forward the view that expecting citizens to have to take an interest in the political co-determination of the country was contrary to the modern understanding of freedom.[10] This argument prepared the ground for the now widely shared notion that modern democracies are based on a "reasonable" pluralism of varying worldviews and ethical convictions, and that this precludes stipulating partici-pation in democratic decision-making as a requirement, or even obligation. Whether one prefers to participate in political debates, sporting events or religious ceremonies is down to the ethical decision of the individual; in the modern constitutional state, there can be no obligation to a particular form of life.

b) John Dewey gave this normative ideal of pluralism a psycho-logical complement, contending that since humans possess such varying interests and pursue such diverse projects, it would be unrealistic to expect them to suddenly agree at some point as to the importance of democratic activities.[11] Viewed from this psychological perspective, it would be rather counterintuitive to hope or believe that the members of modern societies might find solidarity and cohesion in a common commitment to political engagement. The assumption that participation in the mechanisms of democratic self-government could bring citizens together so as to create a common bond involves making a fatal abstraction from the sheer disparity of human interests and preferences.

However, emphasizing each of these shortcomings of the de Tocqueville/Arendt tradition, its neglect of both the normative principle of pluralism and the fact of the pluralism of human interests, by no means entails that we should treat the Marx/ Durkheim tradition as somehow sacrosanct and error-free. The latter has its own weaknesses and restrictions, which I will come to in due course. But I first want to set out the respects in which it is quite clearly superior to the alternative:

a) The greatest advantage of the second conception is, undoubtedly, the suggestion that the source of social integration should be located in a practice or form of activity that is not subject to the free discretion of or to negotiation between the individual members of a society: because each adult individual (or at least each adult male) in a modern "work-based society" is forced to support himself and his family through his own labor, the way in which various forms of work are interwoven within the overall division of labor should guarantee that the members of a society acknowledge their mutual dependence and thus develop a feeling of common belonging. However critically Marx might have regarded the conditions of the division of labor in capital-istic societies, he subscribed to the central premises of this view throughout his life: only through participation in forms of social cooperation – that is: only through the experience of our working for one another[12] – can we acquire an understanding of ourselves as members of a social community.

b) Yet prior to either Marx or Durkheim, it was Hegel who developed a further aspect of the thesis of the division of labor as the source of social integration, an aspect that continues to inform our modern self-understanding: it is to the author of the *Philosophy of Right* that we owe the idea that active participation in the division of labor gives every citizen the opportunity to develop the feeling of being publicly recognized, and thus a sense of their own self-worth.[13] Certainly, the idea that we need social recog-nition and respect if we are to take our place in the public sphere without anxiety or shame has its roots in quite different philo-sophical traditions. It owes a considerable debt not least to Scottish moral philosophy, which recognized the esteem of one's fellow citizens as a presupposition of individual self-worth.[14] Hegel takes up this idea and connects social esteem to the supposition that one contribute to the division of labor in accordance with one's duty. Heavily influenced by Adam Smith, Hegel insisted that only he who is willing to fulfill the tasks assigned him within the division of labor in a dutiful and "upright" [*rechtschaffen*] manner, will enjoy the fruits of social recognition, in particular, a consciousness of his own self-worth. The idea has since become deeply anchored in our culture, which sees validation as an individual in the public sphere as tied to the condition that one contributes, through one's own labor, to increasing the welfare of society as a whole.

c) A third argument in favor of the Marx/Durkheim tradition can best be understood as the negative complement of this Hegelian thesis. To be sure, Hegel's own discussion of the "rabble" shows him following up on the suspicion that involuntary unemployment can bring with it all the psychological dangers concomitant with counting as "superfluous" in one's own eyes. He saw that this can then lead to social deprivation – today, we might instead speak of the dangers of "social death."[15] But it was only later that sociological studies turned these suspicions and speculations into an empirically plausible thesis. Pioneering in this regard was the famous study of "Marienthal" by Marie Jahoda and her colleagues, as it was the first to demonstrate the psychologically drastic consequences of long-term unemployment. Those affected suffered from a gradual deterioration of their sense of time and the increasing loss of the communal solidarity cultivated at the workplace; but the most devastating experience was the sense of becoming "superfluous," of no use, within society at large.[16] It is not difficult to see the findings of this and similar studies as providing empirical support for Hegel's thesis, namely, that we achieve a consciousness of our own self-worth in and through our socially recognized contribution to the division of labor.

    If we take all three points together, it seems reasonable to conclude that the Marx/Durkheim position offers the superior solution to the problem of ascertaining the possible source of integration in modern societies. It is not participation in democratic decision-making, but the division of labor, which has the greatest potential for generating a sense of cohesion amongst members of a society and, thereby, for contributing to the integration of individuals who are otherwise mutually indifferent to one another. Yet before I can turn to the shortcomings and weaknesses of the Marx/Durkheim conception, a further, intermediary step is required: even at this early stage, I should at least indicate why the quality and intensity of democratic participation should depend on the condition of the division of labor in a given society. So far, we have seen, to some extent, why it might be plausible to expect social integration to be a function of incorporation within the division of labor. But it remains completely unclear why this should then have positive effects when it comes to the will and capacity of individuals to participate in the democratic process of deliberative decision-making. For now, a few words should suffice to clarify this connection, at least in its broad outlines.

    The connection I have in mind can be illustrated by means of a shared intuition. Hardly anyone will, from the outset, simply dismiss the contention that nothing influences the will and capacity for democratic participation more than the social conditions that determine one's working life: the slimmer the opportunities for having a say in the shape assumed by one's own labor, the lower one's primary income, and the worse the reputation of the work in question, the weaker the individual's faith in her own "political efficacy." What common sense anyhow suspected has since been confirmed by a variety of sociological studies: the degree to which one believes oneself able to effect some kind of change or exercise some form of influence on prevailing political circum- stances depends to a considerable extent upon one's position within the social division of labor.[17] Given what we know, it is not so much the size of one's income as the social conditions of one's job – employment security, complexity and meaningfulness of work, scope for exercising influence in the workplace – which determines the belief that one's contribution carries weight in the democratic decision-making process. Of course, the strength of this belief is not only, let alone automatically, dependent on one's occupational position within the division of labor; the political- cultural climate of a society also has a considerable influence on how much political heft an individual suspects they might carry. In his autobiographical *Return to Reims*, Didier Eribon gives a powerful description of how, in the 1950s and 1960s, even lowly, unqualified workers in the French province were deeply convinced of their own political strength and power thanks to their represen- tation by the then still powerful communist party. This faith in their political efficacy first began to fade, as Eribon makes clear, when the party gradually started to lose influence, affecting its ability to function as a representative organ of proletarian experiences and concerns.[18] But under historical conditions in which there is no strong labor movement to compensate for the weak sense of self- worth afflicting the industrial and service-sector proletariat, the causal relation I described above can come into effect unhindered. Summarizing a wealth of empirical data, Carol Pateman notes that the lesser one's say at the workplace and the less challenging the activities that define one's occupation, the weaker the faith in one's own political efficacy.[19]

For now, I'll treat these various observations as sufficient support for the thesis that the intensity and quality of democratic participation depends to a considerable extent on how inclusively, transparently, and fairly the division of labor is organized: the more members of a society have the chance to pursue complex tasks at secure places of work, where they can co-determine its character, organization, and goals, the greater will be the degree of political participation in democratic processes. The consequences of this thesis for political philosophy are much broader in scope than may at first be apparent. For as soon as we acknowledge how democracies depend on a rightful and fair organization of labor, it becomes hard to justify the fairly standard decoupling of democratic theory from questions concerning the sociology of labor – indeed, from socioeconomic questions quite generally. The organization of labor in a society is not a matter external to democratic practice. Nor does it represent something like a boundary condition of such practice. Rather, it is an internal component of its functioning. It was authors such as the American pragmatist John Dewey and the British socialist G. D. H. Cole, who time and again pointed out how nonsensical it is for democratic theory to consider the citizen only in terms of his political, but not of his economic, role. For he cannot simply discard his role within the economic process organized around the division of labor as soon as he comes to act as a political subject; and this means that democratic theory has to regard him in terms of the interplay of both functions – an interplay, to be sure, which is characterized by multiple tensions. Before I can pursue the question of what this means for a fair division of labor, I first have to turn to the difficulties of the Marx/Durkheim tradition that I have already alluded to on more than one occasion. Once we have these clearly in view, we will be in a position to take on the question of which normative perspectives need to be borne in mind when it comes to the organization of a division of labor that has the aim of involving a greater number of citizens in democratic decision-making.

2.

If we consider the concept of the division of labor as introduced by Smith and developed in various directions by Marx and Durkheim, a host of shared deficiencies and shortcomings immediately come into view. All three approaches suffer, to differing degrees, from (1) a restricted conception of what has to count as socially necessary "work"; from (2) the deterministic assumption that the dominant form of the division of labor at any given time will be conditioned solely by technological demands; and from (3) committing the mechanistic fallacy, and so categorically excluding the possibility that specific fields of activity might have alternative compositions, and types of occupations quite different boundaries. As I say, all three authors do not commit these errors to the same extent:

Marx, for example, was thoroughly convinced that the future would see much more fluid boundaries between different fields of activity, although his thinking was just as reductionist as Smith's or Durkheim's when it came to the question of which activities should count as "labor" within capitalist societies. In what follows, however, I will abstract from these differences and simply elaborate a little on each of the three deficits listed above. We will then be in a position to see why it is unwise to continue to operate with the traditional concept of the division of labor.

a) As for the question of how to define the very "labor" to be "divided" in modern societies, all three authors seem to share a certain conception: at the heart of this stands industrial, physically arduous wage labor, deployed in large- or small-scale operations that transform raw material into finished products with the aid of machine power. To put the point differently: Smith, Marx, and Durkheim were prisoners of a vocabulary in which "labor" is equivalent to physical effort, is supposed to serve the manufacturing of "material" goods, and is organized in the form of mutually terminable contracts.[20] From the beginning, this notion was far too one-sided and came at a high price, because it tended to bracket out at least the following kinds of socially necessary labor:

- service work in all its organizational forms, from compulsory and indentured labor, to debt bondage, through to contractually regulated wage labor, which, taken together, made up the greatest share of overall employment in the "industrialized" countries of the West at the end of the nineteenth and the beginning of the twentieth centuries;[21]
- all agricultural activities in the various forms it assumed both in the times of Smith, Marx, and Durkheim and, to some extent, still today;
- the residue of slave labor, the merciless exploitation of which, in large segments of Western Europe, created the economic and material preconditions for capitalist industrialization;[22]
- the steadily increasing number of white-collar occupations in the financial sector, law firms, and political organizations, made necessary by the rapid growth of trade and industry;[23]
- and finally, of course, what we now understand as the scandalous variety of physical and psychological labors within the sphere of the household and family, which were carried out for the most part by women and, indirectly, constituted a significant contribution to economic growth.[24]

In light of these omissions, we face the general question of which activities within a society should be designated as "labor" in an economically relevant sense in the first place. It makes little sense to count as labor any kind of performance that pursues a socially useful goal. Doing so means including purely private activities pursued for their own sake – with such a broad understanding of the concept of "labor," the difference between voluntary participation in a choir or performing a spot of DIY in your own house on the one hand and, on the other, gainful employment in the opera house choir or working professionally as a painter or decorator, all but disappears. A provisional route out of these difficulties is the suggestion that we count as "labor" only those activities that are required for the material and cultural reproduction of a society at a given time and so contribute to their added value in a broad sense. All activities and performances that do not facilitate, directly or indirectly, the reproduction of a society in its current state should thus not be categorized as "labor."[25] The problem with such a definition is clear enough: it has to simply prescribe what counts as necessary for the collective maintenance of present society, thereby precluding short-term transformations in cultural self-understanding. Yet the right conclusion to draw from this is only that we should keep the concept of "socially necessary labor" sufficiently open to revision, so that it might incorporate changes in our conceptions of what is and is not indispensable to our form of collective life.

b) The second deficiency contained in the traditional concept is its monocausal view of the factors responsible for a given division of labor. All three of the authors in question simply take for granted that the differentiation between individual performances and their coupling with corresponding items of machinery is conditioned solely by the technological pressures of increasing economic efficiency. Thus, both Smith and Marx were of the view that the transition from the agrarian world of the peasant smallholder to the industrial world of the capitalist is to be understood as a progression from autarchy to economic specialization. But that this was far from being the case, and that this transition was in fact much more complex and socially contested is the central thesis of Michael Piore and Charles Sabel's study of the division of labor at the beginning of the industrial revolution.[26] According to their research, at the beginning of the nineteenth century there were two viable alternatives for an efficacious future combination of human skill with new technologies, namely the mass production of goods through the adoption of highly specialized skillsets and machinery, and the craft production of specialized articles through the use of general resources. In Piore and Sabel's view, the fact that only the first alternative was realized, that of mass production, was not a result of technological necessities, but exclusively of the "distribution of power and wealth": "those who controlled the resources and the return from investment chose from the available technologies the one most favorable to their interest."[27] Accordingly, one should not see the path to Fordism, the dominant form of capitalist production in the twentieth century, as something unavoidable, as though it reflects some iron law of technological progress. Rather, it was the suppression of small-scale craft industries in the middle of the nineteenth century, driven by power and the interests of profit, which led some decades later to standardized assembly manufacturing becoming the dominant model of production. Generalizing on the basis of this historical finding, we can say that the dominant form of the division of labor in a given society is not the necessary consequence of efficiency-driven economic pressures; since at almost any point in time there are comparably efficient possibilities for combining instrumental capacities and technical methods, the decision as to which particular combination is preferable is mostly due to the outcomes of political-economic conflicts. The form in which socially necessary labor is tailored and distributed is co-determined by social struggles and political confrontations; how human capacities, technical rules, and machinery are to be combined are socially negotiated or determined through explicit conflict, not merely through anonymous pressures. This brings me to the third weak spot of the traditional concept of the division of labor, namely its presupposition of an overly mechanistic picture of individual fields of activity and occupations.

c) The complaint that the traditional picture of occupations is too mechanistic refers to its notorious neglect of quite how variously one might draw the boundaries between core individual tasks in both the industrial and service sectors. Depending on the outcomes of political negotiations and conflicts, either more or fewer responsibilities and functions might be assigned to particular fields of activity. A famous example of the indeterminacy associated with individuating different jobs and occupations is the hospital: where the activities and responsibilities of one occupation, of a nurse, for example, end and those of another occupation, of a doctor say, begin, is always a matter of tough negotiations or political decisions. The business of drawing boundaries between the two fields of activity is not conditioned by any kind of inherent necessity or constraint, and is thus always open for revision. Ultimately, these boundaries have to be socially stipulated. And this goes for almost all occupational fields, not just that of the hospital; there are practically always possibilities for reconfiguring the scope of a given occupational domain and its characteristic tasks, for adding certain responsibilities and removing others, or even for creating entirely new bundles of activities. If the critique of determinism targets the false notion that the weighting and distribution of an entire society's modes of labor and production are compelled by the imperatives of economic rationalization, the critique of mechanism takes aim at the misleading idea that individual occupational fields are divided up as they are because the nature of their respective constitutive tasks demands just such a division. We can neither appeal to such "tasks" without a consideration of their socially contested definitions, nor take for granted that they can be discharged solely in the form of given bundles of activities.

Reviewing these various shortcomings, it seems inadvisable to use the traditional conceptions of the division of labor as a framework for posing our guiding question: which form might be both fair and conducive to democracy? As we have seen, they all suffer from a much too narrow idea of what should count as labor, from a deterministic account of why certain modes of production and forms of work dominate at different times, and from an excessively mechanistic view of the constitution of differing fields of activity and occupation. Once we correct for these failures, we attain an essentially more comprehensive and open-ended picture of a society's division of labor: it is not only that we now have to include domains of activity that have thus far been largely excluded, such as domestic and service sector work; in addition, all of these necessary performances also offer much more room for maneuver when it comes to their reconfiguration, reorganization, and recombination than was traditionally assumed. Even if these revisions would require potentially complex and long-term measures, this should not be an obstacle to reflection on divisions of labor that are more conducive to democracy. Sometimes the "strong and slow boring of hard boards" (Max Weber) is necessary for the almost imperceptible, yet persistent redirection of political attention toward those tasks that are truly urgent. On the other hand, whilst the insight into the political constitution of dominant forms of distribution and modes of organizing labor allows for a greater radius of action, this should not be taken as a license to indulge in wild speculations about an ideal world, in which labor is freed from alienation, burdens, and hardship. Such blueprints, drafted in the ivory tower, distract from the need to think about realistic changes; changes which, on the basis of given circumstances, would redistribute socially necessary labor and activities in such a way that every adult gains a greater opportunity to participate in the process of democratic decision-making. In what follows, I would like to attempt to outline a normative perspective that could serve as guiding principle for just such a reorganization of the division of labor. This, to repeat, should not be anything like a normative ideal, but a set of practical requirements, the short- or long-term realization of which would help to bring the world of work into alignment with the demands of democratic equality.

3.

In the tradition of Marxist thought which, willingly or unwillingly, we all inhabit, there is a strong tendency to reflect on future transformations in the world of work using relatively utopian categories, as though that future lies on the far side of a temporal chasm from the present. It is not uncommon to hear talk of a possible future in which labor has shed every aspect of "alienation," in which it is experienced as meaningful, in which, indeed, every worker can freely switch back and forth between different fields of activity as their abilities and desires dictate. Such ideas (bearing, as they do, the idealistic stamp of Romanticism) are certainly attractive. Yet viewed in the sober light of day, they are quite uninformative as to which direction an improvement of our present capitalist division of labor ought to take: the notion of overcoming entirely the alienation of labor is either too vague in its metaphysical premises or far too specific insofar as it continues to be oriented by the self-directed activity characteristic of craft production.[28] The seductive image of a rhythmical transition between contrasting occupations – "hunt in the morning, fish in the afternoon, rear cattle in the evening" – not only severely underestimates the amount of effort and knowledge acquisition required for a vast range of specialized jobs, but also betrays an astonishing tendency to ignore the ongoing persistence of menial, arduous, and degrading work. So if we put our question – *viz.* which changes are needed to bring workers to increased self-consciousness, autonomy, and belief in their own political efficacy? – to the Marxist tradition, their answers may well act as spurs to the imagination, but not necessarily provide sources of illumination.

An alternative to the Marxist legacy is suggested by Émile Durkheim's theory of the normative conditions of a fair division of labor.[29] To be sure, his own efforts in this respect are themselves marked by a series of idealizations and an occasional indulgence in wishful thinking[30]; yet overall, he pays considerably more attention to the real difficulties and constraints that condition the world of work than does Marx. In my view, a sensible way of proceeding if we want to follow in the footsteps of Durkheim's theory is to start from his diagnosis of "anomic" or pathological forms of the division of labor, and to extract some positive criteria that we can use as points of orientation. The advantage of this kind of indirect procedure is that it allows us to set Durkheim's involved justification of his theoretical framework to one side, and concentrate instead on the normative core of his project. His analyses of negative "anomic" forms of the division of labor presuppose positive criteria, and if we uncover these, we derive the following three requirements on fairer, more democratic modes of organization:

a) Durkheim is convinced that society should work toward rendering work more meaningful and cooperative, in such a way that the individual worker, whatever her position, has the chance to understand how her own role fits into the usually opaque whole of interconnected activities that make up the overall division of labor. If this can be achieved, that is, if each worker's station affords her an overview of how her performances are internally connected with those of others, she will acquire a stronger sense of the social value of her everyday activities. Durkheim expects such measures to lead not only to a heightened collective consciousness of recip-rocal interdependence, but also to an increase in each worker's sense of self-worth: learning that one's own activity represents a practically irreplaceable wheel in the overall mechanism of the division of labor should, in standard cases, increase one's pride in one's own accomplishments.[31] Of course, different spheres of activity present different challenges to cultivating a consciousness of such interdependency; the more certain jobs at the lower-paid end of today's service sector, such as various delivery and cleaning services, are individualized, anonymized, and disparaged, the more difficult it might be to even find approaches to investing such occupations with a meaningful role in the overall division of labor.[32] But this only means that the propagation of such forms of work should be resisted by all means possible; and not only because of the inadequate pay, precarious status, and enormous pressures that characterize them, but also because the employees themselves barely have the opportunity to make use of their established right to effective participation in the democratic process. Yet in view of all the spheres of activity in which the very mode of occupation and the very nature of the work contract does not already undermine the claim to democratic participation, it is vital to raise levels of institutional imagination so as to increase collective consciousness of the irreplaceable function of various tasks within the division of labor. The arsenal of possible methods here ranges from the symbolic illustration of reciprocal dependencies, through the expansion of cooperative, team-based work, to the financial and social re-evaluation of fields of activity whose indispensability to social reproduction has previously enjoyed only limited visibility. When it comes to exploring such possibilities, there is much to be learnt from the by now usually forgotten reform projects of both capitalist and former communist countries, that aimed at civilizing the world of work.[33]

b) A second theme that comes to the fore in Durkheim's diagnosis of "anomic" forms of the division of labor bears on the increasing thinning-out and spiritual and intellectual impoverishment of ever more jobs as a result of growing specialization. Like Adam Smith before him – and Harry Braverman after him[34] – Durkheim feared that low-skilled, monotonous work could lead in the long term to a loss of intellectual awareness, a decreasing general curiosity in the world one inhabits, and thus to political disengagement in the case of both white- and blue-collar workers. Having to perform the same small-scale, routinized tasks over weeks, months, and years invites the danger, according to Durkheim, of losing the tools necessary for democratic participation. The suggestion he puts forward for counteracting these tendencies boils down to enriching the functional bundle of activities of individual workers by redrawing the boundaries between different occupations. Lacking a clear understanding of the extent to which the classification and differentiation of various spheres of activity is a matter of political conflict and negotiation, he recommends enriching those sets of tasks that exhibit a particular tendency to restrictedness and one-sidedness. This, too, naturally raises the question of how work today might be enriched, when the recent series of deregulations of the labor market has resulted in the increasing scarcity and isolation of so many occupations (think again of cleaning, delivery, and call-center services). Likewise, we might ask how such considerations should impact upon domains such as housework, which Durkheim had not yet included within the overall network of the division of labor; in such cases too, the relevant kind of labor has traditionally been carried out in conditions of isolation and mostly involved a small set of easily acquired skills. Here, too, the possibility of routinization presents the danger of having a deadening effect and a consequent withdrawal from the democratic process. Of course, for both kinds of occupation, housework and service sector work, there are a series of organizational alternatives which, however, could be implemented only under the conditions of a drastically altered labor regime. In the case of housework, for example, one might think of the example of Kibbutzim, and how the tasks in question could be undertaken in turn by different members of a housing cooperative; and in the case of simple but (for the time being at least) necessary services, one could imagine them being discharged by self-governing groups through teamwork. The only reason why organizational imagination today operates within such narrow boundaries is that the work contract concluded between free legal subjects remains the governing model for all employment relations. And this brings me to the third recommendation we find outlined in Durkheim.

c) In his diagnosis of "anomic" forms of the division of labor, Durkheim's greatest concern is focused on the danger that contracts concluded between employer and employee might be influenced by pressure and coercion. Not unlike Marx, he believed that employees often have nothing at their disposal besides their labor power and, as a consequence, are driven time and again by sheer existential necessity to agree to contractual conditions that they would never endorse in circumstances where they could freely exercise their own volition. Yet unlike Marx, Durkheim supposes that this evil can be combated through political and legal means that are ultimately compatible with the preconditions of a market economy. He sees fiscal policy as the primary means to break the superior negotiating power of the owners of capital, occasionally even recommending the abolition of individual inheritance rights.[35] None of these countermeasures have lost their political relevance in the more than 120 years since the publication of *De la division du travail social*; indeed, in light of the gradual dissolution of labor market boundaries witnessed in recent times, they are no less worthy of consideration than in Durkheim's own day. A frustrating aspect of his recommendations, however, is how they are directed exclusively at creating fairer conditions for concluding contracts between capitalist and worker; he never so much as mentions the possibility that the allocation of work might be undertaken other than via the mechanism of private contracts. For one thing, this exclusion of economic alternatives is historically questionable, suggesting as it does that individual contracts exhausted the possible modes of organizing labor in the late nineteenth century. Yet I've already alluded to how such various mechanisms of allocation as debt bondage, concealed slavery, independent craft production, private domestic labor, and, finally, "freely" entered work contracts all existed beside one another in the capitalist society Durkheim inhabited.[36] Even more significant, however, is that this oversight precludes Durkheim from reflecting on fairer, democracy-promoting forms of the division of labor beyond an amelioration of the contractual conditions of wage laborers. He seems to take it for granted that there could be no other means of organizing labor that might serve the aim of strengthening democratic solidarity.

Thus, one searches Durkheim's analyses in vain for any mention of the possibility that, for example, work could be organized through employee-run, self-governing collectives, or through mandatory public service either for a specific age-cohort or all adult members of a society. Both the present and the past furnish us with models for both alternatives to the labor market and give reason to expect that these would increase both the general willingness and capacity for democratic participation. Several studies and reports show that the inclusion of workers in the operational decision-making processes of industrial concerns, service organizations, or state institutions involves an increase not only in workers' satisfaction and self-confidence, but also in their interest in the political processes of society at large. Quite simply, when one's own views are consulted in organizational decision-making, one feels an obligation to be better informed about wider developments. This applies to a considerably greater degree to participation in self-regulatory operations, be they cooperatively or state owned. A glance at the literature on these kinds of enterprise quickly reveals that there is a strong increase in work satisfaction, political self-consciousness, and democratic engagement as soon as workers acquire a collective responsibility for the fate of an organization.[37]

The allocation of labor via state diktat is, of course, a very different proposition, as we know especially from the context of military service. But if we think instead of, for example, the increasingly important area of elderly care, or of childcare, we see how their effectiveness in enlivening democracy lies less in how they equip people for political participation than in how they communicate knowledge about a society's functional interconnections and the problems they face. It is, to be sure, a radical step, one that is easy to criticize as illiberal, for the state to obligate a specific age-cohort or the entire adult population to perform some service for a specified time-period for the supposed sake of the common good. Such compulsory measures can certainly not be justified by mere reference to gaps in the budget and the need for efficiency savings. A democratically tolerable justification could, however, consist in adverting to how, in light of growing diversification, there is an ever-increasing need to familiarize the population with the everyday demands of social co-existence and the lived circumstances of different classes. An additional, moral, argument could be that certain unavoidable jobs should be performed by all members of the population, perhaps for a set timeframe, rather than their being the permanent occupation of one and the same, usually particularly disadvantaged, group.[38] The first argument appeals to a virtue of democratic participation, the second to an obligation of social justice.

I have not invoked either of these alternatives to the capitalist mode of organization of socially necessary work in order to recommend them as magic bullets that would somehow guarantee a fairer division of labor, one friendlier to democracy. Neither collective self-regulation nor state cooption can, whether in isolation or in combination, recruit all the labor necessary for the reproduction of society in its current state. On the other hand, one ought to avoid Durkheim's error and not simply lose sight of the fact that modern, highly differentiated societies can also offer other means of allocating labor than through the incentive system of the market. State conscription for a limited timeframe, collective self-regulation of enterprises in private or public ownership, producer's coops – all of these various forms of organizing labor, which have all-too-quickly been forgotten in recent decades, present alternatives to common wage labor that merit serious consideration.[39] What is needed today, therefore, is a recovery of the suppressed or failed reform projects of the past, so that, with the right mixture of institutional imagination, political-economic realism, and sociological judgment, we can come up with new, more just forms of the division of labor. The yardstick of all these investigations,

reflections, and experimental tests must be reorganizing the distribution of socially necessary work in such a way that as many
members of society as possible can develop the capacity and
willingness to participate in the democratic process. For, today, at
least so much seems certain: so long as we change nothing in the
current form of the division of labor, so long as we make our peace
with the underpayment, powerlessness, and excessive burdens
of so many fields of economic activity, and so long as we fail to
counter the intellectual and spiritual impoverishment of countless
spheres of work, we will continue the process of precluding a good
half of the population from the actual exercise of their right to
democratic participation.

Translated by Alex Englander

10

Childhood

Inconsistencies in our liberal imagination

For at least the last two decades, literature and cinema have ever more frequently featured neglected children and teenagers who are forced to get by alone. Anyone who saw Ang Lee's *The Ice Storm*, first screened in 1997, will find it difficult to forget the despondent adolescents whose expressions vacillate between bitterness and despair as they wander aimlessly through the frightening darkness of a brewing ice storm the night before Thanksgiving. They have been abandoned by their middle-class mothers and fathers, left alone with their pubescent worries.[1] Richard Ford's *Canada* provides a similar experience: in an irritatingly laconic style, it tells the story of a desperate boy who is suddenly left to his own devices after his parents are sent to prison, and has to grapple with life without caring support.[2] And the rhetorical question put by Boris, the neglected son of a single father, to the protagonist of Donna Tartt's *The Goldfinch*, the thirteen-year-old Theodore Decker, who, in turn, lost his beloved mother in a terrorist attack and cannot count on the support of his father, sounds like a succinct summary of these childhood experiences of neglect and loneliness: "None of us ever find enough kindness in the world, do we?"[3]

Today's novels and films contain countless examples of such depictions of lost and forlorn children. They differ from earlier descriptions of the type – think, for instance, of Dickens's *Bleak House* – mainly insofar as they are set in milieus in which the contemporary ideals of caring families and well-looked-after children are deeply engrained, even if they are not always heeded in daily life. Their protagonists are children or teenagers who, despite the promise of protection and support, are forced at crucial moments to deal with their worries and anxieties alone, without their parents or next of kin. In terms of public visibility and frequency, these depressing depictions of contemporary childhood are outdone only by media descriptions that focus on the experience of sexual abuse. There are countless biographies, stories, and films dedicated to the theme, and hardly a Sunday evening passes by without someone appearing on a talk show, or a character featuring in a whodunnit, whose life has been decisively influenced by an early experience of sexual abuse, be it by a close relative or an authority figure. In 100 years' time, a cultural historian researching the perceptions and treatment of children at the beginning of the twenty-first century will at this rate turn up a pretty ugly result: that childhood in our time was characterized by a degree of neglect, abuse, and deprivation that far exceeds that of previous eras.

In the light of the available empirical information about contemporary childhood, this would, however, be erroneous. Contrary to the imagined future historian's conclusion, we can say – albeit cautiously – that, from a historical perspective, children today receive more individual attention and legal protection than ever before. Historical research in the wake of Philippe Ariès's study *Centuries of Childhood*[4] – a landmark work, even if not convincing in every respect – has taught us that, unlike in earlier phases of history or other cultures, we today understand "childhood" primarily as a time in which the human being needs protection, and in which care and education are required to prepare the child for the role of a mature and autonomous subject. A look at the field of law reveals that today a number of legal instruments exist across the globe, and in particular in liberal democracies, that aim to protect the well-being of children through fundamental rights that can be enforced by the state, most notably the UN Convention on the Rights of the Child.[5] Empirical social research has demonstrated the extent to which attitudes in education have changed in recent decades, at least in Western countries, with individual children being given more communicative attention and free space than in previous times. Martin Dornes summarizes the changes by saying that the parent–child relation has become significantly more egalitarian, even more democratic. From the early years, children are taken seriously as partners in negotiation, and included in discussions of family matters.[6] On the basis of this historical and empirical evidence, there is reason to conclude that children today have more done for their well-being than children in any other culture about which we possess reliable information. We need only remind ourselves of the fairly recent past – the late nineteenth and early twentieth centuries – with its draconian educational methods, authoritarian fathers, and strict gender role identities, and this positive evaluation of the way we treat children seems fully justified.

Yet the examples I mentioned at the outset, even if they seem to contradict the empirical evidence, remain disturbing. After all, they are the result not of overly sensitive individual directors or authors but of a precise, trained, and subtle sense – even if an idiosyncratic one – for ruptures in our routine life practices. One of art's tasks, after all, is to draw our attention to such cracks and chasms in how we understand ourselves, to seek them out and throw a spotlight on them. The works of Ang Lee, Richard Ford, and Donna Tartt carry out this task masterfully. Their sensitive and stirring representations force us, in various ways, to re-examine the subterranean ideas on which our notions of child well-being are based – to ask what their foundation is, and where they might fall short and need to be amended. In what follows, I take up the challenge of exploring, cautiously, the hidden assumptions on which our views about child well-being are based. First, in section I, I try to unfold the various factors that can influence the historically variable experience of children's particular vulnerability and thus, by implication, the corresponding ideals of what constitutes child well-being. We will see that there are always four elements that combine to determine what counts as the well-being of children in different cultures. Then, in section II, against the backdrop of this four-dimensional concept of childhood, I shall seek to determine what our contemporary liberal democratic ideas of child well-being look like in detail. By considering the four elements in turn, this section will examine whether there are ruptures or tensions within our idea of child well-being that might explain the complaints mentioned at the outset of this chapter. My aim could perhaps be described as follows: first, by outlining a concept of childhood that is as general as possible, I distance us from our own relationship with children; this then allows us, second, to discover ruptures and splits that would normally be hidden.

I

We take it for granted today that ideas about what makes a child vulnerable, whether in the context of the family or in other social contexts, have changed radically in the course of human history, and that these ideas continued to change even during modernity. Two examples suffice to remind us of this trivial fact. In some cultures, having young children sleep separately from their parents is seen as harmful, but in the West the practice is almost the opposite. Space permitting, even infants are given a room of their own, so as to help them articulate their own desires and needs as early as possible. Something similar applies in the case of child labor. For much of history, it was seen not only as a necessary means by which the family secured its subsistence but also as a beneficial and pleasant form of cooperation between family members. Today, by contrast, we believe that children need to develop and be cared for, and that having a child do any kind of work is seriously damaging.[7] These examples are meant only to illustrate how significantly ideas about children's well-being vary in accordance with different background assumptions about the specificities of what "childhood" means. If childhood is taken to be a phase of life that is strictly distinct from adulthood, it follows that the child must not be expected to perform any labor. If, by contrast, the transition between these two modes of being is seen as a gradual process, children's contribution to work can be viewed as a valuable first step that prepares them for their later role and gives them the opportunity to experience appreciation early in life. In this way, the culturally valid concepts that attach to "childhood" always determine what counts as injurious for a child and, by implication, what counts as advancing its well-being. Aiming to establish a universally applicable conception of "child well-being" therefore seems a questionable undertaking as it rests on the assumption that there is a general and culture-independent idea of what it means to be a child.

Concepts of "childhood" always consist of very heterogeneous elements. It is only when these elements are taken together that they determine a specific understanding of the nature and status of children. The first of these elements, (a), consists in an answer to the question of whether a human being's early life is a distinct, separate phase of development and, if so, what distinguishes it from later phases. So far as we know, most cultures contrast the first stage of life with all other stages in some way or another, and to that extent they all have a notion of "childhood." The end of this first stage is often marked with initiation rituals, which tell us something about the supposed psychological differences between children and adults. In the West, the issuing of a passport signals the acquisition of the right to autonomy. The collective rituals of other cultures are public demonstrations of someone entering the age of sexual maturity and procreation. But these two examples may give the misguided impression that the psychological specificity of "childhood" must always consist in a lack of "adult" traits. In fact, we can also understand the specificity of adult life as consisting in a lack of certain potentials possessed by children. We need only remind ourselves of Adorno's contention that the child's access to the world involves a mimetic capacity that adults lose as the social reality principle forces them to adopt instrumental forms of thought.[8] Because the concepts of childhood and adulthood refer to one another, a number of alternatives and variations are possible in this context. The specific properties of children are defined with reference to the abilities of adults, and in the same way the specificities of adults are defined with reference to how they differ from the faculties of children. If the older members of a culture are less inclined to view each of their own traits as the apex in the development of a certain quality, they will be more likely to view the attributes of the younger generation not just as the preliminary stages and germs of something to come but as independent and socially enriching abilities in their own right. It will be interesting to see how our societies respond in the longer term to the fact that the growth in life expectancy means that many elderly people will experience a helplessness and dependence that renders them, once again, child-like.

A second element, (b), of any general notion of "childhood" consists in ideas about how closely the young relate to the social environment. Again, there is a range of possibilities here. At one end of the spectrum, there is the idea that the child is exclusively a member of the family, and is thus juxtaposed with society; at the other, there is the idea that the child is from the very beginning a participant in social interactions. The more the conception of childhood leans toward the first possibility, the more the society places all responsibility for the fate of the child on the family group. By the same token, the more that children are seen as participants in social interaction, the more society as a whole is taken to be responsible for children's development. Philippe Ariès's thesis that something akin to a general idea of "childhood" emerged only with modernity, a claim apt to be misconstrued, is certainly made more plausible if we take it to apply just to this second element of the concept. On this understanding, the dissolution of feudal family forms led to a dramatic change in the attitude toward the younger generation because children came to be confined to the space of the new, smaller family unit, which increasingly became emotionally saturated, with children losing their former status as partners in social interaction accordingly. This reinterpretation of Ariès's thesis would have the additional advantage of clarifying the second aspect of his historical reconstruction: the claim that the "familialization" of the child went hand in hand with "pedagogization." This secondary process – the development of schooling – is easier to understand if we see it not simply as a consequence of the "invention" of "childhood" in modernity but instead as a consequence of the child's isolation from society. Where before children acquired knowledge implicitly through their participation in social cooperation, their isolation from society made it necessary to convey this knowledge explicitly and in an artificial form.[9]

Whatever our judgment of Ariès's influential study, it is important to bear in mind that any conception of "childhood" includes an understanding of how tightly or loosely the child is integrated into the social environment. This factor determines not only how the responsibility for the child's well-being is distributed but also the experiences and burdens to which a child can be exposed.

A third element, (c), in all concepts of "childhood" consists in the different characteristics ascribed to the entities involved in a child's socialization – on the one hand the intimate surroundings of the family group, and on the other the more distant world of society at large. There are significant cultural differences in the way these two poles are imagined, and hence in the way the specificity of children and the processes that constitute childhood are understood. It makes a big difference, for instance, whether a society generally assumes that the immediate family unit in which the child grows up is an intrinsically harmonious or an intrinsically conflictual institution. The more the family is seen as a primarily consensual space, the more, surely, the general expectation will be that a child will be well looked after, and therefore will not need any outside support, whether from more distant relatives or from more neutral agencies. If, by contrast, the family is seen as a site of unavoidable, deep-seated conflict, society will be more ready to ensure that the child has some agent, or advocate, to whom the child can turn for help and support. In the extended family units of the past, aunts and uncles were expected to intervene on the child's behalf and mediate in cases of internal family conflict – an institutional role that points in that direction. It is worth briefly mentioning at this point the surprising fact that, 100 years after

Freud's interventions, Western culture has as yet failed to develop comparable mechanisms for the sublimation of family conflict, and instead delegates all such functions to outside institutions such as counsellors and state welfare agencies.

What can be said of the family unit applies equally to the social environment into which the child must, at least to some degree, be integrated. Depending on the culture in question, this space, too, can be imagined either as a harmonious, pacific sphere or as a site of tension and conflict. As with the various characterizations of the family, the differences between the social images of this space will influence perceptions of the child's vulnerability and, accordingly, conceptions of the necessary conditions of the child's well-being. If the social environment in which the child grows up is portrayed as more or less balanced and sound, it may be understood as having little impact on the child's flourishing. But if adults view this environment as a space of inequality, with all the difficulty and misfortune that that entails, it will be understood as a problem to be solved – and this to varying degrees depending on how important the social environment is taken to be for the child's experience of the world. At this point, the second and third elements obviously touch upon each other, for the extent to which a lifeworld rent asunder by severe disparities is seen as something that needs to be changed in the child's interest depends, in turn, on the extent to which social framework conditions in general are seen as influencing the child's development. We can say that, to the extent that one is prepared to acknowledge that influence, one will also be inclined to modify given social conditions that one takes to be damaging to the child.

As if the concept of "childhood" were not already sufficiently multi-dimensional, there is a fourth element, (d), to consider. It is not at all clear – it is often a matter of controversy – what might justify the subjection of children to educational, disciplinary, or instructional authority. There is a broad range of possibilities here, but these possibilities can, again, be captured by considering two opposed poles. At the one end, there is the firm conviction that adults are not justified in subjecting children to any such measures because the child has an individual moral right to autonomy that rules out any tutelage that goes beyond what is strictly necessary. Historically, such a radical idea could be formulated only once all human subjects came to enjoy fundamental individual rights, at which point the question could arise as to why their offspring should not enjoy the same rights.[10] At the opposite end, we find the – historically widespread – idea that children are the property either of their biological parents or of the social community, and that these therefore have a formally unlimited right to exercise power and educational authority over them as they see fit. Over the past two centuries, however, this conception of the ownership of children increasingly fell out of favor as it came into conflict with the emerging idea of fundamental rights. It was not possible to exclude offspring altogether from the scope of these rights, which became the crucial point of reference for the opposite end of the spectrum. Today, we occupy a point somewhere in the middle of the spectrum. Parents and the state share the task of education to varying degrees depending on the child's age, but we do not justify this with reference to property rights, nor do we grant children the right of autonomy. Rather, the asymmetrical distribution of power is justified by a reflexive paternalism, which, in turn, is based on the general assumption that children possess certain psychological properties that distinguish them from adults. These properties are considered the preliminary stages of capacities that older people are generally said to have, such as the capacity to lead an autonomous life or reflect upon the good. This advantage of the older over the younger is meant to justify educational measures that aim to close the gap. With this, our exposition comes full circle. We have returned to the point of departure of our reconstruction of the elements of social conceptions of "childhood": the normatively inflected juxtaposition of children's characteristics with adults' capacities. This juxtaposition is still crucial today, because only it can justify an institutionally far-reaching boundary between two age categories, marking a distinction that is fundamental to all areas of everyday life.

Our reconstruction has shown that every cultural idea of "childhood" contains a bundle of specifications that are related to the most diverse dimensions of social life. These specifications include not only accounts of the properties that distinguish older people from significantly younger ones, but also interpretations of the structure and mutual relations between the worlds of family and society, as well as normative justifications of tutelage and education. In any given culture, the conceptual ideas that result from these four specifications, taken together, determine what counts as potentially damaging to children and, accordingly, what counts as advancing their well-being. We could also put it like this: we could not know what constitutes the vulnerability of younger people, and what therefore should be done to foster their development, if we did not have socially shared concepts that provide us with an intuitive knowledge of the peculiar character of "childhood" and its relation to the social environment. I now seek to apply these findings to the ideas that today guide Western liberal cultures' understanding of "childhood," behind which lies a whole network of social practices. With reference to each of the four conceptual elements I have outlined, I shall reconstruct the background assumptions that inform our current understanding of the relationship between children and society.

II

I have already, at various points, hinted at the fact that I believe there to be weaknesses or deficiencies in the hidden ideas that shape our contemporary Western liberal image of childhood. In what follows, I take up these vague suspicions in more detail, and in so doing find my way back to the literary and aesthetic examples from which I set out. Only if we have a comprehensive overview of the underlying practices can we determine whether these examples are merely empty exaggerations or, rather, keen insights into the painful deficiencies that mark our dealings with children. In providing this overview, we will follow the list of elements identified in the previous section, which will force us to examine components of our culturally specific ideas of childhood to which we do not usually pay attention. We are often unaware of these components because we take them for granted and believe them to be well-justified. My presentation of the individual elements of this image of childhood follows the same sequence as the previous section.

(a) I remarked at the beginning that every cultural idea of "childhood" depends fundamentally on a conceptual distinction between an early and a later phase of human life. Such temporal delimitations, which are a necessary presupposition of any distinction between childhood and adulthood, normally use mutually connoted adjectives that are meant to describe aspects that are characteristic of one of the phases but absent in the other. In the case of our contemporary understanding of this distinction, strict oppositions seem to have increasingly given way to gradual differences. Today, childhood seems to be characterized by the fact that it contains the seeds of all the characteristics and abilities that, following a period of maturation and education, adults are said to acquire. This substitution of a model of gradual growth for a strict opposition certainly has its advantages. There is now not just one homogeneous concept of childhood that requires a single set of educational measures; rather, different phases can now be distinguished, with each demanding its own independent forms of interaction and treatment.[11] Despite its advantages, however, this current model of maturation and development contains a few peculiarities that should give us pause. The child's maturity, for instance, is usually measured exclusively in terms of psychological properties, and all of these properties are variations on just one variable, namely the reflexive capacity for autonomy: the ability to weigh arguments, find moral orientation, and take responsibility. Our youngest relatives may possess the most diverse talents, and we may value all sorts of traits in our children, but according to our cultural standards all such attributes are taken into account only to the extent that they contribute to this kind of reflexive capacity. Given that individual autonomy is an essential – probably even the highest – good in our societies, this narrowness might not be such a problem. But the tendency to look at all stages of childhood as a process of emerging reflexive capacities – this narrowing of the perspective to the intellectual dimension – inevitably means that society fails to recognize or appreciate those properties that characterize the maturing individual, such as imagination, mimetic imitation, and trust, to name just a few.[12] Our modern, liberal concept of childhood, as has been frequently observed,[13] describes the first phase of life exclusively as a gradual "becoming," as a formative process, whereas adulthood, by contrast, is described as a "being," as a matter of permanent capacities that are reliably possessed. As a result of this higher-level juxtaposition of "process" with "result," there is today a tendency to view children and adolescents as merely future adults, and thus to deny them any attributes that are distinct and valuable in their own right.[14] Incidentally, the fact that childhood is increasingly a time of educational pressure, and thus is understood exclusively in terms of the acquisition of adult capacities, may be a further consequence of this diminished perspective. Our culture is certainly "child-friendly," but it lacks the evaluative vocabulary that is necessary to appreciate children other than in terms of a development toward adulthood. Calling children "sweet" and "cute" is not enough, for these terms refer only to behavioral characteristics and not to positive capacities.

But the intellectual bias in the vocabulary with which public discourse describes the properties of adolescents is not the only feature of our gradual conception of childhood that may irk, or perhaps even disadvantage, those thus described. For although we divide early life into temporal stages according to the development of reflexive capacities, our law imposes a non-negotiable end point on the phase of immaturity. Beyond this point the individual at long last achieves autonomy, or, as we say, "comes of age." Here, there is no gradation, no slow maturation, but only a sudden entry into adulthood at a defined age. From the perspective of our background assumptions about "childhood," the capacity for autonomy develops gradually, step by step, over time. From the perspective of our law, this capacity sets in at a stroke, and this moment is recognized through the issuing of certain official documents. The discrepancy between these two perspectives means that a child may be addressed in two highly contradictory ways, and consequently always has to work out which one it is: is the child being addressed as an intellectually advanced, physically developed adolescent, or as a still immature child, dependent on instruction? Some of the trials confronted by Theodore Decker, the hero of Donna Tartt's novel, result from the conflicting messages that this conundrum entails. At one point, he is treated as a mummy's boy, as helpless and in need of therapy, as someone who, in legal terms, is not deemed fit to lead an independent life; at another point, he is an autonomous young man who is supposed to take his life in his own hands. Today, this ambiguity is intensified by the fact that advertisements and the media treat adolescents as consumers who are able to make their own decisions – long before they have reached legal maturity. Our little ones are meant to be mature enough to convey their preferences to their parents, but they have no legal autonomy. There is no other arena in which this contradiction is more blatant than that of sexuality: thanks to the internet and peer pressure, a fifteen-year-old girl is familiar with the full range of possibilities, yet she does not possess the legal right to sexual self-determination. This dichotomy between developmental thinking and the law's binary model can be removed only if the granting of legal maturity is temporally graduated, with the starting points of different phases depending on the specific subject matters concerned.

(b) There is arguably a similar dichotomy at work in the case of the second element, the cultural perception of the child's entwinement with the social environment, although in this case the situation is more complex. This element of the concept of "childhood" can be further divided into two sub-elements. One concerns the degree to which the child is integrated into social processes of interaction; the other concerns the distribution of childrearing responsibilities. The two sub-elements are not, however, independent of each other: the more young people are seen as integrated into the surrounding social world, the more social institutions must take some share of the responsibilities. Let us briefly look at the relationships that this involves on the standard contemporary liberal model. Until children reach the age of compulsory education, they are seen essentially, and exclusively, as members of the biological family, which in the standard case consists of father, mother, and siblings –although no one denies that there are also manifold external influences on children. Because of this restriction to the family unit, a child's interactions are primarily with the parents, who are given the power to take autonomous decisions regarding educational aims, as long as they uphold the fundamental normative principles of child well-being. There are legally determined thresholds for state intervention in this family sphere, which is otherwise understood to be "private." These thresholds are considered to have been crossed when the parents or guardians have seriously violated, or threaten to seriously violate, the socially defined norms for the protection of the child's interests.[15] Once the child has reached the age of compulsory schooling, the educational sovereignty of the parents, which had been protected up to this point, starts to compete with the educational aims of higher level institutions that belong to the social environment. "In schools, to the extent that they are guided by public policy, the young are now confronted with educational principles that may be informed to varying extents by political and democratic intentions or by economic aims." But in either case their source is not a parental decision. On the contrary, they may even be designed to correct, as Kant puts it so well, the potential "family failings" that home schooling often fosters and passes on to the next generation.[16]

There is much to say about this liberal democratic model, which no doubt represents progress compared to earlier educational policies.[17] Here, I limit my remarks to those aspects that seem of particular importance for the question of the potential vulnerability of children. First, it is striking that in this framework children come into regular contact with the social environment at such a late point in time – only once they begin to attend school. If we leave aside kindergarten and prep schools, which have expanded only in recent decades and are obligatory in only a few countries, there are no social institutions that promote the inclusion of the infant in wider processes of social interaction. If we take a step back, this is all the more surprising. Children have not been considered the property of their parents for a long time, and the increase of non-biological parenthood means that any natural justification of such ownership is now definitely obsolete. One would expect that as a consequence there should be a pronounced shift from responsibility based on the act of procreation to responsibility based on social relations. To support such a shift and to allow the youngest to experience themselves as welcomed and cared for by the social community, we would probably require more social institutions that mediate the socialization of children. One example is the American institution of summer camp, which also has the advantage of compensating for the random educational approaches of parents. Without such public spaces for children – incidentally, Oskar Negt pointed out the need for such spaces thirty years ago[18] – the task of socializing the next generation falls to the school alone. When they go to school for the first time, children who did not attend kindergarten or similar institutions are all of a sudden confronted with a completely novel situation. As a result, they are often out of their depth; they have to confront tensions between parents' expectations and the aims of the school, something children find difficult to bear. In the current standard liberal model of the relationship between child and society, all too much relies on the quality of the school and its teaching. The better equipped the school and the more cooperative its atmosphere, the more likely it will be that children develop a feeling for their own role in social interaction and for the problems they may encounter in their social environment – even if they are late entrants into this environment.[19] However, this situation often imposes such excessive demands on schools that they are bound to fail in performing their task, as is demonstrated by the literary and cinematic examples to which I referred at the beginning. In those examples, schools repeatedly appear on the horizon, and the protagonists look to them for support and advice when their parents fail them. But the schools cannot respond to their cries for help: teachers are in short supply, or they do not possess the necessary sensitivities.

If we do not want to limit parental autonomy in educational matters even further – and there are manifold reasons that speak against doing so – then overburdened schools must be complemented with additional institutions that serve the purpose of socializing children and familiarizing them with their social environment, both before and during the time of compulsory education. Kindergarten, nurseries and prep schools are not sufficient. Institutional imagination is required; we need new ideas for how children can participate in social interaction even before school age. The functional argument – that schools are carrying out the task of socialization on their own and that this burden must be shared – is not the only one that speaks in favor of socializing children earlier. Children come to sense that their social environment consists of reliable and trustworthy people only if they enjoy early interactions with members of society from outside their family circle. If they do not have this experience, the risk, as psychologists have repeatedly observed, is that children perceive their own family as well intentioned and the surrounding society as hostile or indifferent, leading to a sometimes lifelong distrust, even fear, of strangers.[20] You might expect a liberal democratic society, whose norms prioritize child well-being over parental autonomy, to ensure that the next generation has ample early opportunities to relate to and interact with strangers.[21] Apart from its being necessary for the development of feelings of social inclusion, earlier child socialization is necessary and desirable for two further reasons, which will become apparent only once we have considered the third element that makes up the concept of childhood.

(c) The third element consists in culturally specific ideas about the constitution and condition of the two institutions that are necessarily involved in the child's socialization: family and society. Despite the bleak image that Freud created, the modern liberal understanding of childhood was for a long time dominated by the view that the nuclear family represents a harmonious space in which the child is safe. This optimistic view has given way to a much more negative one: even if the psychoanalytic claim that family members are, during certain phases, in sexual competition with each other is not the prevailing view, there is nevertheless a widespread suspicion that the nuclear family is a breeding ground for intractable emotional reactions, and that in any case the traditional nuclear family is in a process of dissolution. The empirically misleading – and long since refuted – impression that violence against children within the family has risen dramatically in recent decades is only one of the many strange effects produced by this image of the family.[22] However, setting these wild exaggerations to one side, we are still faced with the sobering fact that the traditional family, the triad of father, biological mother, and child, represents a fertile ground for strong emotional ambivalence and internal discord. The traditional family is beginning to lose its monopoly, and is making way for a plethora of new, hitherto unknown family forms. The result of this gradual "de-institution-alization of the nuclear family"[23] – whether it will be temporally limited parenthood, the patchwork family, single parents, or even a return to bigger family groups – is still unpredictable. It will take a drawn-out phase of experimental exploration to find a good fit for the relation between transformed needs, the requirements of social-ization, and institutional innovations. We cannot anticipate the result of the transformation that we are witnessing, and therefore the future is largely uncertain. However, one thing that we do know for certain is that we would be ill advised to return to the past. Overall, we would be justified in handing more responsibility for the care of children to society, for the emotional ambivalence and attachment disorders with which we are familiar from the past will not disappear during the transitional phase ahead of us – rather, they take on new, as yet unknown forms. Part of the responsibility for the care of the child should therefore be transferred from the new parental elements, howsoever they may be composed, to specialized institutions of the social community. From the child's perspective, this would be preferable, because the traditional concentration of early childcare responsibility in the hands of the parents renders children overly dependent on the arbitrarily distributed willingness of parents to form attachments with their children and provide them with affection. We perhaps under-estimate our children's capacities for emotional adaptation, and their impressive ability to quickly and instinctively accommodate new constellations, but such is their deep-seated dependence that they are always the first to suffer from the discord, uncertainty, and rough treatment that result from parental failings. The handful of novels and films I mentioned at the outset tells us how much the dissolution and splintering of immediate surroundings weigh on a child's mind, but there is an almost endless list of such narratives and short stories that try to depict the child's perspective on what it means to fear for one's own future comfort and security.[24]

These testimonies are fiction, so they depict threats in ways that may only rarely correspond with reality. Nevertheless, these are constant threats that form part of a child's horizon. Because children are dependent on a few attachment figures in their own families for the satisfaction of their desires and attachment needs, their psychological well-being is hostage to the uncontrollable future coherence of the one relational constellation into which they have been born by accident. If that constellation fails, or if for whatever reason the parents are incapable of providing unconditional care, the normal result is insecure attachment, an unclear distribution of responsibilities, and a lack of attention. Given these risks, it seems wise to seek possible alternatives to the traditional two phases of, first, exclusive integration in the family and, second, socialization by the school. Maturing children need to have earlier opportunities to develop a feeling for the fact that social life can be a sphere of emotional support and geniality. Such opportunities should be made available long before the beginning of compulsory schooling, so as not to place all of the burden of providing care on families, which are always fragile and sometimes fractious. To the extent that such childcare, which could begin at the end of the first year, was stable and emotionally reliable and involved many other people, parents would be freed of their onerous responsibilities, and children would be less dependent on their parents fulfilling their duties.[25]

This general suggestion is made more plausible when we turn from one aspect of the third element to the other: the image of society on which our current idea of childhood is based. It is difficult to determine what this image is, because the images of society held by individuals vary widely with social class and ethnic group, and there is hardly any empirical research that is detailed enough for us to say anything with certainty. Overall, however, we may say that in recent years there has been a growing feeling that society is marked by a blatant gap in income and wealth, and so there is in many cases no longer any reluctance to accept the fact that we live in a class society – and the lower one's income, the more likely one is not to deny this fact. Childhood is always seen as located, in some way or other, in a social environment, and so the notion of childhood, too, must be conceived of as part of such "class sociality."[26] Despite this acceptance, however, the necessary conclusions with regard to children have not been drawn, as far as I can see. Many are still reluctant to admit the simple fact that children from the most economically insecure levels of society have only an outside chance of enjoying an open, self-determined future. Yet the social factors that constrain children's ability to shape their futures are no secret, and indeed are well known. If the parents' economic situation is insecure, family life is more likely to be disturbed, and emotional attachments are more likely to be weak. This, in turn, means the children are more likely to suffer neglect, which may ultimately doom any prospect of a better, autonomous future. Of course, this should not be seen as an inevitable sequence of events – only as a statistically well-proven probability. But as the number of children growing up in such precarity rises, so will the number of children whose well-being is under threat. With many empirical indicators currently suggesting a creeping increase in economic insecurity, we must forestall these negative implications for children's welfare. The first action must surely be to introduce social policy measures that offer material support for needy parents, and thus help to create the conditions for a safe family environment. But such measures will never be enough to protect children against the experiences of social deprivation. Mothers and fathers can always end up in situations that rob them not only of material means but also of the psychological resources they need to support their children – with serious implications for the children's future prospects. The examples of alcoholism, drug addiction, sudden economic ruin, or the unexpected death of a parent remind us that, even with the most generous material support, there are cases in which children risk ending up in the downward spiral of social deprivation, neglect, and, finally, the disappearance of any chance at a self-determined future. Given these risks and disadvantages – which grow with economic insecurity – it seems advisable to complement the care offered by the family with state support not only in the form of social benefits but in the form of state-run care facilities for children, offered as early as possible in the child's life. Beginning the social integration of children much earlier, through the care and emotional support offered by appropriately trained and state-financed educationalists, would help to compensate for the disadvantage suffered by children from economically or socially vulnerable families. In this case, the threat to children's well-being derives not from factors inherent in the family, namely the unpredictable threats to its cohesion, but from externally caused deprivation that is not the family's fault. However, in this case, too, the child's well-being is better served by socially provided care that begins much earlier on in life.[27]

(d) We have thus, from several starting points, reached the conclusion that social integration should begin much earlier on in life. What we can say about the fourth element of the concept of childhood follows from this conclusion with an almost organic necessity. Regarding the question of who has the right to provide care and education to children, and on what grounds, our discussion so far suggests that a certain reorientation is required.

In the liberal model, parental paternalism and the parents' almost exclusive responsibility for children's flourishing should be accompanied much earlier on by an equal role for society at large in advocating for children's interests. This attempt to include children in social interaction much earlier is not just a matter of society taking responsibility for long-term care that parents alone, for various reasons, cannot be expected to provide. Rather, the share of the responsibility taken by society also expresses the fact that children, as we should recognize by this point, have intrinsically valuable properties that are independent of the roles they will play in the future as adults. These properties can find public expression only if society limits parents' discretion in deciding on educational aims. In this way, the two corrections to the standard liberal democratic model of childhood suggested here are closely related, and even mutually supportive. First, beginning the social integration of children much earlier will protect them against the vagaries of family-provided care and the possible disadvantages that result from the family's economic situation. But it also provides a protected space for the development of children's specific and intrinsically valuable properties, for it is precisely these properties that are neglected by parents' educational aims, which often focus on performance. From the opposite perspective, the connection between the two arguments could be described as follows. The child's capacity for free, creative play and imaginative interaction can be adequately and publicly honored by society only if society provides multiple spaces that allow these capacities, as soon as they show, to be expressed independently of parental intervention. At the same time, providing such spaces would serve the equally important purpose of releasing children much earlier from their one-sided dependence on the family's fortunes. If we bear in mind Adorno's insight that children's capacities reflect behavioral possibilities that adults often lose as they come under the pressure to perform instrumentally, we can say that these changes would also have a broader social benefit. Society will remember the playful, purposeless potential in children's behavior, which its own bustling economic activity risks eclipsing, only as long as children are given the opportunity to develop their own capacities freely – and perhaps even against the will of their parents. It is in the interest of society as well as parents that children are recognized as fellow inhabitants of our lifeworld as early as their dispositions allow.[28]

Translated by Daniel Steuer

Part III

Sources of Social Freedom

11

Denaturalizations of the Lifeworld
On the threefold use of the humanities

A child growing up in our present society can at an early age identify an airplane in the sky, understand the role of medication in fighting illness, and appreciate the function of a hammer in carrying out repairs. But that is not all. At some point, the child will also learn, whether through direct communication or the media, that all human beings have things called rights; that her hometown has a long history that goes back to its foundation as a center for trade, a center for industry, or the location of some ecclesiastical institution; and that her father and mother often argue about the distribution of household chores. As we may provisionally put it, the eyes of this child are opened not only to technical-instrumental processes but also to the moral-historical elements of her environment. She may still not know exactly what these peculiar entities – rights, moral arguments, and local histories – are, but she probably already suspects that they belong to a different category of facts from that which includes airplanes, medication, and hammers, all of which serve very clearly identifiable purposes. Once the child goes to school, she will learn that she has certain rights against other people, that the names of nearby streets have to do with parts of her hometown's history, and that her parents' arguments represent a much broader public debate in miniature. Even if all that is not covered by the teacher, pupils, in the course of communication with peers, will have to draw these conclusions and generalizations about their moral-historical surroundings in order to position themselves within them. Growing up, we may say, involves learning to understand oneself as a part of this peculiarly immaterial, purely intellectual world, and at the same time already participating in it, despite usually still being a purely passive observer. An adolescent who has not yet come of age cannot take an active part in the process of legislation, nor does she have any input into her hometown's politics of memory. In these cases, she will remain a mere observer. But in the case of her parents' dispute over the distribution of household chores, her involvement is probably so close that she is forced to express her own opinions and thus become a participant.

Once she becomes an adult, she will have fully grown into her moral-historical world. Depending on personal preference and circumstance, she may take part in the social transformation of this world or stick to the perspective of a participating observer. She may still not have a clear conceptual idea of what distinguishes the two categories of facts – the technical-instrumental and the moral-historical. But she will become sufficiently familiar with the differences between them from their different modes of operation – on the one hand, the straightforward application of fixed laws; on the other, social rules that can be changed in cooperation with other people. To move competently in this second world, our new grown-up will have to intuitively draw on a different kind of knowledge from that required to master the first world. In the world of fixed laws, she needs to know which cause-effect relationships make which interventions possible. In the moral-historical world, she needs to know which reasons lead to the formation of which social configurations: that is, which considerations provide the basis for the current state of the law, which intentions are associated with the naming of streets, and which moral considerations motivate the domestic quarrels between her parents. As an adult comes into this second world, she will also want to know whether there are any gaps or one-sided decisions in the chain of justifications and reflections that underlies the status quo: that is, whether the current legal situation can really be explained purely on the basis of the rational interests of everyone involved; whether her hometown's politics of memory reflect the opinion of a minority, rather than the majority; and whether her mother, in the argument with her father, only gave in because she felt dependent and did not want to lose his affection.

A fairly uncontroversial thesis that informs the reflections that follow is that the knowledge that individuals need to take up a position in their social world is derived from those disciplines that are generally referred to as the "humanities," or, in German, *Geisteswissenschaften* (see section I below). When it comes to the large part of our lifeworld that I have called our moral-historical surroundings, it would often be impossible for us to find sufficient orientation, or even impossible to move at all, if it were not for a range of disciplines that render explicit the history and reasons that allow us to understand the social facts of the present. These disciplines form a background that is always available to us. The interplay of the disciplines that make up the humanities informs us, we can say, of the selective chain of rational considerations that has led to the moral-historical world as it presents itself to us in our everyday perception. The roles played by the social, legal and historical sciences are intertwined but all are essential, for each science engages with a particular axis or strand of this formative process, and only taken together can these sciences explain the specific shape of our present lifeworld.

But providing orientation is only one of the functions that the humanities always already perform for us. A second – and one that is generally far more important, although often not recognized by members of the political elite or natural scientists – becomes clear only when we look more closely at the reasons or considerations that give our social lifeworld its specific shape. From the very beginning, the humanities have played a crucial role in the production of the reasons and the fabrication of the ideas that explain the facts of our historical culture. Hardly any of the cultural phenomena that we take for granted in our daily lives – such as legal rights, parental disputes, or street names – would exist at all without the active involvement of various humanities disciplines in generating, testing, and sharpening ideas. The cultural shape of the social world that we take for granted in our daily lives is owed to the laborious work of the generations of theologians, jurists, philosophers, social scientists, and historians who carved it out – sometimes by delving into the nitty-gritty detail of things, sometimes by embarking on daring speculative journeys. The second – and considerably more controversial – thesis of this essay will therefore be that the humanities in fact participated in the production of the reasons and considerations whose importance for the understanding of our present lifeworld the humanities explain to us. We may also say: we would not be who we are, and our social reality would not be what it is, without the prior work of these various disciplines and their separate yet interconnected labor.

If we turn toward the future, we see that the humanities have yet another function. When problems arise in our social world

– when, for instance, there are challenges to the law, when our hometown's politics of memory seems one-sided or when we want to get to the bottom of the ongoing arguments between a father and mother – we almost always look to some of the innovative ideas offered by the humanities for a solution. This usually happens without the individuals concerned being aware of it, for they learn of the proposed solutions only after the proposals have been adopted, through long and convoluted paths, by social movements and political actors. But the source of these productive ideas, before they began their journey through the thicket of public mediation, is almost always the conceptual innovation of a legal scholar, historian, or political scientist who was seeking answers to problems arising within the discipline. The humanities' skepticism toward existing opinions and ideas is not something that has to be introduced from the outside, as if a critical turn were first needed before they can question the reasons that form a particular social reality. Rather, as I hope to show, a delegitimizing, critical attitude is intrinsic to the humanities because, in dealing with reasons under the conditions of a division of labor between the disciplines, they must always question the legitimacy of reasons. My third and final thesis will therefore be that the humanities are always already busy developing reasons, ideas, and consider-ations that, once translated back into public consciousness, reveal possible ways of overcoming problems in social life. Just as these disciplines helped to create today's moral-historical world, they also influence the moral-historical world of the future by devel-oping rational solutions to social challenges. In pursuing these three theses further, I shall continue to refer to the perspective of the child mentioned above. In this way, I hope to ensure that my reasoning does not veer too much toward general argument regarding the theory of science and can be validated against the practical challenges posed by our social lifeworld.

I

It is well established that the emergence of the peculiar concept of *Geisteswissenschaften* is owed to a large extent to the specific condi-tions of the development of philosophy in Germany, where, in the first half of the nineteenth century, the idea that the social-historical world in its totality must be understood as an objectification of spirit asserted itself through the influence of Hegel. Accordingly, the disciplines that deal with this world had to be conceived of as *Geisteswissenschaften*: the sciences of spirit.[1] The peculiarity of this aspect of German intellectual history is revealed by the fact that other intellectual cultures have never coined any comparable terms. Neither in the French nor in the Anglo-Saxon philosophical tradition did that bold idea – understanding spirit on the model of an independently active force that translates itself into reality – ever arise. In these intellectual cultures, the disciplines that concern themselves with the social world were therefore from the very beginning given much more down-to-earth names: the *sciences humaines* in France,[2] and the "humanities," or "human sciences," in the Anglo-Saxon world. However, in terms of their substance, regardless of whether the active source was taken to be the "human being" or "spirit," the terms meant roughly the same thing: they were the collective names for the various disciplines that engage with the world created by human beings and human intellectual activity, as opposed to the natural world. These culturally specific conceptual formations were children of their times, and depended heavily on popular philosophical movements and intellectual preferences. This is clear when we consider the various current counter-movements in the Anglo-Saxon and German-speaking worlds. Such is the dominance of the "philosophy of mind" in the US and Britain that the term *Geisteswissenschaften* might actually be more suitable than "humanities" (because "philosophy of mind" understands the specificity of human history and society in terms of their rootedness in intellectual activity). The opposite process is taking place in Germany, where there have recently been some quite determined attempts to follow common parlance at the international level and replace the term *Geisteswissenschaften* with the term *Humanwissenschaften*.[3] As long as we ensure that the different expressions refer to roughly the same areas of human history and society, these conceptual differences between individual intellectual cultures need not concern us.

Once the various disciplines that address aspects of society and its history were brought under a generic term, and thus related to one another, it soon emerged, in the second half of the nineteenth century, that they differ from the natural sciences not only in their subject matter but also in their methods. In Germany, Wilhelm Dilthey drew this theoretical distinction in the philosophy of science with great clarity in his *Introduction to the Human Sciences*. In France, Ernest Renan pioneered a similar distinction, albeit not with quite the same precision. Both saw the difference between the natural and the human sciences as consisting in the fact that the former aim at establishing causal relations between chains of events, whereas the latter aim to understand processes that are mediated by meanings. On the European continent, this opened up a rift between two realms of knowledge that to the present day remains almost unbridgeable. In Anglo-Saxon countries, thinkers were more circumspect. The differences were seen to lie less in the use of mutually exclusive methods than in the performance of different kinds of tasks. Hence, the differences were not seen as fundamental, but as belonging to a secondary level. It was supposed that the natural and human sciences had a uniform way of proceeding in their search for knowledge; depending on a thinker's epistemological convictions, this either leant toward passive empirical observation or had a stronger emphasis on experimental procedures. The difference was simply that the natural sciences were said to be interested exclusively in the knowledge of natural laws, the human sciences exclusively in knowledge of socially beneficial norms of action. The advantage of this uniform perspective on the sciences over the continental perspective, with its strong emphasis on the opposition between "explaining" and "understanding," was that it brought out much more strongly the practical impulse behind all intellectual endeavors. It also allowed for much greater flexibility in the choice of method: the correct way of solving those burning problems that arise in the pursuit of our knowledge of reality was seen as depending mostly on the context and the human interest being pursued. The various disciplines could thus be placed along a continuum of only gradual differences.[4] This pragmatic approach has proved to be viable and promising, especially in the form given to it at the beginning of the twentieth century by John Dewey's experimentalism. I therefore base my reflections more on Dewey's approach than on Dilthey's theory of *Geisteswissenschaften*, which is still the prevalent one in Germany.

Dewey's experimentalism is, however, not the best starting point when it comes to the first of the three functions I have ascribed to the humanities. Dewey focused so heavily on the practical, problem-solving task of scientific theories that he almost completely ignored their primary role in providing orientation. With regard to this purpose of the humanities, which is often almost taken for granted, we may therefore be justified in turning after all to Wilhelm Dilthey, whose arguments in this area are particularly strong – even if, given the tight connection between understanding and "empathy" he postulates, they must surely be considered outdated.[5] In approaching my first thesis, let us return to the perspective of a person who is growing up and about to take the first steps in her own investigation of her historical and social lifeworld. This young person is now no longer satisfied with simply being told that all human beings have certain rights; she wants to get to the bottom of the issue, and determine what consequences it has for her. Similarly, her curiosity leads her to go beyond her familiarity with the street names of her hometown; she also wants to understand their significance. Finally, she is fed up with enduring her parents' continuing quarrels; she feels that she must now take up a position of her own, and for this she needs to determine what underlies the arguments. Following Dilthey, we can say that the young girl has reached the threshold of the developmental stage at which she learns to understand the "sense" of those intellectual facts [*geistige Gegebenheiten*][6] that are as undeniably a part of her environment as street lamps, kitchen appliances and utensils, and means of transport.[7] The functions or meanings of physical objects can be comprehended much earlier, because they consist in the straightforward consequences of our practical dealings with them at the level of action: street lamps provide illumination at dusk and thus improve visibility; kitchen appliances and utensils help in the preparation of food; means of transport convey people from one place to another. The intellectual objects whose sense the pupil must grasp to move competently in her social world lack any such direct indicators of goal-oriented use. The physical locations of street signs have practical consequences for one's actions, but the names that they typically bear do not. A different kind of effort is therefore required to determine the sense and context of use of these objects. They reveal their sense only in collective consciousness, and do not betray their functions through any of their physical properties.

Our young girl, we may safely assume, will not at once turn to encyclopedias, specialist literature, or sociological studies to find out the significance of the obviously somehow valid – rights, the names of the streets around her, or the motifs behind her parents' domestic quarrels. Normally, her introduction to the meaningful contexts of all these intellectual facts will come by way of oral instruction from relatives, teachers, or friends. This instruction is more likely to be given unintentionally than with an explicit educational purpose. The people providing this information draw on implicit knowledge that they acquired in the same way during their own socialization, and that now ensures their familiarity with the meanings of their moral-historical world. However, the knowledge thus acquired is not always free of gaps; it is often deficient and, given a fast-changing and increasingly complex culture, extremely fragile. When his son asks him who the Alevis are, a father will probably not have an answer ready at hand. When a girlfriend asks her boyfriend about the exact rights of immigrants in Germany today, he will likely be in the same situation. But when they are temporarily at a loss, when their implicit knowledge fails them, they may draw on the written archive of the full breadth of humanities research across all its disciplines.[8] This archive contains in an explicit form – written, and these days also digital – what we need to know about the social meanings of intellectual objects in our everyday life. The archive can therefore help us to close gaps in the horizon of our knowledge. We are now so used to such tools and sources of information that we rarely notice that we draw on them more or less continuously in the course of our social life. Our young pupil will therefore be orally introduced not only to the tradition that is sedimented in her moral-historical environment but also, at the same time and imperceptibly, to the cultural techniques that enable her to make good use of the humanities archive. Taking her parents, trusted acquaintances, and teachers as a model, she learns how to expand her knowledge about the surrounding intellectual reality on her own by using dictionaries, history books or the daily press. In this way, when the network through which tradition is implicitly transmitted threatens to break down, when the people in the young person's social environment come to the limits of their knowledge of the historical meaning of certain street names, or her parents become tight-lipped when asked about the cause of their argument, the young girl will become an active researcher. She starts to compensate for the deficiencies of oral tradition by actively appropriating parts of the corpus of written knowledge, and thereby gradually increases her understanding of the meanings that make up her intellectual environment.

People are often quick to dismiss this compensatory function of the humanities – their role in complementing our knowledge of intellectual-cultural contexts of meaning – as an aspect of a conservative worldview. It is only if we do not trust oral tradition at all – because of an exaggerated skepticism toward modernity – that the process of education through the medium of writing can have such an elevated status. This objection overlooks the fact that, today, all action-guiding knowledge is handed down in a way that depends to a large extent on constant access to written sources. Our cultural orientation relies on encyclopedias, studies, and papers whose informational content has been shaped by enormous amounts of humanities research that is not necessarily explicitly mentioned. Most of all, however, the accusation of conservatism ignores how important, even indispensable, the results of work in the humanities are for the educational formation of young people. Only when our young person comes across and registers sociological insights – whether through her own reading or in conversation with others – will she realize that the true cause of her parents' argument is the idea, now generally accepted, of equality between the sexes, which requires, among other things, a fair distribution of household work. Only with the help of the findings of local historians – again, whether read by herself or related to her by others – will she find out that local street names still reflect the inglorious past of her hometown during the time of national socialism, and that they are therefore the expression of the convictions, intentions, and feelings of a specific era. Finally, she will at some point learn, through direct or indirect engagement with discussions of legal policy, that the laws of her country now even protect her against physical punishment by her parents.

By providing orientation the humanities always at the same time serve an enlightening function. By informing us about the traditional meanings of the intellectual objects in our environment, they allow us to autonomously develop these senses further, to push them in a direction that transcends established cultural self-understandings. The humanities, as mediators, have this double effect in relation to the first function only because of the internal dynamic and disruptive power of the ideas and reasons themselves whose meaning for the cultural situation the humanities teach us. Looking back, these ideas and reasons show us what were considered the right solutions to the social and cultural challenges of the past. Looking to the future, however, they may at any time turn out to be means of only limited suitability for the solution of newly arising problems. We must now shed more light on the temporal dimension of the reasons, considerations, intentions, and feelings that inform the purely intellectual objects in our environment, and that are revealed by the humanities. It is only when we look at this temporal dimension, the relationship of the ideas objectified in our present society to the past and future, that the other functions that the human sciences perform for us and our lifeworld will become visible.

II

As we saw, our protagonist can orientate herself in her socio-cultural environment only to the extent that she understands the significance not only of technical artefacts but also of purely intellectual facts. It is not enough that she knows how to use public transport or apply a plaster; over time, she must also find out the significance of the objects that exist only in the intersubjective consciousness of her contemporaries.[9] In the case of both technical artefacts and intellectual facts, the gradual process of developing an understanding of the meanings involved will consist in recognizing the consequences for our actions that are intrinsically related to a given entity. But in the case of purely intellectual objects, learning about this meaning is considerably more difficult, because the consequences for our actions follow only from the ideas or reasons that exist in a non-physical form within these objects. The acquisition of technical-instrumental knowledge rarely requires the support of the natural sciences, but the development of an understanding of the meanings in our cultural environment almost always requires the mediation of the humanities. It is thanks to their preparatory work that the reasons and ideas currently expressed in intellectual entities remain publicly available. The humanities' function in providing orientation is expressed most clearly in the efforts our young girl makes in deciphering the meaning of her parents' arguments, of her legal rights, and of her hometown's street names. When she reaches the limits of common knowledge, when she exhausts the insight of friends and relatives, when she wants to find out more than she knows from hearsay, she must draw on ancillary sources of information, such as websites, newspapers, or encyclopedias, all of which are filled with the more or less properly digested results of humanities research.

Let us assume that our protagonist is a curious soul, and therefore wants to delve deeper into the background sources of the phenomena in her social environment. She now knows the reasons and ideas behind the intellectual facts, and thus also their meanings, which were hitherto opaque to her. But she is no longer satisfied with the knowledge that rights are meant to protect individual autonomy, including her own well-being within the family, that some of the streets in her hometown are named for historical figures who supported national socialism, or that her parents' conflict results from differing opinions about how best to implement the idea, welcomed in principle, that housework should be distributed fairly between the sexes. What our pupil wants now to find out is the true origin of all these reasons and ideas, which explained the phenomena that were previously difficult for her to understand. So far she has relied on the common knowledge of her friends and others, knowledge that is underpinned by the work of the humanities, but in pursuing her new interest she is far more dependent on her own amateur research. For the purposes of our argument, the detail of what she may discover in this pursuit is of less interest than a general point she will notice: the birth of every idea, whether good or bad, that becomes the basis for some cultural fact – whether individual civil rights, the normative principle of gender equality, or a town's dubious street names – involves the activity of scholars and intellectuals from the fields of the humanities.

We may lend our pupil a hand by granting her an understanding of John Dewey's experimentalism, with which she will quickly be able to make sense of her historical observation.[10] In general, Dewey assumes, we move within our environment on the basis of "intellectual habits" that have formed as a result of successfully tackling problems we encountered in adapting and coordinating our actions. As long as we continue to behave in these ways, and thus follow habitual intellectual patterns, we perceive in the objects exactly those properties that we have isolated and identified in the course of the intellectual effort to remove interruptions to the flow of our actions caused by various disturbances. According to Dewey, this tendency to presuppose an already disclosed world that is experienced in terms of elements that have been uncovered in the course of previous problem-solving activities can be found in both intersubjective behavior and in behavior toward nature. In social interaction, we usually follow normative points of reference that are already part of our institutions, having been laid down in them as a result of previous attempts at the moral regulation of our behavior. In our treatment of nature, we generally consider as given those objects that have previously turned out to be conditions for successful control. In these certainties of our lifeworld, concept and intuition, intellectual operations and sensual impressions, are combined into a qualitative unity,[11] but according to Dewey these certainties dissolve as soon as we encounter new and unforeseen problems when we use them to guide action. At that point, we are forced to enter a phase of reflexive distancing. In this phase, we rearticulate the previously habitual intellectual patterns into their conceptual-theoretical and sensually perceivable elements, and in this way, through repeated attempts to find an appropriate readjustment of these elements, we restore the disrupted flow of action.[12] This is, to put it somewhat pompously, when the natural scientist or the humanities scholar steps on to the historical stage. Whether the context in which the disruption arises has more to do with the regulation of our social interaction or more with our treatment of nature, certain new ideas, concepts, or justifications must be found and integrated into the environment, such that possible solutions to the problems that have interrupted the flow of action become visible. This development of knowledge in response to the dissolution of our cognitive certainties may be illustrated by returning to those intellectual facts whose meaning so exercised our young girl. The idea that individual freedom of opinion must be protected against those in power was a product of various social movements during the turmoil of the European wars of religion. But the powerful idea that it became – namely that this protection must be guaranteed by the state as a fundamental right – was the product of various philosophers who kept working away on natural law. Our pupil's discovery that the protection of her well-being is a fundamental right is thus the provisional end of a path that was first trodden when scholars in the humanities were forced, in a time of cultural transformation, to look for a new way of regulating social action – for a conceptual innovation that took those changing conditions into account. The normative idea that underlies the ongoing dispute between the girl's parents is a similar case. It was probably the resentment of a growing number of women that led initially to the questioning of traditional ideas of marriage and family. This commotion in the lifeworld led feminists with social scientific skills to formulate the courageous suggestion that it was perhaps time to think about remuneration for housework, and thus about a fundamentally new division of labor between the sexes. Of course, in the decades that followed, this proposal was not adopted. Nevertheless, it was an idea that grew out of the sociological tradition, namely the idea of looking at the private sphere from an economic perspective, that got the ball rolling and prompted the intellectual search for new forms of moral regulation. Finally, we know that the naming of new streets and the renaming of old ones in the post-war era – a time of the collapse of all previous certainties – involved some real luminaries from the field of the humanities. The fact that their proposals and arguments reveal a worrying lack of sensitivity in the exercise of political-moral judgment goes to show, yet again, the extent of the repression of the past among the historians and constitutional lawyers at the time.

Beyond our protagonist's sphere, there are numerous similar examples of the contribution of the humanities to the formation and provision of meaning in our lifeworld. The fact that we all explain everyday behavior that is incomprehensible, irrational, and self-destructive with reference to a subjective source that we call the "unconscious" has its sole source in Freud, who proposed this ingenious and philosophically charged concept in response to the failure of traditional explanations of a number of new pathological symptoms. One might dismiss that example on the grounds that it reveals only the worryingly superficial extent to which science infiltrates our lifeworld, but we can easily cite cases that lie further back in history. For instance, when at the end of the eighteenth century the educated bourgeoisie in German-speaking regions began to talk of "friendship" as a new kind of relationship based on mutual trust and affection, they were unwittingly taking up a concept that was originally developed by the Scottish moral philosophers decades earlier. These scholars, who were all trained in philosophy or the humanities, formulated the ground-breaking, and still influential, idea that the looming expansion of market-based interactions had to be counterbalanced by social forces, and friendly relationships among like-minded people were seen as a model for such forces.[13]

These cases demonstrate how important humanities scholars – whether philosophers, jurists, philologists, or, later, sociologists – were in the creation of ideas and concepts that helped to replace everyday practices that had stalled – or were idling, so to speak – with new habitual forms of action that were better suited to changed circumstances. To begin with, there was always a protracted experimental process of adapting the innovative ideas to the new material of experience before the new, historically superior certainties finally fully emerged. It was possible to speak of a successful establishment of new intellectual habits only after a phase of practical testing to make sure that concept and intuition, intellectual innovation and changed impressions, could really be made to agree. But as far as the theoretical dimension of this experimental transformation was concerned, that is, the provision of creative, liberating ideas and reasons, humanities scholars were at the forefront at times of crisis in our social-moral habits. Their training in intellectual history and their conceptual imagination allowed them, at times of cultural disorientation, to suggest strains of thought that could productively be linked up with earlier ones.

John Dewey suggests that we conceive of the overall historical sequence of such intellectual revisions as a process by which reality is constantly enriched with new phenomena. Faced with transformed challenges, we develop new ideas, and we must attune these ideas to the artificially isolated data of our perception in an experimental process. Once concepts and intuitions have been aligned again, we are confronted with new facts or entities, which may be understood as previously undiscovered aspects of the world. This process of discovery may not be continuous, but in the longer term it cannot be halted, and for Dewey it represents a simultaneous denaturalization and intellectualization [*Vergeistigung*] of our reality. With every corrective step we take in our intellectual habits, a part of the world's pure naturalness is taken away, and a product of our intellectual activity is added.[14] In this sense, from the very beginning, the work of the humanities was part of the denaturalization of our social lifeworld. As their suggestions for new ways of regulating interaction, justified on an interdisciplinary basis, migrate into social reality via a phase of experimental testing, they destroy the seeming naturalness of social reality, and instead enrich it with facts that reflect our own intentions. The cultural phenomena of our daily lifeworld are therefore to a large extent the products of the past intellectual efforts of experts who used their conceptually disciplined imagination to find ideas to avert crises that were about to occur in our forms of interaction. The rights we enjoy, the moral disputes to which we are party, or even the street names that annoy us – these exist in large part because jurists, philosophers, sociologists, and literary scholars contributed to the formation of their intellectual content.

Dewey repeatedly stresses that such cultural facts are never stable. They are constantly under pressure to change, simply because expressions of discontent and moral doubt can appear at any time and at any point in the established system of convictions and deprive it of its legitimacy. The ideas of the past that justified the now doubtful convictions must then be subjected to a reflexive revision in the present to adapt the system to an as yet unknown future. For Dewey, all intellectual facts, any established system of cultural practices, therefore represent no more than a transitory stage in our ongoing intellectual attempt to adapt to a permanently changing environment. This shift in perspective from past to future reveals yet another function performed by the humanities. For they now no longer appear as a bundle of disciplines that have played a decisive role in creating today's lifeworld and help to maintain our awareness of the ideas on which it is based. Rather, they appear as an intellectual force that is engaged in the development of future possibilities of thought.

III

Let us return to our protagonist. In the meantime, she has aged two or three years, and is now looking forward, with some but not too much ambition, to finishing her secondary education. Although she has not yet come of age, she thinks of herself not as someone who merely interprets her socio-intellectual environment but rather, along with her peers, as someone who thinks about its legitimacy, and how it might be improved. She has for some time been aware of the questionable nature of some of the street names in her hometown – adults dropped some hints – but the shape of the German legal system and her parents' arguments are also increasingly occupying her. Her doubts are fueled not only by the teaching of humanities subjects in the classroom, which now focuses much more on problems of recent history and literature, but also by frequent conversations with her friends. The questions that most exercise them concern the conditions for a harmonious multicultural society and the possibility of combining professional and family life.

In this phase of her life, our pupil's encounters with the humanities are still of an only indirect nature. As before, she consults summaries and surveys of certain topics in encyclopedias to satisfy her curiosity, but the impetus behind her research is now a different one: she is interested not so much in being instructed and informed, but in examining and questioning. She therefore notices something interesting about these second-hand summaries of the knowledge of various disciplines, something that she had not previously perceived at all: the reasons that the articles mention as justifying certain rules or moral stances are rarely presented as fixed once and for all. Rather, they seem to point toward better or more comprehensive solutions. Often, this progressive internal dynamic becomes apparent because the articles suggest alternatives to existing rules, and sometimes it is made clear by remarks about the need for further clarification. But in every case this dynamic is conveyed by the fact that reasons, interpretations, and ideas are never presented as undeniably correct or indisputable. To our reader, it seems that each individual discipline wants to unsettle any feelings of certainty, and to strengthen the sense of possibility.[15] This characteristic of the articles, which she had not noticed at first, now reveals to her what I have described as the humanities' third function. Each discipline adopts a subversive perspective on the intellectual facts of the present – in whose emergence they played a crucial role – and looks for reasons and arguments that one might reasonably expect to invalidate those facts in the future. In legal studies, literary studies, or the social sciences, the accepted meaning of law, literature, or social phenomena is bracketed, or placed in doubt, so as to examine the extent to which we might rationally hope for more perfect solutions, better interpretations, or more widely accepted rules. To refer back to Dewey's experimentalism, we might say that this function of the humanities anticipates possible questions that could be raised about the ideas contributed by humanities disciplines in the overcoming of crises in the lifeworld. From the perspective of these disciplines, no intellectual habit is so stable or certain as to be excluded from such anticipatory examination in light of an uncertain future. Such anticipatory critique tests established reasons and ideas for rational reliability, and it may reveal to public consciousness objections that are latent but not yet socially realized. In this third function, then, the humanities serve as a reflexive institution that is charged by the reasoning public with investigating possible issues that might speak against continuing with established intellectual habits.

To reiterate the point, discharging this function does not require there to have been a criticism or accusation actually raised in the social sphere. The humanities do not need to wait for explicit doubts about the existing solutions for social integration to be articulated before beginning their critical, future-oriented work. Rather, it is part of their basic method that they look at agreements that have been reached in their area and ask whether they would withstand potential future objections. For instance, in the study of literature, scholars might ask how a certain cultural minority would view a particular text even though this group does not yet have a voice in its interpretation. In legal studies, similarly, scholars may examine how existing basic rights could be transformed or expanded so as to take into account the interests of peoples who so far do not have any role in decision-making processes, yet are affected by the decisions taken. And in the social sciences, finally, many theoretical discussions can be properly understood only when we appreciate that researchers are considering social facts with a view to how people potentially affected may in future respond to those facts.[16] In all these cases, the implications of intellectual facts that are as yet unestablished are anticipated by an imagination that is controlled by the principles of a discipline, and in this way scholars consider, on behalf of the public, which of our interpretations, laws, or social rules we might revise to achieve a more comprehensive solution. If an informed public is convinced by the arguments, they can then seek to implement whichever reforms seem necessary in light of the possibilities laid out. The humanities thus appear in our lifeworld as a force of reflexive denaturalization along three temporal dimensions. In the past, they were a driving force in the rationalization of behavior that was initially taken as natural. In the present, they are an institution that counteracts the ideological naturalization of our circumstances by making us aware of contexts of meaning. And with respect to the future, they serve to undermine our blind acceptance of the status quo as natural.

Let us return one last time to our pupil. She is now more or less grown up. Although she has indirectly learned a great deal from the humanities in the course of her intellectual development, she will not necessarily choose to study one of the disciplines in the field. Perhaps after finishing school she will decide to pursue her interest in sports, or in medicine, and the study of philology, history, or sociology will be out of the question. But if at some point in her studies she hears in the news that there are, again, political attempts to cut funding for the humanities, she will probably react with suspicion, or even anger. These are the disciplines to which she turned when she was growing up, to which she owes her increasing familiarity with the world of intellectual facts, her social self-understanding and her distinct sense of as yet unrealized possibility. Why should they be worse off than the natural sciences, which are accepted as a matter of course? We might hope that our young person will, as a grown-up citizen, continue to support the humanities through thick and thin.[17]

Translated by Daniel Steuer

12

Is There an Emancipatory Interest?

An attempt to answer critical theory's most
fundamental question

1. Introduction

The idea that human beings have a deep-seated interest in overcoming dependencies and heteronomy has always been a hallmark of the tradition of critical social theory deriving from Marx. Some of the Left Hegelians already held that in the absence of such an emancipatory interest on the part of the entire species, the demand for social progress would remain a merely moral "ought," lacking any support in historical reality. Marx was convinced that under capitalism, this interest was represented by the proletariat, forced by its particular situation to fight on behalf of all of humanity for fully noncoercive and nondominating social relations.[1] When Georg Lukács took up this thought in the early 1920s, even surpassing its original ambitions through a bold appropriation of Fichtean ideas, the revolutionary ethos of the working class had already been in decline to such an extent that his construction received little acclaim even from those sympathetic to it.[2] Max Horkheimer was therefore cautious enough to rely in his development of a critical social theory only on the claim that such an emancipatory interest was revealed in the ineradicable human tendency to revolt against structures of domination. Without attempting to provide a more detailed argument for this assumption, he thereby reiterated on a more abstract level the Marxian thesis that the epistemological foundation of his theory would have to lie in its connection with "critical conduct."[3] It was only with Jürgen Habermas's path-breaking monograph *Knowledge and Human Interests* that new life was breathed into this century-old idea. Through original re-interpretations of Kant, Fichte, and Hegel, Habermas develops the thesis that we as human beings have an interest in dissolving previously unrecognized dependencies and "pseudo-objectivities," and he finally draws on Freud to fully rehabilitate the thesis as amounting to an anthropology of knowledge.[4] Even though Habermas has in the meantime distanced himself from some of the book's central assumptions,[5] it is still a good point of departure for thinking through the theoretical intentions associated with the idea of an "emancipatory interest" and for understanding what is at stake in dispensing with this idea. In what follows, I will therefore start out from this book and recapitulate its central argument. In a second and third step, I will endeavor to salvage its fruitful central idea by supplying it with a new and less vulnerable foundation.

2

In *Knowledge and Human Interests*, Habermas pursues at least two theoretical goals, which are intertwined to such an extent that a neat demarcation between them is barely possible. On the one hand, the book aims to undermine the epistemological basis of the "positivist" methodology prevalent at its time of publication, by showing that both the sciences and the humanities are "functionally" or "transcendentally" rooted in encompassing anthropologically given practical aims whose pursuit determines the methodologies of those types of inquiry. Habermas's first thesis is that because mainstream philosophy of science does not attend to this constitutive dependency of these two branches of knowledge, it remains wedded to a "positivist" misunderstanding and fails to adequately comprehend the constitutive connection between "Knowledge and Human Interests," between the construction of theories and social reproduction.[6] But independently of this, Habermas also seeks to defend a second and more far-reaching thesis, which aims to provide an epistemological foundation for critical theory itself. According to this second thesis, the type of theoretical pursuit known since Marx as "social critique" is itself rooted in a distinct third form of human practice, whose aim is to overcome pseudo-natural dependencies and whose methodology must therefore rely on entirely different sorts of procedures.[7] Both these explanatory goals of *Knowledge and Human Interests* are closely related in that the functionalist or transcendental

derivation of the natural sciences and the humanities from underlying and invariant epistemic interests serves as the model for
searching for a similarly foundational and anthropologically basic
practical interest with regard to social critique. Moreover, the first
thesis turns out to presuppose the second, because the postulated
emancipatory epistemic interest is supposed to first supply us
with a way of understanding the interrelation between social
reproduction and scientific practice that Habermas asserts against
the positivist doctrine. However, in what follows, I will leave to
one side the entire part of the book devoted to the epistemological
critique of positivism and focus only on the second thesis, that
is to say, the claim that there is a self-standing epistemic interest
in emancipation rooted in invariant features of a specific human
practice.

What pushed Habermas toward this thesis will easily be
apparent independent from any familiarity with the theory of
human knowledge held by Habermas at that time, sometimes
characterized as "transcendental anthropology." If the respective
"epistemic interests" underlying the natural sciences and the
humanities can be properly understood only by tracing them back
to forms of activity necessary to the goal of social reproduction –
activities whose rational improvement those kinds of inquiry serve
– then the so-called critical science too requires a demonstration of
their practical sources if they are to be something more than just
a combination of the methods proper to the two other branches
of inquiry. In order to vindicate the methodological autonomy of
the kind of science properly termed "critical," its methods must
be derivable from a distinct type of epistemic interest as fundamental to our human form of life as the other two interests, that
is, the interest in material reproduction through labor and the
interest in symbolic reproduction through linguistic communication. Habermas's argument in support of such an emancipatory
epistemic interest will therefore have to proceed in at least three
independent steps. First, he needs to identify a specific form of
human activity that is as invariant as labor and interaction, but
which in contrast to them serves the overcoming of heteronomy
and previously unrecognized dependencies (Step a). Second, he
must show that this further practical interest gives rise to a specific
type of knowledge that is sufficiently distinct from the kinds of
knowledge latent in labor and in communicative action (Step b).
Third, he has to demonstrate that rationally satisfying this "third"
epistemic interest requires a methodology of its own, rather than

just a combination of methods taken from the sciences and the humanities (Step c). As far as one can tell from the text, Habermas clearly recognizes all three of these tasks, but he has a harder time discharging some of them than others. I will briefly comment on his proposed solutions in the order just named, in order to identify the most pressing problems faced by the approach developed in *Knowledge and Human Interests*.

(a) In my view, the first of the three tasks presents Habermas with the most serious problems. The ambitious goal here is to show that in addition to labor and interaction, we human beings necessarily engage in a third invariant type of activity, which in contrast to the other two is founded on an interest in questioning and combating existing social orders insofar as they are characterized by relations of domination. One could also put it as follows: This third type of activity must allow us to grasp the interrelation of social reproduction and practical critique in such a way that it becomes apparent why societies can be maintained only through social conflicts and social struggles. This is indeed what Max Horkheimer must have had in mind when he referred in his famous essay to what he termed "critical conduct,"[8] which he viewed as in some manner furnishing the epistemological foundation of Critical Theory. It seems probable that he too was concerned with the thesis that any established social order gives rise to some form of resistance or struggle which shakes the foundations of that social order but which finally results in its being reproduced in a different shape or at a higher stage of development. But if Horkheimer did not succeed in offering persuasive arguments for the claim that there is an internal connection between social reproduction and practical critique, neither does Habermas in *Knowledge and Human Interests*. So far as I can tell, Habermas fails to discharge this self-imposed task because in explaining the role of struggle in the process of social development, he chooses psychoanalysis as his model. Taking the psychological development of individuals as his example, he intends to show how the presence of unconscious dependencies and constraints generates an internal struggle on the part of each individual, resulting in a desire to be healed by being liberated from inner heteronomy. To a certain extent, he thereby manages to show how the successful development of an individual can be conceived of as a process of recurring struggles against the danger of newly emerging constraints on an individual's self, and how these "struggles" are an intrinsic part of any normal process of self-formation. Yet the drawback of using the process of individual formation as a model in this way is that doing so gives rise to the misleading idea that in the case of social dependencies and heteronomies, the struggle is internal to the human species understood as a collective "subject," rather than taking place among different social groups. The struggle or conflict that was supposed to constitute a third basic form of human activity is thus understood as a type of self-estrangement rather than as a genuinely practical struggle between two opposing parties. There may of course be some use in conceiving of an individual subject's intentional self-affection as a form of activity, but in that case, there is no longer any connotation of an external intervention in the world. That Habermas is inclined toward this kind of conception, and thus toward viewing the third type of social activity not as an activity proper but rather as a mental process writ large, becomes apparent at the point in his book where he offers a first synopsis of his three invariant forms of activity. He there writes that the three "cultural preconditions of our existence" are "labor," "language," and "power." It is striking that the third item is "power" rather than struggle, conflict, or disagreement, as one might have expected.[9] Habermas thus points to the social structure to which conflictual activity may be a response, rather than to the pursuit of that activity itself. He hesitates to place struggle as a third and equally fundamental type of activity alongside labor and interaction. As a consequence of this neglect, which results from his focus on the model of conflict developed by psychoanalysis, Habermas finds himself in a difficult position right at the beginning of his project of deriving a third, specifically critical epistemic interest. He is unable to tie it back to a pragmatic motive, to some fundamental practical interest, in the way he had done with regard to the other two branches of knowledge. Instead, the third kind of epistemic interest seems from the very outset to be characterized primarily as a type of cognitive striving without any apparent motivational basis in worldly goals or activities.

(b) When it comes to discharging the second task, that is, to identify the specific type of knowledge that is supposed to emerge from the third of the invariant practices proper to our form of life, this shortcoming of the first step leads to an odd reduplication. Instead of a real, substantial practice, we were offered a self-referential struggle of the human species with itself, a certain kind of collective mental process. Habermas is now unable to conceive of this already cognitive activity as the basis of some further and distinct epistemic achievement. The initial definition, according to which the third kind of practical interest aims at a "mental" liberation from self-imposed but unrecognized dependencies, is then merely reduplicated. This tendency becomes apparent in the way in which Habermas derives the third, emancipatory epistemic interest from the notion of an "interest of reason" found in Kant and Fichte. He begins by criticizing Kant's introduction of the idea that reason as such may have an interest in its own realization by charging this approach with a failure to overcome the division between theoretical and practical employments of reason. Habermas grants that by claiming that a feeling of "respect" could allow the faculty of reason to affect our sensibility, Kant had offered an argument for the view that rational guidance by the moral law could be motivationally efficacious. But because Kant did not extend this line of thought to the case of theoretical knowledge, the demonstration of an internal connection between reason and human interest had remained incomplete.[10] In Habermas's view, only Fichte succeeded in overcoming this weakness of the Kantian derivation of an interest of reason, and he did so by resolutely subordinating theoretical reason to practical reason. What allowed Fichte to do this, according to Habermas, was his assumption that the human self or "I" has an essential interest in mustering all its rational powers – the theoretical no less than the moral ones – in order to emancipate itself from all determinations not produced by itself and thus eventually to be able to conceive of itself as completely "free."[11] We can leave it open whether Habermas is right to claim that Fichte managed to demonstrate an "interest in the self-standingness of the self inherent in the very operation of reason" or whether what he demonstrated was rather human beings' interest in the comprehensive use of their rational faculties, or in other words, whether the interest identified by Fichte belongs to reason itself or rather to human subjects. The crucial point regarding Habermas's method is that he intends to appropriate Fichte's line of thought to some extent in order to employ it for his own project of identifying an "emancipatory epistemic interest," even while adhering to "materialist assumptions."

Regarding the second of his three tasks, then, his proposal is that this cognitive interest prompts a process of self-reflection aimed at a recurrent liberation from various sorts of dependency and heteronomy that had remained invisible during previous developmental stages of the human species.[12] As Habermas

himself admits, the particular kind of knowledge in which we
human beings here take an interest is identical with the activity
already adverted to in relation to the first task. The second characterization of this interest, as a cognitive interest in emancipation,
adds nothing to its first characterization as a practical motive,
because both are eventually supposed to coincide. In retrospect,
this central step in Habermas's argument only serves to bring out
the fact that the third fundamental practice inherent in human
culture, in addition to labor and interaction, cannot be conceived
as an "activity" in the proper sense at all. In contrast with labor
and interaction, it is not the case here that there is first a pressure
toward a certain practice and then, on a further level, an interest
in acquiring some methodologically secure type of knowledge.
Instead, with respect to emancipatory resistance and struggle,
Habermas conceives of the relevant activity as being identical with
the attempt to acquire methodologically secure knowledge of the
previously undiagnosed dependencies whose gradual elimination
would successively render the "self" of the human species more
and more free. But this sort of conception of the emancipatory
epistemic interest means that his first problem – his lack of a robust
conception of social struggle – is complemented by a second,
closely related one. The bearer of this interest in understanding the
conditions of one's own heteronomy must be the human species as
a whole, as though the diversity of conflicting interests regarding
the type and content of the desired knowledge were merely
apparent. Where there are no social conflicts, there can be no
conflicting epistemic interests. Both problems result from the way
in which Habermas's attempt to characterize our emancipatory
interest is guided by the model of psychoanalysis. In the first step,
this theoretical orientation had led him to a conception of social
conflict as a subject's reflexive struggle with itself. In the second
step, it leads him to the dubious claim that, like an individual
subject, the human species has a common interest in some unitary
type of emancipatory knowledge. Neither of these two assumptions enables us to see why human history should give rise to a
type of activity whose success requires the attainment of a specifically critical sort of knowledge.[13]

(c) Even though the model of psychoanalysis thus turns out
to stand in the way of developing a satisfactory answer to the
first two questions, it is surprisingly helpful in solving the third
problem. The task here is to identify the characteristic methodology
of those kinds of knowledge that serve to satisfy the emancipatory

epistemic interest in a systematic way. I am not going to dwell on this topic at any length, because it is of secondary importance for the question with which I am concerned here, that is, whether there is such a thing as an emancipatory interest at all. The methodological particularity of the critical sciences only becomes an issue once it has been established that there is some distinct epistemic interest that makes it possible for such sciences to exist in the first place. As we have seen, Habermas justified the existence of such a third class of sciences by way of an "anthropology of knowledge," arguing that the human species, just like individual subjects, has a deep-seated interest in liberating itself on an ongoing basis from previously unrecognized dependencies and pseudo-natural constraints, so as to attain a condition of intersubjectivity free from coercion and domination.

As in psychoanalysis, the practical realization of this interest consists in coming to recognize unconscious determinants of one's own agency and in using that knowledge in one's relation to oneself. And satisfying this interest in a more advanced fashion requires organizing it into a methodologically controlled discipline, which is to say, institutionalizing it as an autonomous science. The general knowledge this science is meant to yield, like the knowledge of psychoanalysis, must aim to understand the causes of those unrecognized dependencies that have hitherto posed obstacles to human interaction. And like psychoanalysis, this critical science must combine explanatory and hermeneutic methods in such a way that it employs an idealized model of the "normal" developmental process of the human species so as to identify the "deviations" from this process that have given rise to undesirable dependencies and thereby to defective forms of interaction. But the mere identification of such pathologies of social development does not yet complete the project of critical science. Again like psychoanalysis, it needs to take the further step of presenting its findings to the relevant parties in such a way that they are enabled to overcome or remove the obstacles thus identified. Critical science has reached its emancipatory goal only once this has been accomplished, only when those to whom it is addressed have effectively transcended a given stage of previously unrecognized dependency. This conception of the method of a critical theory, clearly derived from the model of psychoanalysis, has been widely criticized in the literature on many points, which do in fact invite misunderstanding. This includes the following charges: First, unlike for the case of psychoanalysis, there are no clear criteria on which social analyses can rely for a meaningful distinction between developmental successes and failures. Second, with regard to whole societies, there is nothing that corresponds to the psychosexual problems of individuals in determining their future development. Third, there is a suspicion that in the model under discussion, theorists claim to possess some form of secure knowledge that is immune to the uncertainties involved in understanding one's own present. In short, transposing the psychoanalytic method onto the practice of critical social theory must fail because the latter stands in an altogether different sort of relation to their object than the analyst does to his or her patient.[14] Yet there is something in the methodology outlined by Habermas that seems to me to be worth preserving. It is the thought that critical social theories should proceed in a "reconstructive" fashion so as to identify idealized developmental paths that can be conceived of as actualizations of already accepted norms and which can then be used to diagnose the deviations that mark de facto developmental processes.[15]

As I said before, I want to set aside the further problems arising in this context and turn instead to the two previous basic assumptions of Habermas's project. His claim was that we can think of critical social theory as a distinct type of science only if we can show that it is rooted, like the natural sciences and the humanities, in a distinctive form of human activity, and only if the latter gives rise to a distinctive epistemic interest. My goal was to show that Habermas does not offer sufficient support for either of these two claims because his adherence to the psychoanalytic model led him to conceive of the relevant type of activity as consisting in a cognitive self-affection of the human species as a whole and thereby to sever the connection between practical critique and an opposition between groups or classes. Those who would like to adhere to Habermas's starting intuition are therefore confronted with two basic challenges that need to be addressed separately. First, can we identify a uniform type of action or activity that is characteristic of our form of life and that, contrary to Habermas's conception, is in fact bound up with a "struggle" or conflict among groups? Second, can we say of this type of activity that it contains a distinct epistemic interest that might serve as the foundation of an autonomous group of sciences? In the remaining two parts of my talk, I will suggest positive answers to both questions, in order to outline an alternative to the theoretical project pursued in *Knowledge and Human Interests*.

3

Against the background of contemporary social ontology, the first of the two questions just mentioned could be reformulated as follows: Are we justified in treating conflict or struggle among social groups as a type of social action that is an ineliminable explanatory element of any viable social theory?[16] Looking back at the history of social philosophy and political thought, one quickly comes across a number of strands that have suggested a positive answer to this question. Numerous past thinkers were convinced that social conflict is an invariant element of all social life. At the same time, there is considerable variation in the reasons that have been given for this assumption, ranging from claims about the psychological disposition of human beings to explanations appealing directly to social tensions. To approach this difficult territory, let me point to four typical sorts of explanation to consider the plausibility of the respective arguments.

A first position – which we could call the Rousseau-Kant view – asserts that a tendency toward permanent strife is intrinsic to our form of life because human individuals constantly seek to prove their own superior standing and value relative to others, resulting in a "vain" and interminable struggle for superiority. Kant holds that the "unsociable" aspect that is inseparable from human sociability consists in individuals' striving to distinguish themselves from others through actions or accomplishments that are meant to elicit special esteem.[17] The second position – which we could call the Freudian view – also explains the inevitability of social struggle by appealing to a psychological disposition, but does so by focusing on a quite different sort of desire. It holds that adult human beings necessarily experience some degree of internal resistance and hostility to authority because their early relationship with their parents is inevitably marked by hatred as well as love. According to Freud, social life can never reach a state of equilibrium but will always give rise to new conflicts and struggles because each of us is psychologically forced by his or her early childhood experiences to rebel against being governed by others, even where such government has been democratically authorized.[18] The third position – which I will call the Marxian view – explains the inevitability of social struggle by appealing not to psychological dispositions but to social tensions. The reason why conflicts remain an ineliminable feature of all forms of human sociality is here said to lie in the fact that the relations between different social classes must be marked by conflict and strife as long as the relations of production make one class predominant and provide it with greater opportunities to realize its own particular interests.[19] But the further remark that class struggle is inevitable only "for the time being" indicates that this third view is not strictly speaking a thesis in social ontology. According to Marx, social conflict will be a thing of the past once the revolution, which is to be expected sooner or later, has brought about a classless society. By contrast, the fourth position I would like to mention – and which for a lack of undisputed proponents I am going to call the Hegel-Dewey view – advances a thesis that belongs to social ontology in the strict sense. This fourth view asserts that social conflict is inevitable in all societies simply because the norms accepted by their members will again and again give rise to new moral claims that cannot be satisfied under existing conditions and whose frustration will therefore result in social conflicts.[20] Here, the explanatory burden rests on the thought that the interpretation of socially valid norms is an essentially unfinished process, in which one-sided interpretations and resistance to them take turns with each other.

Even though there may be yet other views that treat struggle as an ineliminable component of human social life – such as social Darwinism or Georg Simmel's famous doctrine that social strife is a mode of social integration[21] – I will leave it at these four proposals. The key concepts employed by them, in the order in which I mentioned them, are *amour propre* or vanity, affective ambivalence vis-à-vis authority, conflicting economic interests, and the hermeneutic openness (*Geltungsüberhang*) of the norms of social integration, which contains a potential for collective social protest. Because we are in search of a class of actions that will lead to a struggle among social groups in the context of any social structure whatsoever, it seems to me that the first two explanations are off the table. The first one asserts, more clearly in the case of Kant than in the case of Rousseau, that the motive for recurrent revolts against established normative orders is individuals' desire to assert their superiority or preeminence over other members of their society. There is no reference to a conflict between two groups here, only to a struggle of individuals with respect to the public opinion of others, to whom they desire to demonstrate their own virtues and abilities. Moreover, Rousseau's own interpretation of *amour propre* suggests that this psychological feature may be a product of cultural forces, whose "toxic," conflict-enhancing effects may be reduced or altogether eliminated given a future state of social equality.[22] The Rousseau-Kant view thus seems ill-suited for explaining a struggle among groups as an invariant feature of social action. The same is clearly true of the Freudian view. This view, too, locates the motive for resistance in the dispositions of individuals. Although these dispositions can sometimes find an outlet in various forms of collective reaction, from the cult of the charismatic leader to Freud's so-called "patricide," the Freudian view comes no closer to demonstrating the necessary recurrence of collective strife than does the view that focuses on the dissatisfactions generated by our vanities.

Things are different with respect to the third view, which I have subsumed for the sake of simplicity under the Marxian doctrine of class struggle. It is central to this view that history has throughout been characterized by a struggle for economic predominance waged among social classes. In this regard, the Marxian view is indeed committed to the idea that past social structures cannot be adequately described without reference to conflicts between collective agents. But not only does this social fact lack a proper ontological foundation because it obtains only up to the threshold of a classless society. There is actually a further limitation to this Marxian doctrine that makes it unsuitable for our purposes: we are given no convincing reason to believe that the relevant struggles were only ever motivated by economic interests. This claim certainly seems to be false with regard to those past social structures in which economic action was embedded in the social lifeworld in such a way that their economic concerns did not form a separate social sphere at all.[23] But even regarding our capitalist present, it is more than doubtful whether we can really understand conflicts among social groups as caused primarily by opposing economic interests. The Marxian doctrine of class struggle fails above all because it views all conflict among groups or classes as economically motivated, whereas historical reality suggests that experiences of injustice and of frustrated hopes have had far greater motivating power.[24]

This brings me to the fourth of the views according to which conflict is a necessary aspect of all forms of sociality. Everything that remains underemphasized in the Marxist tradition takes center stage in the context of this fourth position. In the tradition that includes Hegel and Dewey as its main exponents, the source of recurrent social struggles is thought to lie in the fact that any disadvantaged social group will attempt to appeal to norms that are already institutionalized but that are being interpreted or applied in hegemonic ways, and to turn those norms against the dominant groups by relying on them for a moral justification of their own marginalized needs and interests. We should distinguish between two aspects of this complex thesis, which need to be argued for independently of each other. First, it needs to be shown that the norms regulating social interaction do in fact always lend themselves to being called into question by pointing to their one-sided interpretation. Second, it must be shown that groups who experience exclusion or discrimination due to hegemonic interpretations of norms do in fact tend to call these interpretations into question and to rebel against existing social orders. If these two claims can be defended, they will support the claim that social reproduction necessarily includes practical critique or a struggle among groups. In what follows, I will make only some brief suggestions about how one might argue for both of these theses.

The first thesis requires that the norms that enable social integration are by their own nature sufficiently open as to admit recurrent re-interpretation appealing to previously neglected needs or interests. A corollary of this claim is that any such norm always stands under the proviso that it has hitherto only been interpreted in a one-sided, hegemonic way. We can see that this is indeed so by considering the fact that the norms enabling social integration result from a reciprocal empowerment on the part of all individuals to be liable to others' criticism for misapplications of these norms. We cannot understand what it even means for such norms to exist except by reference to a reciprocally granted right to object to deviations from them.[25] And we can expand this observation by adding that in guiding themselves by these norms, agents must treat each other as subjects who possess the authority to criticize others' application of those norms. Insofar as social action is possible only on the basis of shared norms,[26] it is always informed by agents' mutual expectations that they are recognized as members of a community in which everyone is licensed to criticize the normatively guided activity of others. These fundamental enabling conditions of social norms explain why we can treat any given interpretation of a social norm as essentially contested or conflictual. It is always possible that someone will offer reasons to doubt that a given norm is applied or interpreted in a way that is consistent with the underlying expectation of mutual recognition. It is thus intrinsic to the constitutive norms of any given society that they can be criticized for being insufficiently responsive to the concerns or interests of particular individuals or groups.

In contrast with this first thesis, which can be supported by a conceptual explanation of the essential properties of social norms, the second thesis is much more difficult to establish. What is now required is evidence for the steep assertion that previously disadvantaged groups regularly and recurrently rely on the interpretative openness of social norms in attempts to win recognition for their own neglected interests by way of re-interpretation. So what is at issue now is the question what empirical grounds there are for the claim that social reproduction generally involves a type of practical critique that yields a subversive re-interpretation of existing norms with the aim of expanding the reach of mutual recognition. The argument has to proceed indirectly, because it would border on the presumptuous to attempt an inductive proof here. It may be that we can find attempts by some historians and historical sociologists to establish general propositions concerning the logic of the oppositional practices of oppressed groups,[27] but none of these are likely to be sufficient for our purposes. What we might do instead is to consider what alternative forms of action are open to disadvantaged groups, other than to advance transformative re-interpretations. As soon as we frame the issue in this way, it becomes evident that the options are very limited here. When individuals realize that not they alone but an entire group of similarly positioned people are denied appropriate recognition within some structure of socially practiced norms, their only recourse will normally be to call into question the established interpretations of those norms by articulating creative and more inclusive re-interpretations guided by their own particular concerns. Relatively well-studied cases such as the slave revolts in both the Americas, the civil rights movement in the United States, the European workers' movement, and the British suffragette movement serve to show that this was often the procedure of choice.[28] Regardless of how violent or peaceful, how illegal or how legal were the means taken to these various ends, they were justified both outwardly and inwardly by pointing to the fact that they would have to be considered legitimate under a morally sound, expansionary re-interpretation of already existing norms. Even if this "revisionist" approach was sometimes subsequently abandoned because the available norms proved to be too restrictive to accommodate the relevant demands, giving rise to a desire for altogether "new" ideals of social life, we can nevertheless consider it the standard case of the genesis of practical critique.

People's experience that institutionalized norms are inexplicably inapplicable to their own social situation and position leads them to re-interpret these norms in a cooperative hermeneutic effort in order to then be able to draw on them as a normative resource for the legitimation of socially transformative goals.

In order to derive a general model of the dynamic of practical critique from the relatively contemporary examples just named, we need to abstract from them in two or three steps. First, it would need to be demonstrable for all social formations that they recurrently witness the emergence of social groups who are disadvantaged or discriminated against, relative to the expectations of recognition embedded in the established norms of social integration. Second, it would have to be the case that such groups sooner or later develop a sense of dissatisfaction or indignation about the disappointment of these legitimate expectations. Third, this collective outrage would have to lead the relevant groups to initiate struggles involving the attempt to invest established norms with a new, expansive interpretation suitable to justify their demand for social change. In generalizing from our cases in this way, we rely above all on the assumption that social groups will not permanently submit to states of affairs in which they are manifestly disadvantaged by the lights of widely accepted social norms. If this assumption is true, that is, if we can expect sentiments of injustice to manifest themselves on a regular basis, then it seems to me that we are warranted in accepting the dynamic model of practical critique as capturing an essential element of all social reproduction.

4

Even though I have not presented a conclusive proof for this thesis, I am going to rely on it from now on. Perhaps it is sufficient if I have shown that it is not far-fetched to regard what Horkheimer called "critical conduct," that is, the transformative re-interpretation of established social norms, as a recurring practice of oppressed social groups in all societies. In continuing the project of taking up the theoretical aims of Habermas's *Knowledge and Human Interests* even while giving them a different twist, we next need to consider whether the practice just described involves some epistemic interest that is recognizably different from other cognitive concerns we have. If that is the case, that is to say, if social struggle entails an interest in a distinct type of knowledge, it might be that on further scrutiny this prescientific knowledge could turn out to be an epistemic source of a critical theory. Before I can turn to this problem, I should first guard against a misunderstanding that might be invited by what I have said so far. If, as I have done, we think of critical behavior as a cooperative practice of interpretation, this could be taken to suggest that I think of the struggle among social groups as a purely intellectual business, as simply a matter of argument rather than a tangible conflict.[29] This misleading impression arises when the part is mistaken for the whole, as though it was being claimed that the relevant sort of conflict is exhausted by a process of critical and creative re-interpretation. But that is not so. So far, I have merely asserted that such a normative-interpretative practice must be one component of critical behavior, if this behavior is to be intelligible to those engaged in it. Whether in setting fire to buildings, in occupying factories, or in erecting barricades in the street – all of them activities that may become part of a social struggle – those who are fighting in this way must be able to give at least a minimal account of the point and appropriateness, the goals, and the legitimacy of what they are doing. My thesis is that this internal aspect of their activity, the work of persuasion that they perform vis-à-vis themselves as well as others, consists in a cooperative re-interpretation of existing norms. This is no idealizing reduction of social struggle to intellectual activity. Rather, I proceed on the assumption that any social struggle involves conceptual and normative operations as well as outwardly directed resistance, insurrection, or rebellion. Both aspects belong together and should not be artificially isolated from each other.

With this conceptual clarification out of the way, I can now turn to the question whether there is anything to be said in favor of reading a distinct epistemic interest into these sorts of struggles. Do those who participate in the practice of cooperative re-interpretation have some cognitive interest that is clearly distinct from the dominant types of inquiry belonging to the established social order? The beginnings of an answer can be found in the chapter on "Lordship and Bondage" in Hegel's *Phenomenology of Spirit*, however overused that chapter may be.[30] The relationship between lord and bondsman (or master and servant) is there presented as one in which both parties are initially limited to incomplete forms of self-consciousness. The master is lacking in self-consciousness because he is related to the objects he desires only indirectly through his servant and hence has no experience of their fluid and changeable nature. The servant, on the other hand, is unable to attain full self-consciousness because his goals remain dependent on the master, and he is therefore unable to experience himself as a self-determining agent. Thus, each of these two characters fails to meet a certain necessary condition for the attainment of self-consciousness that is satisfied by the other. The master remains in a relationship of dependency vis-à-vis the world of external objects because he is incapable of transforming objects through labor. The servant remains in a relationship of dependency vis-à-vis his master because he is subject to the latter's will and is unable to influence it. In using Hegel's line of thought as a point of departure for my attempt to answer the question at hand, I am going to set aside all the further complications of this famous chapter. The servant's fear of death and the master's hedonism are not going to play any role in what follows. The only thing relevant for my purposes is the contrast between the two protagonists regarding their respective relations to the world of external objects. Whereas the master experiences his external surroundings only as an in-itself whose structure and modifiability remain unknown to him in his passive stance, the servant forced to execute the tasks imposed on him relates to external objects in the mode of "formative activity"[31] and thus turns them into something that is "for-him." If we now think of the relevant external object as consisting in the social norms established at some moment in time, Hegel's reflections will have helped us make some progress. For now, we can think of the master as someone who remains in a position of passive dependency vis-à-vis those norms, whereas the servant encounters them as objects of his own formative activity. This transposition of Hegel's scenario may perhaps appear forced or arbitrary, but it helps us understand the respective reasons for two quite different attitudes toward an existing set of norms. Those who experience no need to be skeptical of the dominant interpretations of shared social norms because they themselves derive advantages or privileges from them will tend to accept those norms as an "in-itself," as something unchangeably given. But those who are forced to call those interpretations into question because their own claims or desires are not reflected in them will seek to conceive of those norms as existing merely "for-them" and relate to them with a formative and transformative attitude. I would now like to use this contrast as a key to understanding whether the intellectual side of social struggles entails an interest in a distinctive type of knowledge.

Let us begin by considering the situation in which oppressed or disadvantaged groups generally find themselves. Initially, the sense that the existing conditions are somehow unjust because they block the satisfaction of seemingly legitimate concerns will only be shared within relatively small circles. Even at this initial stage, individuals relate to the established norms in an interpretative mode, because those norms are relied on as reasons both for regarding the needs articulated by the group as morally legitimate and as perceiving the frustration of those needs as an injustice or a wrong. Without some such reference to norms shared by all the members of a society, it would be difficult to apply the terminology of "justice" and "injustice" in a way that is publicly intelligible and open to public scrutiny. At the same time, at this early stage, it is not yet understood that the existing norms are in need of re-interpretation. Their established and institutionally embodied interpretation is still treated as fully authoritative, and what is questioned is only the fairness or justice of their application. Only at a second stage does the oppressed group raise doubts regarding the hegemonic interpretation of the established norms. It seems to me that this would be the point at which those involved become aware of an interest in a type of knowledge that is distinct from the existing, official forms of knowledge developed in their society. For what exactly is the sort of knowledge that the disadvantaged group must acquire in order to undertake the work of expansive re-interpretation? It seems to me that the step from reliance on a traditional interpretation to its questioning and transformative expansion requires at least two insights for which there seems to be no use within the practices of an established social order. First, agents need to learn that any existing norm is amenable to a range of quite different interpretations, because it does not itself specify to whom and exactly in what way it is to be applied. Second, they need to develop an understanding of why, or on the basis of what interests, specific interpretations are dominant within an existing social order. Taken together, the awareness of the plasticity of social norms and the awareness of the reasons for their one-sided interpretation amount to what is known as "emancipatory knowledge." The thesis, in short, is that oppressed groups have an interest in acquiring this type of knowledge insofar as their goal is to change interpretations of existing norms in their own favor.

The two cognitive elements just identified as the components of emancipatory knowledge need to be described in some more detail if the thesis is to be convincing. We already saw earlier that the norms enabling social integration are only ever valid in a qualified way, in that their previous interpretations through social practices can always turn out to have been partial or one-sided. It is a fundamental property of such norms that those whose actions are governed by them may always bring complaints regarding their current interpretation. To jointly follow a norm is to accord to one another the authority to criticize others for their application of the shared norm. But between this basic fact and actual critique lies a considerable step, which requires that implicit knowledge turns into explicit practical knowledge. It is this cognitive step that I am claiming oppressed groups must be able to take when they come to revolt against a dominant social order. Before a disadvantaged or oppressed group starts engaging in the cooperative re-interpretation of some established norm, it first needs to have become aware that such norms admit a far greater range of interpretations than is suggested by the congealed form they have assumed in a given institutional environment. The semblance of naturalness that in everyday life attaches to any established interpretation first needs to be ruptured before agents can then jointly explore which new and creative interpretation is most suited to accommodate their hitherto excluded interests and concerns. This de-naturalization of hegemonic interpretations of norms is one type of knowledge in which those engaged in social struggles have an essential interest. In acquiring it, they are able to draw on an intuitive kind of knowledge, which is shared by all the members of a society but which the members of dominant groups lack any motive to articulate explicitly. The latter cling to the semblance of naturalness that accompanies habituated interpretations, and they do so because those interpretations lend legitimacy to their institutionally entrenched advantages and privileges. By contrast, those who rebel against those privileges need to be able to reveal the semblance for what it is in order to make room for a re-interpretation of the same norms.

But the groups engaged in a social struggle also have an essential interest in a second type of knowledge. It is not enough for them to pierce through the pseudo-objectivity of existing interpretations of social norms. In addition, they must be capable of determining which interests underlie people's attachment to those dominant interpretations. This second cognitive step is required because in its absence, it would be impossible to cite reasons for attacking the one-sided interpretations on which the established social order is based. The demonstration that such an interpretation is designed to legitimize the partisan interests of some can lend moral urgency to the demand that the shared norms be given a new interpretation. It is one thing to identify an existing interpretation of a norm as insufficient by pointing to the fact that it is unresponsive to one's own interests and concerns. But such a demonstration becomes a positive reason to replace the given interpretation by a better and more inclusive one only once this demand itself has been cleared of the suspicion of partisanship, by uncovering the way in which the current interpretative practice is bound up with an interest in domination. In an oppressed group's struggle for hermeneutic authority, the interest in understanding the interpretative openness of social norms thus goes hand in hand with an interest in the type of knowledge known as ideology critique. Both the de-naturalization of hegemonic interpretations and the deciphering of the interests underlying them are forms of knowledge whose motivational roots are found in the process of social struggle. Social groups that rebel against an established social order because their own concerns are not adequately reflected in it must necessarily take an interest in both these types of knowledge.

In conclusion, I would like to relate this thesis back to Habermas's project in *Knowledge and Human Interests*, which I outlined in the beginning. In this early work, Habermas proceeded from the assumption that all types of human knowledge serve the function of enabling or facilitating actions or activities that are ineliminable elements of our social reproduction. From this starting point, he was led to the thought that the "transcendental" role of the natural sciences is to serve our interest in controlling nature, whereas the humanities serve our interest in intersubjective communication. What remained unclear in this sketch was what place might be assigned to the so-called "emancipatory" sciences whose epistemological roots were after all the main object of Habermas's inquiry. One way of approaching this problem was by drawing on the model of psychoanalysis, whose methodology was to show how the development of a theory can serve to provide individuals with the means to liberate themselves from the self-perpetuated type of dependency embodied in neuroses. I tried to show that the transposition of this theoretical model from the case of individuals to the analysis of whole societies gave rise to some fundamental difficulties that could not properly be addressed within the framework developed by Habermas. Not only did his approach produce the misleading impression that the human species could be viewed as a single, large-scale individual, it also failed to establish a connection with some type of human activity and thus with the alleged transcendental source of all branches of knowledge. To avoid these calamitous implications, it therefore seemed natural to me to approach Habermas's original problem from the opposite direction and to start out by examining whether in addition to labor and interaction, there might be a third type of human activity that could serve as the "functional" source of "emancipatory" forms of knowledge. In pursuing this line of thought, I follow the traces that Habermas himself, following Horkheimer, had laid out when he occasionally spoke of "struggle" as a possible candidate for the practical context in which critical theory might be embedded.

The result of my investigation of this proposal, nascent in the recent philosophical tradition, and of various alternatives to it, was that we can conceive of such an activity of "struggle" as a permanently recurring feature of social reproduction only if we see it as connected to the essential interpretative openness of social norms. We found that the norms that enable social integration can always be scrutinized with regard to the question whether the interpretations prevailing at a given time live up to the promise of recognition implicit in all such norms. It is therefore very likely that oppressed or disadvantaged groups will periodically attempt to deepen or expand the semantic content of those norms through creative re-interpretation. To its participants, this sort of struggle therefore always has an ineliminable conceptual and normative dimension, whereas the representatives of the established order experience it as an insurrection and a confrontation that may, depending on circumstances, show a violent face. Provided that the occurrence of such struggles is indeed an ineliminable feature of our social life, the crucial task for my purposes was then to find out whether there is some essential and distinct form of epistemic interest inherent in them. Or to put it in a slightly different and more functionalist way, I could say my task now was to show to what extent this sort of struggle requires its agents to acquire certain understandings and insights that are not straightforwardly available within the dominant epistemic culture. My proposal for a solution was to distinguish between two kinds of epistemic achievement that any group fighting for its emancipation would each need to aim for in order to succeed in its practical goals: First, such a group must develop an awareness of the essential inter-pretative openness of established norms, in the face of a stubborn tendency toward their naturalization. Second, it must gain an understanding of the interests that account for the entrenchment of the existing, institutionally embodied interpretative practice. And, to repeat, both of these epistemic achievements amount to forms of knowledge in which groups struggling for social inclusion must take an interest insofar as they increase the chances that their efforts will meet with success.

These conclusions bring me back to the considerations with which I began my talk. I said at the outset that the tradition of critical theory was committed because of its inception to viewing its own scientific activity as nothing but a methodologically disci-plined extension of epistemic efforts undertaken by oppressed groups in their daily struggles. Horkheimer was still guided by this idea when he developed his groundwork for a critical theory, as was Habermas in his *Knowledge and Human Interests*, albeit without complete success. The only remaining question for today then is whether the concept of social struggle that I have outlined is better suited to establish the often asserted but never sufficiently explained connection between a prescientific epistemic interest and the discipline of critical theory. Can my proposals about the two forms of knowledge and their functional role within social struggles be read as pointing to the cognitive interest proper to a critical social analysis? I am hoping that it will not appear presump-tuous if I give a cautiously affirmative answer to this concluding question. In my view, it is indeed the case that critical theory is nothing but the continuation, by means of a controlled scien-tific methodology, of the cognitive labor that oppressed groups have to perform in their everyday struggles when they work to de-naturalize hegemonic patterns of interpretation and to expose the interests by which these are motivated. The insights generated in this way, quite without any reference to standards of scientific inquiry, are the undisciplined germ which a critical theory should bring to fruition within the sphere of the established sciences. In the end, what has been offered over time under the rubric of social critique has always consisted in advancing plausible historical accounts as scientific proof of the fact that a tangible interest in domination generally ensures that socially prevailing norms are given scandalously one-sided interpretations. Taken together, the de-naturalization of hegemonic patterns of interpreting social norms and the uncovering of these motivating interests forge a path along which a critical theory can proceed toward its goal of furthering the process of social emancipation by means of scientific inquiry.[32]

Translated by Felix Koch

13

A History of Moral Self-Correction
Tracing European solidarity

For Claus Offe on the occasion of his eightieth birthday

Scarcely a day goes by without a terrifying report on the impending disintegration of the European Union. In one country, there is a torturous, months-long debate about the conditions under which it will leave the EU, in another country European civil rights are being trampled on, and in yet another a radical right-wing party is busy mobilizing large swathes of the electorate behind an anti-European manifesto. For someone who grew up during the time of Franco-German reconciliation, and of enthusiasm for the European idea, it feels like a nightmare. For the first time since the end of World War II, Europe seems to be going in reverse. Where before there was a process of growing unification, containment of market forces, and progressive social policy, there is now a sudden backlash, and a return to rivalry among states, nationalist sentiment, and capitalist competition.

We are witnessing a political reversal in Europe, one that takes the form of a return of the nation state and a reduction of the welfare state. Its causes are by now well known, and have been succinctly summarized by Claus Offe in his study *Europe Entrapped*. The introduction of the euro was meant to facilitate economic cooperation by removing national obstacles to the flow of capital and smoothing access to labor markets, but the introduction was ill-considered and rushed. Before long, the common currency led to dramatic differences between the gross domestic products of member states. Because of the new exchange conditions, the rich exporting countries, foremost among them Germany, grew their profits

from exports, while the weaker economic regions, particularly in
southern Europe, suffered massive losses. Add to this economic
imbalance the global financial crisis and the growing stream of
refugees from the war-torn and poverty-stricken countries of the
Middle East and Africa, and the result is the mood of discontent
we observe in Europe today. Many Europeans are concerned about
economic and political injustice, and the blame for this injustice
is increasingly laid at the door of a bloated, centralized administration in Brussels.[1] In the space of just a few years, a Europe that
was unified and proud of its social and cultural achievements has
been transformed into an edifice of states held together in no more
than a makeshift fashion. It seems as though one final push is all it
will take to let it collapse.

The question of what to do in the face of this threat exercises
all those who have not yet given up hope for a democratic, united
Europe. There is only one point upon which all those in this
shrinking camp agree: stopping the backslide in the European
project and offering a sustainable and inspiring perspective for the
future to the demoralized alliance of states will require objective
and subjective factors, both functional changes and motivating
reasons. Functional changes will be needed because any successful
plan for the democratic renewal of Europe will have to include, at
the very least, political measures that remove economic disparities
and strengthen the legal and governmental authority of existing
institutions. No vision of a democratically united Europe, however
attractive, will have any chance of success if it does not provide a
sober and robust solution to the problem of promoting social well-
being under current socio-economic circumstances. But for any such
social and economic reform plan to be effective, it would first have to
capture the hearts and minds of the European citizenry. Regardless
of its merits, it will not be possible to implement it without this
subjective factor: the convictions, opinions, and preferences of
all those whom the institutional channels of will-formation must
win over. The thorny question is how the objective and subjective
factors, the necessary functional changes and the individuals'
motivations, can be linked up in a coherent vision of a revitalized
Europe. As things stand, and given that the EU has thus far shown
itself to be too inflexible, overly bureaucratic, and sclerotic, I do not
believe that a plan for the economic and political reform of the EU
will be persuasive if it is not accompanied by *historical* arguments
that spell out why citizens should place their hopes in the institution. Even the most well-meaning efforts to respond to both

challenges, that is, to mobilize individuals to support objectively necessary changes, have failed to instill a renewed passion for the European idea. The very common invocation of the Christian values that supposedly once gave Europe its cultural unity is unlikely to be successful in bringing about the necessary social and economic reform, and announcements of new plans for political and social reform at the European level do not make clear why individual nation states should not be better placed to take care of their citizens' economic well-being.[2] However, the shortcomings of these two approaches – a mere invocation of cultural tradition and a sober appeal to individual interest – are instructive. They reveal what an inspiring perspective on Europe's future would require: it would need to reconstruct the history of these states, which have been linked to each other, in good times and bad, over centuries, in such a way that the historical narrative itself would be enough to convince European citizens that they must seek ways of bringing about greater well-being and more justice within the context of a common alliance. In the current crisis, what is usually called European solidarity can be revived only if all citizens can be convinced that their common history demands that a supranational legislature should be entrusted with the protection and defense of their legitimate interest in social improvement. In what follows, I take the first steps toward such a normative reconstruction of Europe's conflict-ridden history. I hope to be able to show that the idea of a struggle for recognition, as I have developed it following Hegel, can provide valuable inspiration when reflecting on the possible sources of European solidarity.

I

The greatest error in many of the current efforts to promote European solidarity is the assumption that cohesion can be based only on a positive common ground and shared past glory.[3] The presupposition is that human beings will stand by each other and share burdens cooperatively only if they can look back at a successful common history. The idea that only positive experiences can generate feelings of solidarity is deeply mistaken, as we can see by considering the sources of family cohesion. The members of a family support one another's well-being not because of a shared history of splendid success but because of a sequence of crises and catastrophes that they overcame together: illness and death, quarrels, and personal failures. The root of a family's spirit of solidarity is quite often not a series of positive experiences but a series of calamities that they suffered, lived through, and overcame together. And what goes for individual families applies even more to a political community. If there is solidarity in such a community, it rests on a common history in which negative events, disputes, and conflicts were overcome. That said, there is a significant difference here: in political communities, these decisive events are often not strokes of fate that were passively suffered but violations of norms that were approved or actively pursued by the community itself, such as wars or crimes.

When seeking the sources of European solidarity, we can draw a first conclusion from this insight into the often negative foundation of solidarity: we should reject the mendacious and brazen claim that usually forms the starting point for well-meaning narratives of the history of Europe, namely that the cultural cohesion of this alliance of states is based on the civilizing, even moral, achievements they brought about in their mutual exchange over past centuries. Nothing could be more wrongheaded, nothing could do more harm to the search for sources of European solidarity, than this kind of moral loftiness. Many have rightly accused Europe's political and intellectual elites of cultivating a moral self-image that bizarrely contradicts the historical facts. Such grand expressions as "European values" are belied by historic abominations whose egregiousness should make anyone blush: for many centuries, the slave trade was practiced on the European continent and on the island of Britain, a number of European countries brutally colonized Asia, Africa, and South America, the industrial workforce of the nineteenth century was exploited mercilessly, and Nazi Germany carried out the genocide of the Jews. The values, or rather moral principles, of individual freedom, tolerance, popular sovereignty, and the welfare state are each tainted ineradicably by injustice and bloodshed. None of these normative ideals came about innocently, as if they were merely noble suggestions for human self-improvement. Rather, they are, without exception, the results of intellectual endeavors that aimed to tame the destructive forces of brazen presumption and repression, and to avoid the worst excesses of strife and war. Any reconsideration of European solidarity must therefore begin with this bitter acknowledgment: that our history is first and foremost one of grave misdeeds, serious crimes, and flagrant violations of norms. Beginning with the crusades, moving on to the bloody wars of religion, the unscrupulous slave trade, colonial conquest, exploitative industrial capitalism, and ending with the Holocaust, the European continent has been home to the most serious wrongdoing the world has ever seen, and each crime has further eroded the foundations of civilization.[4]

This history of wrongdoing and extreme norm violation represents, however, only one side of the historical process to be reconstructed. This negative side already reveals the moral reasons that underlie the obligations that today's European association of states has toward large parts of the global community: returning artworks to their original and legitimate owners; granting asylum to people affected by war, genocide, or poverty; or spending a portion of gross national product on developmental aid. These duties have now been made legally binding. European states are compelled to accept them because of the atrocities and norm violations they committed in the past. But recollecting the dark, criminal side of European history does not tell us why European citizens should trust one another and stand by each other in the interests of their common well-being. Europe's past crimes, which, if they were not always jointly committed, were at least mutually tolerated, place the EU under moral and legal obligations toward the rest of the world, but they do not provide the foundation for a commitment to solidarity within Europe itself.

The origin of such *obligations* between European citizens becomes clear when we consider the fact that Europe's crimes have always also pulled Europe into a dynamic of self-questioning and moral self-correction – a process that is still ongoing. I already hinted at this second side of European history, which is inseparable from the first, when I referred briefly to the peculiar genesis of European values. These normative ideals came about because of the constant effort to bring destructive forces under control through trying out new theoretical designs for moral principles of social life and, finally, through the institutionalization of such principles. It is this fateful interweaving of norm violations and moral self-examination, of crimes and reflexive attempts to work through them, that has shaped European history in such a way that it is possible today to find within it the sources of solidarity among European citizens.[5] The members of the European Union owe each other help and support because it is only through cooperation that Europe can continue the learning process carried out by previous generations: that of finding institutional corrections for moral injustices and working together to create a more equitable community.

Before I consider in more detail the birth of European solidarity out of the common mastery of self-inflicted harm, I will first discuss a few examples that further illustrate the peculiar interweaving of wrongdoing and moral self-correction in European history.

II

As I have indicated, the history of Europe has been anything but a happy story of moral progress and civilizing achievement. To think that Europe's past is a shining history of ever-expanding justice and freedom is to grossly deceive oneself about the crimes that stretch from the wars of religion, colonialism, and "primitive accumulation" to the Holocaust. Most instances of moral progress in this region of the world followed some atrocity, and took the form of a reflection on the moral principles that could have avoided it. However, these processes of moral improvement did not consist in a straightforward introduction of whichever normative principles seemed appropriate to moderate or control particular destructive forces. Rather, the moral self-examination was typically a drawn-out conflict in which different parties waged a discursive battle over the appropriate normative and institutional revisions. The back and forth between these parties over which moral rules would make society less harmful, and thus more just, lent the process of Europe's intellectual formation its particular character. There was never just one correct solution, but always several possible ones, and in this way the European continent inadvertently, and despite its regressive tendencies, became a laboratory for the testing of normative provisions for the improvement of human life. I will look at three decisive turning points in European history in order to discuss the extent to which the reflexive process of working through past injustices took the form of a drawn-out conflict over the better argument. In particular, I want to demonstrate that this battle over the pros and cons of particular suggestions has not come to an end: it continues in the form of ongoing discussions about alternative, more equitable forms of communal life.

A sensible starting point for a reconstruction of major turning points in the history of Europe's self-understanding is the aftermath of the wars of religion and the intellectual attempts to come to terms with them. The effort to reflexively understand the causes and consequences of these catastrophic events saw, for the first time, something like political and philosophical communication across the borders of individual countries. The key figure in the quickly developing debate was Thomas Hobbes, the founder of modern political philosophy, who was born in the west of England in 1588. Hobbes offered a surprisingly simple solution to the problem of how to suppress religiously motivated civil war. The attraction of his solution lay in its promise of reconciling the individual's desire for liberty with the requirements of an authoritarian form of rule that could secure peace. Hobbes argued that if all citizens had a rational insight into the threat posed by an unregulated social situation, they would submit to a sovereign with absolute power, and thereby would preserve their "natural" liberty within a secure social system that would be pacified from above. For Hobbes, this liberty in any case consisted merely of the ability to do whatever one liked, as long as external obstacles, including the sovereign's law, did not prevent one from doing it.[6] This narrow, negative definition of liberty soon found intellectual resistance in groups that were opposed to the English monarchy. They drew on conceptions of the state from older Greek and Roman traditions in the pursuit of a republican solution to the civil war. According to these thinkers, individual liberty required not only the absence of obstacles to the ends pursued by individuals but also the ability of individuals to formulate their intentions without coercion, influence, or domination by others.[7] Although this conception of liberty also remained in a certain sense "negative" – because the presence of liberty is always a matter of the absence of something else[8] – it nevertheless helped to establish an understanding of the legitimacy of the political order that was opposed to the Hobbesian understanding. The legitimacy of the state was no longer to be measured against its ability to secure peace and social order, but against its ability to protect the individual from dependency on third parties by giving the individual the right to participate in the formation of law.

To avoid misunderstanding: the regulative ideas of these two models of liberty did not, of course, put an end to the wars of religion. That happened only with the Peace of Westphalia, a transnational peace accord between the warring states, the normative implications of which had far more influence on the future of international law than did the debates over the legitimacy of the state. But the war itself, the fact that blind religious faith had led inadvertently to the destruction of countless lives, made it necessary, even while the brutality was still unfolding, to reflect on the extent of and the limits to the individual citizen's liberty. Through these

intellectual efforts at normative self-control, two conceptions of
the legitimacy of political systems emerged in Europe, and while
they contrast with each other, they inform our views to the present
day. On the one hand, there were the more conservative groups
that, in the interests of political stability and security, sought to
understand individual liberty as a legally protected space of purely
private purposes.[9] On the other, there were forces that sought
to understand individual liberty in terms of participation in the
law-making processes of a republican state. Their interest was in
overcoming the authoritarian state and political tutelage, and they
were viewed as more progressive even at the time. But it took more
than another 100 years before Rousseau and Kant developed this
idea far enough that it could become the intellectual foundation of
the democratic revolutions on the continent.[10] Individual liberty,
whether expressed in a negative or positive form, was understood
as the right to self-legislation, a right that in political matters,
that is, matters affecting all citizens, could be exercised only by
everyone in common. For normative reasons, this right therefore
required a democratic form of government. Although with this
victory the republican side of the argument had finally won the
battle for hegemony in Europe, the advocates of a Hobbesian
authoritarianism never gave up hope, and they continued to be
successful in finding support, whether in the form of antidemo-
cratic movements or even attempts at dictatorships. In a certain
sense, the two answers to the religiously motivated civil war of the
sixteenth century have thus remained present within Europe. To
the present day, the legitimacy of political rule is based either on
the state guaranteeing security, stability, and order, or on the conditions for democratic political will-formation.[11]

Something similar is true of another turning point in the history
of European efforts at controlling its own destructive forces and
defeating the causes of disorder, war, and injustice. Some 200–300
years after the religiously motivated civil wars, the chief injustice
was no longer the repression and persecution of heterodox believers
but the exploitation of the proletariat and the deprivation of their
rights. Friedrich Engels's famous book *The Condition of the Working
Class in England*, published in 1845, was merely the stylistic high
point of a plethora of reports that described the devastating
consequences of the unscrupulous exploitation of the emergent
industrial proletarian class.[12] These reports of child labor, lengthy
working days, and starvation wages caused such widespread
outrage across Europe that there soon emerged a sense of moral

urgency about finding a solution to the "social question."[13] As with the wars of religion, there were a variety of proposals for moral provisions to alleviate these scandalous social ills. At one end of the fierce debate were those who agreed with Marx and the early socialists that the misery of the working class could be remedied only by the abolition of private ownership of the means of production, and thus by the removal of the capitalist economy. The middle ground was occupied by an equally large group that believed in the possibility of reforming the capitalist market from within through legal measures to improve the working conditions, social security, and living standards of the industrial proletariat. And at the opposite end of the spectrum was a group that was small in number but powerful in terms of its negotiating position. This group wanted to convince the public that the extreme precarity of the industrial workforce was only a temporary price that had to be paid to increase the wealth of all over time – an argument that, 100 years later, would be summarized in the catchphrase "trickle-down economics."[14]

As with the intellectual effort that followed the wars of religion, it is not difficult to identify the normative point around which the theoretical debates and political battles about the social question turned. The question was what form the economic system should take in order to prevent the harm and suffering of those whose labor maintained economic wealth. In the twentieth century, after bitter and drawn-out conflict, the moderate wing of the labor movement won out for a time. In almost all European countries, the state now legally regulates the capitalist labor market in a way that takes into account employees' legitimate demands regarding safety at work, basic economic security, and limited working hours.[15] However, these significant achievements of social policy and the welfare state should not blind us to the fragility of the social consensus on which they rest today. The new form of capitalism that has developed over the past four decades as a consequence of the massive deregulation of markets and the unparalleled rise of finance capitalism makes it unmistakably clear that the welfare state can never be taken for granted.[16] Current debates about the advantages and disadvantages of capitalist markets strikingly resemble those of the nineteenth century. There is, again, a faction that wants to overcome capitalist economic relations in the name of social justice, another that considers it possible to civilize the capitalist market, and a third that propagates a far-reaching deregulation on the basis of the alleged benefits this would have for all.

At this point, a preliminary conclusion might be that Europe's intellectual engagement with its self-inflicted harm and injustice has always led to the formulation of norms that conflict with each other. These remain present even today, in the form of alternative proposals for one and the same social area. The political order can be judged either according to the level of security and stability it provides, or according to the extent to which it enables a democratic form of political will-formation. The economic system can be judged either according to its economic efficiency, or according to the level of social justice it generates. As we have seen, the second of each of these alternatives has prevailed in the social battle: the modern state based on the rule of law is expected to enable a formation of the political will that includes as many citizens as possible, and the capitalist market is meant to be tempered by regulation and the welfare state. But it does not follow that the alternatives have disappeared. Rather, at every moment of political destabilization or economic crisis, it is only a matter of time before the opposite norms are forcefully advanced, and revisions to the institutional order demanded in their name. Before continuing this train of thought, I will touch on a further turning point in the history of Europe's self-understanding, which will bring us right up to the threshold of the present.

Unlike the first two moral disasters, in the case of this third European crime the reflexive working-through is still a long time coming – a very long time. The colonialism practiced by various European countries over centuries has still not been normatively dealt with or expiated in an appropriate way. For decades, the unscrupulous conquest and exploitation of countries on the African, Asian, and South American continents were either justified with the racist argument that they brought civilization to backward cultures, or endorsed as the perfectly legitimate side effects of the economic expansion of the major European powers. In either case, the violent appropriation of foreign lands, their natural resources, labor power, and cultural goods were not seen as moral abominations or crimes.[17] Occasionally, of course, there were complaints in Europe when the exercise of colonial rule was deemed to exceed a level of brutality that was considered normal, and in these cases certain methods of rule were suddenly called into question. But even thinkers as sensitive as Alexis de Tocqueville or John Stuart Mill, despite their fundamentally universalist convictions, found reason to justify more moderate practices of colonial conquest. Diderot, and possibly also Herder, were the laudable exceptions to the phalanx of defenders of "enlightened" colonialism.[18]

Only with the pressure exerted by anti-colonial liberation movements from the 1950s onwards did we see the first faltering attempts by Europeans to address the moral guilt of colonialism.[19] And in this case, again, two opposed sets of norms were mobilized in trying to account for Europe's colonial past. One party sees it as a historical injustice of such grave dimensions that its economic, political, and cultural consequences can be felt to the present day. The miserable condition of many of the former colonies is seen by this party as a symptom of a continuing, subcutaneous dependence that can be overcome only through sustained reparations of various kinds.[20] The other party forcefully rejects the claim of enduring guilt. Once the former colonies became sovereign states, this argument runs, the former colonial powers ceased to have any responsibilities toward them. Sometimes, preferential treatment is granted to the citizens of former colonies who want to immigrate to the countries of former colonial powers, but any further demands, whether for compensation, development aid, or reparations, if made on the grounds of former injustice, are flatly rejected.

As with the first two examples of processes of moral improvement, coming to terms with colonial injustice has led to a tense relationship between two normative perspectives. However, this recent chapter in the long history of European self-questioning has not yet progressed far enough for a stable system of alternative proposals to emerge in this area. Nevertheless, the three turning points in Europe's history that we have considered suffice to justify a conclusion whose significance for the search for sources of European solidarity can hardly be overstated. The cultural unity of Europe does not consist in a moral orientation whose values are shared across borders, and it certainly does not consist in a common history of great civilizing achievements that have delighted the rest of the world. Rather, if we can speak of such unity at all, it consists in a surprising ability to work through and reflexively come to terms with our various atrocities, calamities, and norm violations through a discursive process at the end of which there is, at least, an understanding of the moral legitimacy of different perspectives. The cultural foundation of Europe is not consensus, and not harmony, but a tacit agreement about the substance and purpose of moral conflict.[21] I will next discuss in more detail what these ongoing tensions between negative and positive freedom, democracy and *raison d'état*, enlightenment and counter-enlightenment, and welfare state and economic liberalism mean for the prospect of European solidarity.

III

Europe's current desolation might well lead us to long for a return of the optimism of Marcel Mauss's philosophy of history. The great anthropologist's posthumously published study *La nation* confidently developed the thesis that the social forces pushing for the socialization of the economy would necessarily also promote the removal of borders between states, and thus internationalism.[22] We have lost this faith in socialism's power to unite people and overcome national borders. It has become very difficult to hope that a shared desire for social control of the conditions of production might revive the spirit of European solidarity any time soon. I have already hinted at more realistic alternatives: instead of searching for sources of solidarity in religious traditions or supposedly great achievements, we should rather look toward the history of crises and conflicts that were mastered together. The suggestion is that it is not so much the invocation of a positive shared past but the remembrance of a collective response to negative events that leads people to stand by and support one another. In what follows, I substantiate this idea further as I prepare to answer my original question.

The idea that solidarity is the result not of harmony and consensus but of civically resolved conflict is not new to sociology. Among the classical practitioners of the discipline, it was primarily Georg Simmel who believed that "conflict" creates commonalities among people and thus contributes significantly to the integration of social groups. However, he bases his thesis on an argument that is of little help for my present purposes because, drawing on Nietzsche, it emphasizes the vitalizing and energizing function of discord or conflict in counteracting cultural ossification.[23] Nor do Albert Hirschman's reflections, which take up Simmel's idea in a slightly modified form, fully correspond to what I have in mind when I speak of the socially integrating effect of normative conflict. In one of his last essays, the American sociologist developed the interesting thesis that in democracies political conflict supports social integration because it forces the members of society to relate to each other and, in spite of their differences, to remain mindful of the common good. Hirschman, however, sought to limit the validity of this claim to conflicts about the distribution of socially shared goods, because in these cases it is frequently necessary to find temporary compromises. The claim therefore does not apply to situations that are unresolvable in principle.[24] The conflicts I have in mind are of an altogether different kind. They do not result from incompatible values, nor do they simply concern the just distribution of goods. Rather, they are the result of different views about how to atone for injustice so that the solution benefits all affected. In such cases, conflict is preceded by the emergence of a "we"-perspective. Differences of opinion arise only because there is already a tacit acceptance that certain events constitute wrongdoing, and that – as everyone is responsible for this wrong-doing, either directly through their action or indirectly through a failure to act – it can only be rectified jointly by everyone. The comparison with the family, although it should not be taken too far, again allows us to see a similar genesis of feelings of solidarity. At the outset, the family members are united by the spontaneous but often not explicitly formulated agreement that a negative event poses a challenge to them all: everyone is affected in the same way, and therefore all must help to find a solution. The family members may then come into conflict over the best way to face the challenge. This is likely to further strengthen their existing cohesion, for everyone is aware that they have a common goal – the substance of the conflict – that makes the conflict worth having. In a way, such conflicts may be seen as a variation on Hegel's "struggle for recognition." From a common perspective of those affected, a battle takes place between various parties over who offers the most inclusive and beneficial solution to a crisis that is experienced by all as existential.[25]

This notion of conflict differs from both Simmel's and Hirschman's. On this view, a conflict or argument has an integrating effect if all involved are more or less clear about the reasonable goal to be achieved, and if that goal is seen by all as the right one. There is, so to speak, a "second order" agreement: all agree, at least, on what the disagreement is about, and all agree that that is something worth fighting over.[26] In short, to modify a well-known expression coined by John Rawls, these conflicts are cases of "reasonable disagreement." If we understand the smoldering, centuries-long moral disputes in Europe on this model, they reveal the first, tentative signs of European solidarity. Since the wars of religion, scholars and laymen everywhere – from London to Paris, Riga and Saint Petersburg – have argued about which moral measures might weaken and finally extinguish the causes of the ever-present tendencies toward exploitation, war, repression, and exclusion. This hidden but continuous discourse has shaped the history of the European mind more profoundly than any other controversy. While it may not have produced a first-order agreement, it has established a second-order agreement: quite apart from all the ferocious arguments about whether a political system should guarantee security or democratic participation, whether the economic system should be geared toward growth or the needs of workers, or whether colonialism must be understood as an injustice that demands redress today, there is agreement about the "whys" and "wherefores" of each debate.

This creation of community through discord and conflict merely prepared the ground for a possible future European solidarity. The ongoing controversies over alternative ways of normatively disciplining social behavior created an open-minded interest in the attitudes prevalent in other countries, and they perhaps even produced feelings of belonging, but they did not lead to a pronounced willingness to engage in mutual aid in the pursuit of shared goals. The transition from an enduring but loose unity to a state of obligatory solidarity was, again, triggered by a negative event. This time it was of such monstrous proportions that far more substantial, even qualitatively different, efforts seemed to be needed in response. World War II was itself a clear symptom of uncontrolled forces of destruction, and with its end came the harrowing realization that the worst crimes in human history had been committed by a highly civilized country in the heart of Europe. The Holocaust was planned and executed by Nazi Germany, but it was also tolerated for far too long by neighboring countries that were not altogether free of antisemitism themselves. It represented a new kind of turning point in Europe's self-understanding. The response to this moral catastrophe in Western Europe was not just a further step in the ongoing process of moral self-questioning and institutional correction. Rather, it was a fundamental transformation that changed the form that debates and controversies concerning the destructive potential of Europe's own culture would take thereafter. Such is the importance of this moment of transformation in the process of Europe's self-disciplining, which began to take shape with the foundation of the European Economic Community in the 1950s, that it merits more detailed analysis.

The first attempt to draw some conclusions from the disaster of World War II involved no more than the intensification of economic cooperation between certain Western European countries. In accordance with the old doctrine of *doux commerce*,[27] mutually beneficial economic policy was seen as the best means of maintaining peaceful relations between the states. But even these early steps toward European integration already contained the seeds of the far more ambitious aim of creating, in the long term, a transnational alliance of states that would reliably coordinate all important political matters. On a generous hermeneutic reading, we might perhaps say that those involved had already begun to acknowledge the idea that debates about how to civilize one's own culture should not be left to uncontrolled and accidental encounters and controversies. The intention was to give a stable, centralized organizational form to the process of self-examination and self-control, which had hitherto taken place in a relatively haphazard and uncoordinated fashion. From this perspective, it is no exaggeration to say that the intention behind these first tentative steps toward European unification was the establishment of a kind of collective super-ego. Instead of leaving the task of taming Europe's destructiveness, exploitativeness, bellicosity, and xenophobia to the vagaries of the various controversies and – hopefully successful – compromises, it was to be given to a higher-level institution with binding authority. Of course, talk of a "collective super-ego" is misleading insofar as it suggests an entity that, even if established by many, speaks with one voice. It would be more precise, but linguistically cumbersome, to speak of the creation of a discursively operating "super-we." Even in the early years, the intention to someday create a democratic polity out of this alliance of states was clear from all official announcements and plans. The decisions of this polity were supposed to be dependent on a process of will-formation involving all the citizens of the participating nation states. Whatever the member states decided about the precise form the transnational community would come to take, and whatever its organizational structure,[28] there was from the very beginning an agreement on its minimum moral function: to promote the transition to a supranational democracy that would guarantee, once and for all, that the discursive process of normative self-control on the European continent would be grounded in a rule-based and centrally directed dialogue of all citizens. The central idea behind the foundation of a European community was the replacement of discord and uncontrolled conflict over alternative plans for the civic improvement of Europe with institutionalized, fair, uncoerced discussion on all such matters.

Understanding the political integration of Europe from the perspective of the negative aim of preventing further wrongdoing and norm violation on European soil through a mechanism of discursive self-control also changes our perspective on possible sources of European solidarity. European solidarity does not have its roots in agreement on positive goals, nor in shared cultural traditions, but in a shared will to prevent the worst from happening, and this through the introduction of a democratic institution that interrogates the moral conscience of Europe. The memory of Europe's long history of war, expulsion, exclusion, and genocide, passed down from generation to generation, is the foundation of the social cohesion of the European citizenry. The obligation to stand by and support one another derives from the lesson that this history teaches us: that Europe's destructive and rapacious tendencies can be kept in check only through cooperative processes for the control of moral behavior.

If this supranational form of governance is to be experienced as aiming at solidarity, and not as something heteronomous, it must conform to institutional conditions that are protected from changes in majority opinion. Regardless of majority decisions, all citizens of the European Union must be guaranteed an equal opportunity to influence the process of common will-formation. This point brings me, finally, to the functional necessities that a vision for a regenerated Europe needs to take into account.

IV.

We are conceiving of European unity not in terms of consensus, as many often do, but in terms of dissent, that is, basing it on the perennial differences of opinion regarding alternative ways of dealing with the self-inflicted injustices whose effects are still with us today. Doing so allows us to draw some conclusions about the institutional organization of the new polity. The economic policies that began the unification process after World War II were merely a way of facilitating, by way of trade and exchange, an initial rapprochement between states that were previously only loosely connected – and even then connected mainly through conflict. But the real, hidden purpose of the emergent transnational alliance was to create the institutional conditions for a centralized and open-ended debate about the best way to control the continent's regressive tendencies, and in the long term to develop more civilized social behavior. For that to happen, the institutional borders between states had to be overcome. As I have mentioned, it was only through the institutionalization of cross-border debate about the merits of different means of moral self-discipline that Europe – inadvertently – became a laboratory for the investigation of more equitable ways of living. From the very beginning, this required that the organizational formation of the new polity be constructed in such a way as to make ongoing discursive reflexion possible in the long term. In this way, from its inconspicuous beginnings in the late 1950s, the European Union was, in fact, designed so that pan-European democratic will-formation would become possible in the future. Any agenda less ambitious than this goal of supranational democracy would be a betrayal of the deeper sense and purpose behind the original decision to begin disman-tling the borders between the European nation states. To reiterate, the intention back then was to create transnational institutions that would give the existing "second order" consensus the lasting form of a centralized, cross-border discourse. Debates over how to control Europe's tendencies toward imperiousness and authoritari-anism, which for centuries had taken place in more or less obscure, haphazard, and disorganized ways, were now to be conducted in a centrally organized European public sphere. The hope was that this institutionalization of democratic self-questioning would provide means of mutual control and consultation, and would thus contain the continent's politically regressive inclinations, or, in the long run, even eradicate them altogether.

Today, however, we are even further away from the realization of the necessary conditions of this project than we were, say, twenty or thirty years ago. Back then, there was still some hope that, within a reasonable period of time, the institutional conditions for such a form of democratic self-control could be created. Today, that prospect has vanished into an unforeseeable, unpredictable future. There are no initiatives that aim to develop the essential founda-tions for a pan-European public sphere, despite the fact that we know very well what is required: the Europeanization of political parties, and transnational channels of communication in the form of newspapers, broadcasting stations, and, yes, even the obligatory introduction of an official second language by all member states.[29] All this is public knowledge, but efforts to take even initial steps in this direction are nowhere to be seen. It seems as though the actors who are charged with this task – the political parties, the press, radio and television broadcasters, and ministries of education – have long since lost faith in the feasibility of these elementary requirements. But even if the development of a European public sphere were more advanced than it is, it would count for little as long as some countries still experience severe poverty, high unemployment, and fiscal crisis, while others enjoy adequate levels of wealth, economic growth, and healthy state revenue. In these conditions, even the finest means of public communication and the best democratic institutions would not be able to bridge the huge social divide and bring about the formation of a common public opinion and will. The leveling of social and economic conditions across Europe therefore takes precedence over the creation of the conditions for a European public sphere.

With this, I have, of course, returned to the ideas with which I began my argument. I spoke of two factors that had to be taken into consideration in any attempt to produce an inspiring perspective on the future of Europe. I said that, as well as the subjective reasons that motivate individuals to work toward a common Europe, there was an "objective" factor to be taken into account: namely, that to preserve the European Union, no task is more urgent than that of equalizing individual opportunities between the various member states. I also pointed out, however, that these two factors had to be coordinated, so that the individual motivation to support a unified Europe is affirmed and strengthened by the requisite socio-economic measures. We might also say that it would make little sense to demand solidarity among the citizens of Europe if that solidarity hindered, or even undermined, the project of creating more equal living conditions. I believe that the narrative I have offered of the difficult process of Europe's unification, born out of and pushed forward at every step by misery and remorse, allows for such an integration of functional requirements and individual motivations. The citizens of Europe owe duties of solidarity to one another because only together can they contain the continent's politically regressive tendencies and find means of moral improvement, and they can properly discharge those duties only if they enjoy roughly the same opportunities in life. Only someone who can raise his or her voice free of the shame of personal hardship and the fear of economic dependence, and uncoerced, can participate in the communicative exploration of more equitable social relations as an equal among equals.

Good advice on how to achieve this is hard to come by. No one seems to have a masterplan for a swift, non-bureaucratic way of reducing economic inequality within the European Union. I am not enough of an expert to come up with my own proposals, but nor do I want to conclude without mentioning an example from the past that could serve as a model for this urgently needed reform. When the US was facing imminent economic collapse in the early 1930s, a time referred to as the Great Depression, the team around President Franklin D. Roosevelt, a member of the Democratic Party, drew up a plan, a new social contract, to stop large parts of the population falling into poverty: the so-called "New Deal." This comprehensive plan included state-run work programs and public investment to combat growing unemployment; regulation of industry through the introduction of minimum wages, the strengthening of trade unions, and measures to prevent the formation of monopolies; and, finally, sweeping reform of the financial sector through state support for ailing banks, combined with strict limits on high-risk speculation. This bundle of measures was later referred to as the three "Rs": "relief," "recovery," and "reform."[30] More recently, renowned historians have identified some weaknesses and unintended consequences of Roosevelt's massive reform program, not least among them an astonishing reluctance to nationalize banks and large transport companies, the implicit racism of some of the program's elements, and the consolidation of the central powers of the state.[31] But it is not doubted that the overall effect of the New Deal was highly beneficial for the labor market, social security, and public welfare. The gap between rich and poor diminished within a few years, the working population was soon back in safe and better-paid jobs, and the volume of public assets increased significantly and rapidly.

I remind us of the New Deal not, however, because I am chiefly interested in the detail of the economic policy, but rather because I am interested in its formal properties. Its performative as well as its rhetorical dimensions were remarkable, even astounding. There was an aura of moral promise around the words Roosevelt used when he announced his economic measures. They aimed, he said, to ensure that there would be a "more equitable opportunity to share in the distribution of national wealth," and he ended by declaring that the plan was "more than a political campaign," that it was "a call to arms," emphasizing again his determination to create greater social justice with the help of the American people.[32] We are probably justified in taking these emphatic words as an evocative appeal to a popular front. Both elements here seem to me to have been crucial in producing the broad support enjoyed by the New Deal: the promise of a new social contract that would primarily help the economically disadvantaged, and the general appeal for all to come together, with courage and shared will, to realize this new contract in the interests of justice. For me, this raises the question of whether a plan to reduce economic inequality in the member states of the European Union should not also have something of this spirit of an appeal to engage in the creation of a more just society. Perhaps what is needed is a comprehensive set of economic policies with a name that clearly and evocatively expresses the intention to create a new social contract that works in favor of the poorer member states. Whatever the details of such a plan, among its essential elements would be an immediate end to austerity policies, complemented by a program of public investment in European infrastructure projects, with corresponding job creation schemes. Without a willingness on the side of the wealthy EU countries to shift a generous portion of their gross domestic product toward the south and east, such a new deal for Europe would be doomed to fail.

Of course, the conundrum remains: the populations of the richer member states would probably accept such a redistribution only if the spirit of solidarity advocated here had already been revived, but this spirit will come alive again throughout Europe only once such redistribution has already had a beneficial effect in the poorer member states. To initiate both developments simultaneously, and so that they gain the support of each other, would require something like the flash of inspiration that Roosevelt had ninety years ago: an invocation of a proactive solidarity through a recollection of the European citizenry's common historical experience, and the provision of this solidarity's material conditions as that invocation begins to have its performative effects.[33]

Translated by Daniel Steuer

Notes

Preface

1 Axel Honneth, *Freedom's Right: The Social Foundations of Democratic Life*, Cambridge: Polity, 2014.
2 The first attempt of this kind was made in 1994, republished in: Axel Honneth, "Pathologien des Sozialen: Tradition und Aktualität der Sozialphilosophie," in: *Das Andere der Gerechtigkeit: Aufsätze zur praktischen Philosophie*, Frankfurt am Main: Suhrkamp, 2000, pp. 11–69. English translation: Axel Honneth, "Pathologies of the Social: The Past and Present of Social Philosophy," in: David M. Rasmussen (ed.), *The Handbook of Critical Theory*, Oxford: Basil Blackwell, 1996, pp. 369–98.
3 See Axel Honneth, "Erwiderung," in: Magnus Schlette (ed.), *Ist Selbstverwirklichung institutionalisierbar? Axel Honneths Freiheitstheorie in der Diskussion*, Frankfurt am Main: Campus, 2018, pp. 313–37; esp. pp. 315f.
4 Jürgen Habermas, "Erkenntnis und Interesse," in: *Technologie und Wissenschaft als "Ideologie,"* Frankfurt am Main: Suhrkamp, 1968, pp. 146–68. English translation: "Knowledge and Human Interests: A General Perspective," in: *Knowledge and Human Interest*, Boston, MA: Beacon Press, 1971, pp. 301–17.

Chapter 1: The Depths of Recognition

1 Ernst Cassirer, *The Question of Jean-Jacques Rousseau*, trans. Peter Gay, New York: Columbia University Press, 1954.
2 Ibid., pp. 104–28.
3 Elements of such a critique of Cassirer, with a particular view to the

wide divergence between Rousseau's and Kant's concepts of history, can be found in George Armstrong Kelly, "Rousseau, Kant and History," *Journal of the History of Ideas*, 29/3 (1968), 317–64.

4   Rousseau, *Discourse on Inequality (DI)*, pp. 111–222.
5   Rousseau, *Emile, or On Education*, trans. Allan Bloom, New York: Basic Books, 1979.
6   Rousseau, *Social Contract (SC)*, pp. 39–152.
7   N. J. H. Dent, *Rousseau: An Introduction to His Psychological, Social, and Political Theory*, Oxford: Blackwell, 1988.
8   Frederick Neuhouser, *Rousseau's Theodicy of Self-Love: Evil, Rationality and the Drive for Recognition*, Oxford: Oxford University Press, 2008. See also Honneth, "Die Entgiftung Jean-Jacques Rousseaus. Neuere Literatur zum Werk des Philosophen," *Deutsche Zeitschrift für Philosophie*, 4 (2012), 611–32. Independently of Neuhouser, Barbara Carnevali too has attempted to present Rousseau as a theoretician of recognition: see her *Romantisme et reconnaissance. Figures de la conscience chez Rousseau*, trans. Philippe Audegean, Geneva: Droz, 2011.
9   Rousseau, "Discourse on the Arts and the Sciences," in *DI*, pp. 1–28; *Oeuvres Complètes (OC)* III, pp. 1–30.
10 Rousseau, *Politics and the Arts: Letter to M. D'Alembert on the Theatre*, trans. Allan Bloom, Ithaca, NY: Cornell University Press, 1987, p. 79; *OC* V, pp. 72–3.
11 *Letter*, p. 80; *OC* V, p. 73. On Rousseau's critique of the theater and its consequences for his understanding of democracy, see the excellent study by Juliane Rebentisch, *Die Kunst der Freiheit. Zur Dialektik demokratischer Existenz*, Frankfurt am Main: Suhrkamp, 2011, ch. 5.
12 *DI*, pp. 152, 153, 167, 174; *OC* III, pp. 154, 156, 171, 174.
13 *DI*, p. 218; *OC* III, pp. 219–20.
14 *DI*, p. 218; *OC* III, p. 219.
15 Cf. Adam Smith, *Theory of Moral Sentiments* (1759), ed. D. D. Raphael and A. L. Macfic, Indianapolis, IN: Liberty Fund, 1984, p. 110: "We endeavour to examine our own conduct as we imagine any other fair and impartial spectator would examine it. If, upon placing ourselves in his situation, we thoroughly enter into all the passions and motives which influenced it, we approve of it, by sympathy with the approbation of this supposed equitable judge."
16 Cf. Neuhouser, *Rousseau's Theodicy*, p. 34.
17 Rousseau, *DI*, p. 167; *OC* III, p. 171.
18 Cf. Neuhouser, *Rousseau's Theodicy*, p. 76.
19 Rousseau, *Emile* in *OC* IV, pp. 444–5, 453–4, 522–42.
20 Rousseau, *Emile* (trans. Bloom), p. 252; *OC* IV, p. 547.
21 In relation to this "egalitarian form" of *amour propre*, and following the pioneering study by Dent, see Joshua Cohen, *Rousseau: A Free Community of Equals*, Oxford: Oxford University Press, 2010, pp. 101–4. Cf. Neuhouser, *Rousseau's Theodicy*, pp. 57–70 (including a critique of Cohen's views).

22 On the notion of recognition in Adam Smith, see Christel Fricke and Hans-Peter Schütt (eds.), *Adam Smith als Moralphilosoph*, Berlin: De Gruyter, 2008, esp. the contributions by Stephen Darwall and Robert C. Solomon, pp. 178–89; 251–76.

23 The normative limitations imposed by Rousseau on the general will can also be understood from this perspective as attempts, through the elimination of fundamental power asymmetries in society, to deny an individual the acquisition of high esteem at the expense of others' freedom. Cf. Neuhouser, *Rousseau's Theodicy*, pp. 162–6.

24 Besides a few loci in *Emile*, which Neuhouser mentions (*Rousseau's Theodicy*, p. 67), the main reference here is the chapter on civil religion in the *Social Contract*, extolling the advantages of a state that fosters "the ardent love of glory and of fatherland" (*SC*, IV.8; *OC* III, p. 466).

25 Neuhouser, *Rousseau's Theodicy*, pp. 166–71.

26 See Sharon R. Krause's study on Montesquieu and Tocqueville, *Liberalism with Honor*, Cambridge, MA: Harvard University Press, 2002. Unfortunately, Rousseau's works receive hardly any attention in this excellent study, for it is committed from the outset to a one-dimensional reading of *amour propre* (p. 60).

27 This impact of Rousseau on Kant's early moral philosophy is clearly apparent (Manfred Kuehn, *Kant: A Biography*, Cambridge: Cambridge University Press, 2001, pp. 131–2); yet it becomes manifestly volatile with his development of the distinction between the factual and the ideal, even if some basic insights are maintained. See Jerome B. Schneewind, *The Invention of Autonomy*, Cambridge: Cambridge University Press, 1998, pp. 487–92.

28 See, in the most exemplary and striking manner, Kant's *Religion within the Boundaries of Mere Reason*, ed. Allen Wood, George di Giovanni, and Robert Merrihew Adams, Cambridge: Cambridge University Press, 1998, esp. pp. 45–73.

29 Honneth, "The Irreducibility of Progress: Kant's Account of the Relationship between Morality and History," in: *Pathologies of Reason: On the Legacy of Critical Theory*, trans. James Ingram, New York: Columbia University Press, 2009, pp. 1–18. Additionally, see the groundbreaking study by Yirmiyahu Yovel, *Kant and the Philosophy of History*, Princeton, NJ: Princeton University Press, 1980, pp. 146–51 (without reference to Rousseau but with a preliminary link to Hegel).

30 Kant, "Idea for a Universal History with a Cosmopolitan Purpose," in *Political Writings*, ed. Hans Reiss and H. B. Nisbet, Cambridge: Cambridge University Press, 1991, pp. 41–53; esp. the fourth proposition, pp. 44–5.

31 On the impact of Rousseau's *Social Contract* on Hegel's intellectual development up to his philosophy of right, see the excellent article by Hans Friedrich Fulda, "Rousseausche Probleme in Hegels Entwicklung," in *Rousseau, die Revolution und der junge Hegel*, ed. Hans Friedrich Fulda and Rolf-Peter Horstmann, Stuttgart:

Klett-Cotta, 1991, pp. 41–73, esp. pp. 62ff.; see also Patrick Riley, "Rousseau's General Will," in: *The Cambridge Companion to Rousseau*, ed. Patrick Riley, Cambridge: Cambridge University Press, 2001, pp. 124–53. It may be that Fichte too follows the pattern of Rousseau's general will; see the notable essay by Georg Gurwitsch, "Kant und Fichte als Rousseau-Interpreten," *Kant-Studien*, 27 (1922), 138–64. However, neither contribution discusses explicitly the authors' debt to Rousseau's insight into the conditions of *amour propre*; in my opinion, the opportunity to explore further these deeper contexts arose only with the publication of Neuhouser's monograph.

32   This split in the notion of recognition is particularly manifest in the instances of the *Philosophy of Right* where Hegel conceives individual craving for acknowledgment as the consequence of the failure of an established, "moral" relations of recognition. See, for example, G. W. F. Hegel, *Elements of the Philosophy of Right*, ed. Allen Wood and H. B. Nisbet, Cambridge: Cambridge University Press, 1991, §253, pp. 271–2. Moreover, it seems to me not inappropriate to understand Hegel's design of a morally demarcated market economy as a response to Rousseau's diagnosis of the decay of civil society, as Jeffrey Church suggests in "The Freedom of Desire: Hegel's Response to Rousseau on the Problem of Civil Society," *American Journal of Political Science*, 54/1 (2010), 125–39.

33   Cf. Neuhouser, *Rousseau's Theodicy*, pp. 67–70.

34   This other form of recognition, aimed at individual distinction rather than at equal respect, was related to the category of "esteem" (*Wertschätzung*) in my study *The Struggle for Recognition: Moral Grammar of Social Conflicts*, trans. Joel Anderson, Cambridge: Polity Press, 1995, Part II, ch. 5. As Neuhouser would later do, I relied there on the now renowned article by Stephen L. Darwall, "Two Kinds of Respect," *Ethics*, 88/1 (1977), 36–49.

35   On some occasions Adam Smith presents the "impartial spectator" as generalized to such an extent that he becomes a "vicegerent of God within us" and even identified with the principles of reason (Smith, *Theory of Moral Sentiments*, p. 166). Kant would take up this point in order to endow this sum of the principles of reason with transcendental aspects. On the significance of Smith's moral theory in this context, see Ernst Tugendhat, *Vorlesungen über Ethik*, Frankfurt am Main: Suhrkamp, 1993, pp. 282–309.

36   In Rousseau's later, autobiographically framed works, one can find an increased number of such statements, where he describes the intersubjective structure of *amour propre* as dependence on the establishment of facts about one's own qualities and behavior. As evidence, the following citation from his posthumously published work *Rousseau, Judge of Jean-Jacques* would suffice: "Should he speak of himself with praise that is merited but generally denied? Should he boast of the qualities he feels he has but which everyone refuses

to see?" (Rousseau, *Judge of Jean-Jacques: Dialogues*, ed. Roger D. Masters and Christopher Kelly, Hanover, NH: University Press of New England, 1990, p. 6; *OC* I, p. 665.

37 A separate study is required to substantiate this thesis about the deeply ingrained dependence of French currents of recognition theory on Rousseau's epistemological model. Here I limit myself to indicating a few loci which highlight the extent to which Sartre, Lacan, and other French thinkers saw the danger of a "cognitive" failure of recognition as the consequence of any act of recognition: Jean-Paul Sartre, *Being and Nothingness*, trans. Hazel E. Barnes, New York: Washington Square Press, 1992, pp. 349–55; Jacques Lacan, "The Subversion of the Subject and the Dialectic of Desire in the Freudian Unconscious," in: *Écrits: The First Complete Edition in English*, trans. Bruce Fink, New York: W.W. Norton & Co., 2006, pp. 671–702; Pierre Bourdieu, *Pascalian Meditations*, trans. Richard Nice, Cambridge: Polity, 2000, pp. 164–7.

38 For an account of these "Stoic" positions and their critique, see Avishai Margalit, *The Decent Society*, Cambridge, MA: Harvard University Press, 1996, pp. 22–7. An impressive defense of such positions is undertaken in Ernst Tugendhat, *Egozentrizität und Mystik. Eine anthropologische Studie*, Munich: Beck, 2003, esp. chs. 2 and 4.

39 See particularly the fifth walk in Rousseau, *Reveries of a Solitary Walker*, trans. Russell Goulbourne, Oxford: Oxford University Press, 2011, pp. 49–58; *OC* I, pp. 1040–9. For a brilliant reading of this significant chapter, see Heinrich Meier, *Über das Glück des philosophischen Lebens. Reflexionen zu Rousseaus Rêveries in zwei Büchern*, Munich: C.H. Beck, 2011, Book I, ch. 4.

Chapter 2: On the Poverty of Our Freedom

1 The original German (rendered here as "ethical system") is *Sittlichkeitslehre* and implies the teaching (*Lehre*) of "ethical life" (*Sittlichkeit*). In English usage, the terms "ethics" or "ethical" are more or less synonymous with "morality" or "moral." This is not the case with Hegel. His concept of "ethical life," with which this chapter is principally concerned, refers to the freedom conferred by participation in social institutions, or in Hegel's own words, the "concept of freedom developed into the existing world" (G. W. F. Hegel, *Outlines of the Philosophy of Right*, trans. T. M. Knox, New York: Oxford University Press, [1820] 2008, section 142). (Translator's note.)

2 Throughout this essay, the original German is included in parentheses where a standard translation does not exist or in cases that warrant reference to Hegel's original terminology. (Translator's note.)

3   I. Berlin, *Four Essays on Liberty*, Oxford: Oxford University Press, 1969.
4   R. Geuss, "Freedom as an Ideal," *Proceedings of the Aristotelian Society* Supplementary 69 (1995), 87–100.
5   Hegel, *Outlines of the Philosophy of Right*.
6   D. Henrich, "Zerfall und Zukunft. Hegels Theoreme über das Ende der Kunst," in: *Fixpunkte: Abhandlungen und Essays zur Theorie der Kunst*, Frankfurt: Suhrkamp, 2003, p. 65.
7   Cf. D. Emundts and R.-P. Horstmann, *G.W.F. Hegel. Eine Einführung*, Stuttgart: Reclam, 2002, pp. 69–75.
8   Berlin, *Four Essays on Liberty*.
9   Hegel, *Outlines of the Philosophy of Right*, p. 33.
10 Ibid., section 29.
11 A. Hirschman, *Exit, Voice and Loyalty*, Cambridge, MA: Harvard University Press, 1970.

Chapter 3: The Normativity of Ethical Life

1   For a summary exposition, see Terry Pinkard, "Das Paradox der Autonomie: Kants Problem und Hegels Lösung" [The Paradox of Autonomy: Kant's Problem and Hegel's Solution], in: Thomas Khurana and Christoph Menke (eds.), *Paradoxien der Autonomie* [Paradoxes of Autonomy], Berlin: August Verlag, 2011, pp. 25–60.
2   Jürgen Habermas, *Moral Consciousness and Communicative Action*, Cambridge, MA: MIT Press, 2001, p. 210.
3   Immanuel Kant, "Groundwork of the Metaphysics of Morals," in: Immanuel Kant, *Practical Philosophy*, Cambridge: Cambridge University Press, 1996, p. 56 (fn.).
4   Cf. Ludwig Siep, *Anerkennung als Prinzip der praktischen Philosophie. Untersuchungen in Hegels Jenaer Philosophie des Geistes* [Recognition as a Principle of Practical Philosophy: An Inquiry into Hegel's "Jenaer Philosophy of Mind"], Freiburg and Munich: Karl Alber Verlag, 1979; Andreas Wildt, *Autonomie und Anerkennung. Hegels Moralitätskritik im Lichte seiner Fichte-Rezeption* [Autonomy and Recognition: Hegel's Critique of Morality in Light of his Reception of Fichte], Stuttgart: Klett-Cotta, 1982.
5   Titus Stahl, *Immanente Kritik. Elemente einer Theorie sozialer Praktiken* [Immanent Critique: Elements of a Theory of Social Practices], Frankfurt am Main: Campus, 2013, ch. 4, pp. 191–255.
6   Cf. G. W. F. Hegel, *Elements of the Philosophy of Right*, Cambridge: Cambridge University Press, 1991, §§161–2.
7   These considerations are directed against Robert Brandom, who tends to reduce the idea of recognition to the mutual granting of a single type of deliberative autonomy. Cf. Robert Brandom, *Reason*

in Philosophy: Animating Ideas, Cambridge, MA: Harvard University Press, 2009, chs. 2 and 3 (pp. 52–109).

8   Cf. Axel Honneth, *The Struggle for Recognition: The Moral Grammar of Social Conflicts*, Cambridge, MA: MIT Press, 1996, ch. 5 (pp. 92–130).

9   G. W. F. Hegel, *Die Philosophie des Rechts. Vorlesungen von 1821/22* [The Philosophy of Right: Lectures from 1821/22], Frankfurt am Main: Suhrkamp, 2005, p. 157.

10 Hegel offers several different characterizations of this requirement on all ethical action, but generally he holds that it must be possible for the natural needs of individuals to be "molded" by objective spirit through processes of ethical formation; cf., for example, Hegel, *Elements of the Philosophy of Right*, §187. Elsewhere he seeks to capture the same condition by saying of "ethical substantiality" that its "universal" includes "the end which moves [the ethical character]" (§152).

11 Cf. Hegel, *Elements of the Philosophy of Right*, §148.

12 The assumptions that form the premises of Hegel's philosophy of history are discussed in a very convincing essay by Rolf-Peter Horstmann, "Der geheime Kantianismus in Hegels Geschichtsphilosophie" [The Concealed Kantianism in Hegel's Philosophy of History], in: Rolf-Peter Horstmann, *Die Grenzen der Vernunft* [The Limits of Reason], Frankfurt am Main: Suhrkamp, 1991, pp. 221–44. Cf. also Emil Angehrn, "Vernunft in der Geschichte? Zum Problem der Hegelschen Geschichtsphilosophie" [Reason in History? The Problem in Hegel's Philosophy of History], *Zeitschrift für philosophische Forschung*, 35 (1981), 341–64. Martin Saar argues that when the relevant passages are properly taken into account, Hegel's philosophy of history can also be seen as independent of objectivist premises: Martin Saar, "Fortschritt im Ruckblick. Zum Zusammenhang von Geschichtsphilosophie und Philosophiegeschichte bei Hegel" [Progress in Retrospect: On the Relation of Philosophy of History and History of Philosophy in Hegel] (unpublished MS). This converges with my own suggestion further below.

13 As Yirmiyahu Yovel has persuasively shown in his *Kant and the Philosophy of History* (Princeton, NJ: Princeton University Press, 1980), Kant's heuristically intended construction of world-historical progress already relies on certain conceptual elements of a struggle for recognition, though he conceives of this struggle – following Rousseau – as essentially consisting in a conflict fueled by vanity and pride. The goal of my own proposal is to combine such a heuristic explanatory scheme with a notion of struggles for recognition that assigns them an ineliminably normative dimension. This is what is meant by the suggestion that we retrace the path back from Hegel's philosophy of history to Kant's, by relying on ideas found in Hegel's work itself.

14 This idea was at the basis of the reconstructive method I employed

in the empirical and historical sections of *Freedom's Right: The Social Foundations of Democratic Life*, Cambridge: Polity, 2014.

15 These formulations are rather provisional. Their intention is to suggest that the theory of recognition offers an interpretation of the world-historical process that many modern thinkers – foremost among them Hegel and Durkheim – have described as a process of "individuation" or "individualization." The basic idea is that the aforementioned conflicts over the interpretation of institutionalized principles of recognition serve to increase the extent to which individual motives and particularities can be understood and owned up to. Those conflicts themselves force us to acquire a better understanding of such individual motives, so as to be able to cite them in our normative arguments.

Chapter 4: Hegel and Marx

1 Clear evidence of this is found in the debate about the extent of Kant's influence on Marx, which goes back to the late nineteenth century. See H. J. Sandkühler and R. de la Vega (eds.), *Marxismus und Ethik*, Frankfurt am Main: Suhrkamp, 1970.

2 See, e.g., H. Marcuse, "Neue Quellen zur Grundlegung des Historischen Materialismus," in: *Schriften, Vol. 1*, Springe: zu Klampen Verlag, 2004 [1932].

3 A useful overview is offered by J. Habermas, "Literaturbericht zur philosophischen Debatte um Marx und den Marxismus," in: *Theorie und Praxis. Sozialphilosophische Studien*, 2nd edn, Frankfurt am Main: Suhrkamp, 1971, pp. 387–463, esp. pp. 402–13.

4 L. Althusser, *For Marx*, New York: Verso, 1969.

5 See, especially, C. Taylor, *Hegel and Modern Society*, Cambridge: Cambridge University Press, 1979.

6 A. Honneth, *Kampf um Anerkennung. Zur moralischen Grammatik sozialer Konflikte*, Frankfurt am Main: Suhrkamp, 1992; M. Quante, *Die Wirklichkeit des Geistes. Studien zu Hegel*, Frankfurt am Main: Suhrkamp, 2011, pp. 231–52.

7 For a concise but very accurate summary, see D. Emundts and R.-P. Horstmann, *Georg Wilhelm Friedrich Hegel. Eine Einführung*, Stuttgart: Reclam, 2002, pp. 32–7.

8 G. W. F. Hegel, *Vorlesungen über die Philosophie der Geschichte. Theorie-Werkausgabe, Vol. 12*, Frankfurt am Main: Suhrkamp, 1970, p. 32; J. McCarney, *Hegel on History*, London: Routledge, 2000, ch. 8.

9 There is an ongoing debate about whether Hegel's philosophy of history is in fact best read as asserting that world history exhibits an "objective" teleology ensuring the realization of freedom (G. W. F. Hegel, *Grundlinien der Philosophie des Rechts. Theorie-Werkausgabe, Vol.*

7, Frankfurt am Main: Suhrkamp, 1970). Many of the relevant passages also admit of a more Kantian interpretation to the effect that such a teleology is found in human history only when the latter is regarded from the perspective of a philosophical outlook committed to reason. This becomes especially clear in G. W. F. Hegel, *Enzyklopädie der philosophischen Wissenschaften, Vol. 3. Theorie-Werkausgabe, Vol. 10,* Frankfurt am Main: Suhrkamp, 1970, pp. 347–52.

10 On Hegel's ambitions in this book, see A. Honneth, "Anerkennung als Ideologie. Zum Zusammenhang von Macht und Moral," in: *Das Ich im Wir. Studien zur Anerkennungstheorie,* Berlin: Suhrkamp, 2010, pp. 103–30 and A. Honneth, "Das Reich der verwirklichten Freiheit. Hegels Idee einer 'Rechtsphilosophie'," in: *Das Ich im Wir. Studien zur Anerkennungstheorie,* Berlin: Suhrkamp, 2010, pp. 33–50.

11 K. Löwith, *Von Hegel zu Nietzsche. Der revolutionäre Bruch im Denken des 19 Jahrhunderts,* 7th edn, Hamburg: Meiner Verlag, 1978, pp. 78–136; D. Brudney, *Marx's Attempt to Leave Philosophy,* Cambridge, MA: Harvard University Press, 1998, pp. 6–12.

12 See, especially, K. Marx, "Auszüge aus Mills 'Éléments d'économie politique'," in: *Werke, Suppl. Vol. 1,* Frankfurt am Main: Suhrkamp, 1968, pp. 445–63, esp. p. 462, and K. Marx, "Ökonomisch-philosophische Manuskripte aus dem Jahr 1844," in: *Werke, Suppl. Vol. 1,* Frankfurt am Main: Suhrkamp, 1968, pp. 467–588, esp. pp. 510–22. More generally on this topic, see Brudney, *Marx's Attempt to Leave Philosophy,* ch. 5.

13 M. Tomasello, *A Natural History of Human Morality,* Cambridge, MA: Harvard University Press, 2016, ch. 3.

14 See Marx's famous dictum that "the history of industry" is "the open book of man's essential powers" (Marx, "Ökonomisch-philosophische Manuskripte aus dem Jahr 1844," esp. pp. 510–22).

15 See the reference to the "most revolutionary role" of the "bourgeoisie" in the *Communist Manifesto* (K. Marx and F. Engels, *Manifest der Kommunistischen Partei,* in: *Werke, Vol. 4,* Frankfurt am Main: Suhrkamp, 1972, p. 464).

16 J. Habermas, "Arbeit und Interaktion," in: *Technik und Wissenschaft als "Ideologie,"* Frankfurt am Main: Suhrkamp, 1970, pp. 9–48.

17 Hegel's own use of the term "society" (*Gesellschaft*) is limited to the "system of needs" (*System der Bedürfnisse*), to which he also refers as "bourgeois society" (*bürgerliche Gesellschaft*) in his *Philosophy of Right.* What he has in mind by these latter terms, following Adam Smith, is the historically recent structure of a capitalist market society (see F. Rosenzweig, *Hegel und der Staat,* ed. F. Lachmann, Berlin: Suhrkamp, 2010, pp. 391–401; P. Vogel, *Hegels Gesellschaftsbegriff und seine geschichtliche Fortbildung durch Lorenz, Stein, Marx, Engels und Lassalle,* Berlin: Pan-Vig, Rolf Heise, 1925). In the present context, when I speak of Hegel's concept of society, I have in mind what Hegel calls "objective spirit" (concretely represented in particular

"national spirits"), that is to say, the most general unit to which processes of social differentiation can be attributed.

18 K. Polanyi, *Ökonomie und Gesellschaft*, Frankfurt am Main: Suhrkamp, 1979, ch. 2; K. Polanyi, *The Great Transformation: The Political and Economic Origins of Our Time*, Boston, MA: Beacon Press, 1957, esp. chs. 4–5.

19 For example, M. Mauss, *The Gift: Forms and Functions of Exchange in Archaic Societies*, London: Norton, 1969.

20 See J. Searle, *The Construction of Social Reality*, New York: Free Press, 1995. An interesting comparison, along with a critique of Searle from a Hegelian perspective, is offered by S. Ostritsch, "Hegel and Searle on the Necessity of Social Reality," *Rivista di Estetica*, 57 (2014), 205–18.

21 The model for this explanation is Hegel's interpretation of Sophocles's *Antigone* in his *Phenomenology of Spirit* (G. W. F. Hegel, *Phenomenology of Spirit*, trans. A. V. Miller, Oxford: Oxford University Press, 1977). On the interpretation proposed here, see, more generally, A. Särkelä, "Ein Drama in drei Akten. Der Kampf um öffentliche Anerkennung nach Dewey und Hegel," *Deutsche Zeitschrift für Philosophie*, 61 (2013), 681–96.

22 Following Hegel, an explanation of this sort was offered by J. Dewey, *Lectures in China, 1919–1920*, Honolulu: University of Hawaii Press, 1973, pp. 64–71.

23 See, among others, C. Castoriadis, *Gesellschaft als imaginäre Institution. Entwurf einer politischen Philosophie*, Frankfurt am Main: Suhrkamp, 1984, ch. I.2.

24 See, especially, K. Marx, *Zur Kritik der politischen Ökonomie*, in: *Werke, Vol. 13*, Frankfurt am Main: Suhrkamp, 1971, pp. 8ff.

25 On the tension between these two interpretative models, see Castoriadis, *Gesellschaft als imaginäre Institution*, pp. 52–9.

26 Marx and Engels, *Manifest der Kommunistischen Partei*.

27 See F. Neuhouser, "Marx (und Hegel) zur Philosophie der Freiheit," in: R. Jaeggi and D. Loick (eds.), *Nach Marx. Philosophie, Kritik, Praxis*, Berlin: Suhrkamp, 2013, pp. 39f.

28 F. Neuhouser, *Foundations of Hegel's Social Theory: Actualizing Freedom*, Cambridge, MA: Harvard University Press, 2000.

29 See K. Marx, "Zur Judenfrage," in: *Werke, Suppl. Vol. 1*, Frankfurt am Main: Suhrkamp, 1968, pp. 347–77. For more detailed commentary, see A. Honneth, *Die Idee des Sozialismus. Versuch einer Aktualisierung*, Berlin: Suhrkamp, 2015, pp. 60ff.

30 Neuhouser, "Marx (und Hegel) zur Philosophie der Freiheit."

31 At the same time, Hegel faces great difficulties in establishing that the state, too, is a sphere of intersubjectivity that is enabling of freedom. These difficulties have been treated, with impressive precision, by M. Theunissen, "Die verdrängte Intersubjektivität in Hegels Philosophie des Rechts," in: D. Henrich and R.-P. Horstmann (eds.), *Hegels Philosophie des Rechts*, Stuttgart: Klett-Cotta, 1982, pp. 317–81.

32 H.-C. Schmidt am Busch, *"Anerkennung" als Prinzip der Kritischen Theorie*, Berlin: de Gruyter, 2011, part III.
33 K. Marx, *Das Kapital, Vol. 1*, in: *Werke, Vol. 23*, Frankfurt am Main: Suhrkamp, 1971a, pp. 181–91.
34 Ibid., pp. 56–61.
35 Ibid., pp. 531–41.
36 Ibid., pp. 85–98.
37 See H. Reichelt, *Zur logischen Struktur des Kapitalbegriffs bei Karl Marx*, Frankfurt am Main: Suhrkamp, 1973; V. Çidam, *Die Phänomenologie des Widergeistes. Eine anerkennungstheoretische Deutung von Marx' normativer Kritik im Kapital*, Baden-Baden: Nomos, 2012.
38 I have put forward a proposal of this kind in "Die Moral im Kapital," in: R. Jaeggi and D. Loick (eds.), *Nach Marx. Philosophie, Kritik, Praxis*, Berlin: Suhrkamp, 2013, pp. 350–63.
39 See, for instance, W. Streeck, *Gekaufte Zeit. Die vertagte Krise des demokratischen Kapitalismus*, Berlin: Suhrkamp, 2013; D. Kotz, *The Rise and Fall of Neoliberal Capitalism*, Cambridge, MA: Harvard University Press, 2015.
40 Habermas, "Literaturbericht zur philosophischen Debatte um Marx und den Marxismus;" J. Habermas, *Theorie des kommunikativen Handelns, Vol. 2: Zur Kritik der funktionalistischen Vernunft*, Frankfurt am Main: Suhrkamp, 1981, ch. VIII, 2.
41 On these difficulties regarding the foundational concepts of the traditional theory of social differentiation, see U. Schimank and U. Volkmann, "Ökonomisierung der Gesellschaft," in: A. Maurer (ed.), *Handbuch der Wirtschaftssoziologie*, Wiesbaden: Springer, 2008, pp. 382–93.
42 L. Herzog, *Inventing the Market: Smith, Hegel and Political Thought*, Oxford: Oxford University Press, 2013.
43 Some initial suggestions can be found in Honneth, "Anerkennung als Ideologie."
44 My thanks to Juliane Rebentisch and Ferdinand Sutterlüty for helpful comments and suggestions.

Chapter 5: Economy or Society?

1 Louis Althusser, *For Marx*, London: Verso, 2005.
2 On this stage in his life, see Gareth Stedman Jones, *Karl Marx: Greatness and Illusion*, Cambridge, MA: Harvard University Press, 2016, chs. III and IV.
3 Ludwig Feuerbach, *The Essence of Christianity*, London: Trübner & Co., 1881.
4 These can be found in Karl Marx, *Early Writings*, London: Penguin, 1992: "On the Jewish Question," pp. 211–41; "A Contribution to the Critique of Hegel's Philosophy of Right. Introduction," pp. 243–57.

On the project of the "Franco-German Yearbooks," see Gareth
Stedman Jones, *Karl Marx*, pp. 144–50.

5   See Karl Marx, "On the Jewish Question," pp. 219ff.; here: p. 220.
6   Karl Marx, *Grundrisse: Foundations of the Critique of Political Economy*,
    London: Vintage, 1973, p. 84. The full sentence runs: "The human
    being is in the most literal sense a ζῷον πολιτιχόν, not merely a
    gregarious animal, but an animal which can individuate itself only in
    the midst of society."
7   Karl Marx, "On the Jewish Question," p. 228.
8   For a critical assessment of the analysis in "On the Jewish Question,"
    see Frederick Neuhouser, "Marx (und Hegel) zur Philosophie der
    Freiheit," in: Rahel Jaeggi and Daniel Loick (eds.), *Nach Marx*, Berlin:
    Suhrkamp, 2013, pp. 25–47. Some of the material covered in this
    article can also be found in Frederick Neuhouser, "Marx and Hegel
    on the Value of 'Bourgeois' Ideals," in: Jan Kandiyali, *Reassessing
    Marx's Social and Political Philosophy: Freedom, Recognition and Human
    Flourishing*, London: Routledge, 2018, pp. 149–62.
9   Karl Marx, "On the Jewish Question," p. 229.
10 Ibid.
11 Ibid.
12 Ibid., p. 227.
13 Karl Polanyi, *The Great Transformation: The Political and Economic
    Origins of Our Time*, Boston, MA: Beacon Press, 2001 [1944].
14 Karl Marx, "On the Jewish Question," pp. 232f.
15 Ibid.
16 In a certain sense, Marx's position is the direct opposite of that
    developed by Hannah Arendt 100 years later. Where Marx saw
    the withdrawal of economic activities from the sphere of public
    interest as the social pathology of modernity, Arendt suspected that
    the pathology was rather the opposite process: economic interests
    constantly threatening to intrude into political public life. See
    Hannah Arendt, *The Human Condition*, Chicago, IL: The University of
    Chicago Press, 1998 [1958] and *On Revolution*, London: Penguin, 1990
    [1963], ch. 2. This obvious discrepancy between Marx's and Arendt's
    perspectives makes it impossible, I believe, to reconcile their inten-
    tions or see their analyses as complementary.
17 On this trait in Marx's early writings, see the still extremely worth-
    while study by Karl Löwith, *Max Weber and Karl Marx*, London:
    Routledge, 2003 [1960], pp. 102–8.
18 On this phase, see Gareth Stedman Jones, *Karl Marx*, pp. 171–80.
19 Karl Marx, "Economic and Philosophical Manuscripts (1844)," in:
    Early Writings, pp. 279–400.
20 See ibid., p. 281, where Marx calls Feuerbach's works "the only
    writings since Hegel's *Phenomenology* and *Logic* to contain a real
    theoretical revolution." By far the most accurate study of the
    relation between Marx and Feuerbach is Daniel Brudney, *Marx's*

Attempt to Leave Philosophy, Cambridge, MA: Harvard University Press, 1998.

21 Karl Marx, "Economic and Philosophical Manuscripts," p. 324.

22 Ibid., p. 319.

23 Karl Marx and Friedrich Engels, *The German Ideology*, New York: Prometheus, 1998. Karl Marx and Friedrich Engels, *The Communist Manifesto*, New York: Appleton-Century-Crofts, 1955. For *Grundrisse*, see fn. 6.

24 See Louis Althusser, *For Marx*, pp. 33–9.

25 See Karl Marx, *Grundrisse*, p. 505, one of the many places where he explicitly draws a distinction between the "history" and the "conceptual development" of "capital."

26 Ibid., pp. 471f.

27 Ibid., p. 485.

28 The idea that at this stage of common property the environment is still a "laboratory" in which the individual producer tests his powers can be found in several places in the text. See, e.g., pp. 492 and 497 (transl. modified). Another formulation favored by Marx is that of the objective conditions of production as the worker's "extended body," e.g. ibid., p. 491.

29 Ibid., p. 499.

30 Ibid., pp. 497–500.

31 On the idea of a "negative development" ["*negative Modification*"], see ibid., pp. 491, 493, 500. The crucial passage is: "If human beings themselves are conquered along with the land and soil as its organic accessories, then they are equally conquered as one of the conditions of production, and in this way arises slavery and serfdom, which soon corrupts and modifies the original forms of all communities, and then itself becomes their basis. The simple construction is thereby negatively determined." Ibid., p. 491.

32 Ibid., pp. 500f. and 485.

33 Ibid., p. 507.

34 Ibid., pp. 221–6.

35 Ibid., p. 507.

36 Ibid., pp. 504, 507, and 512.

37 Ibid., p. 505.

38 Ibid., pp. 504–7.

39 Ibid., p. 276.

40 Ibid., p. 222.

41 For the most impressive of these passages, see pp. 221–6.

42 On the problems with Marx's concept of work, see Ernst Michael Lange's classic study *Das Prinzip Arbeit: Drei metakritische Kapitel über Grundbegriffe, Struktur und Darstellung der* Kritik der Politischen Ökonomie *von Karl Marx*, Berlin: Springer, 1980; esp. ch. 2. Short, but impressively clear, is Will Kymlicka, *Political Philosophy Today: An Introduction*, Oxford: Oxford University Press, 2002 ("Marxism").

43 See, e.g., Karl Marx, *Grundrisse*, pp. 474f. and 491–4.

44 See, e.g., ibid., pp. 277f. and 489f.

45 See the remarks on the emergence of psychological attitudes such as "greed," "greed for money," money as "*the* object of greed [*Bereicherungssucht*]" in the course of money becoming established as the universal equivalent in economic exchange, ibid., pp. 221–6. Forty years later, Georg Simmel seems to take up these reflections when he tries to determine the psychological dispositions that arise with "money" as a "pure means." See his *The Philosophy of Money*, London: Routledge, 2004, esp. ch. 3, part II: "The psychological growth of means into ends," pp. 228–32.

46 There were major debates about Marx's inclination toward reductionism in the circles around Max Weber, and this topic was later picked up by many others, among them Jürgen Habermas, *Zur Rekonstruktion des Historischen Materialismus*, Frankfurt am Main: Suhrkamp, 1976 (some of the essays from this volume can be found in Jürgen Habermas, *Communication and the Evolution of Human Society*, Boston, MA: Beacon Press, 1979) and Cornelius Castoriadis, *The Imaginary Institution of Society*, Cambridge: Polity, 1987; esp. part 1.

47 G. W. F. Hegel, *Elements of the Philosophy of Right Or Natural Law and Political Science in Outline*, Cambridge: Cambridge University Press, 1991, part 3, section 2, §§182–256, pp. 220–74. "'State' and 'Civil Society': Linguistic Context and Historical Origin," in: *Between Tradition and Revolution: The Hegelian Transformation of Political Philosophy*, Cambridge: Cambridge University Press, 1984, pp. 129–58.

48 Karl Marx, *Grundrisse*, p. 276.

49 Ibid., pp. 831–3.

50 Ibid., p. 831.

51 Georg Lukács, "Reification and the Consciousness of the Proletariat," in: *History and Class Consciousness: Studies in Marxist Dialectics*, Cambridge, MA: MIT Press, 1971, pp. 83–222. Theodor W. Adorno, *Negative Dialectics*, London: Routledge, 1973, p. 406. See also Theodor W. Adorno, "Late Capitalism or Industrial Society?," in: Volker Meja, Dieter Misgeld, and Nico Stehr (eds.), *Modern German Sociology*, New York: Columbia University Press, 1987, pp. 232–47.

52 Karl Marx, *Capital Volume I*, London: Penguin, 1990.

53 See Gareth Stedman Jones, *Karl Marx*, pp. 389ff. On January 16, 1858, Marx wrote to Engels: "What was of great use to me as regards *method* of treatment was Hegel's *Logic* at which I had taken another look by mere accident, Freiligrath having found and made me a present of several volumes of Hegel, originally the property of Bakunin." Karl Marx and Frederick Engels, *Collected Works Volume 40: Marx and Engels Letters 1856–1859*, London: Lawrence & Wishart, 1983, p. 249.

54 Karl Marx, *Grundrisse*, p. 276.

55 See Georg Lohmann, *Indifferenz und Gesellschaft: Eine kritische Auseinandersetzung mit Marx*, Frankfurt am Main: Suhrkamp, 1991.

56 In a recent study, William Clare Roberts has presented the interesting thesis that Marx was strongly influenced by the first part (Inferno) of Dante's *Divina Comedia*. See his *Marx's Inferno: The Political Theory of Capital*, Princeton, NJ: Princeton University Press, 2017.

57 Karl Marx, *Capital Volume 1*, p. 257.

58 Ibid., pp. 163–77.

59 Ibid., pp. 164f.

60 Georg Simmel says as much in his *The Philosophy of Money*, p. 495: "The fact that the product of labour in the capitalist era is an object with a decidedly autonomous character, with its own laws of motion and a character alien to the producing subject, is most forcefully illustrated where the worker is compelled to buy his own product if he wishes to have it."

61 On the internal inconsistencies of Marx's critique of commodity fetishism, see Marco Iorio, "Fetisch und Geheimniss: Zur Kritik der Kapitalismuskritik von Karl Marx," *Deutsche Zeitschrift für Philosophie*, 58 (2010), 241–56.

62 Karl Marx, *Capital Volume 1*, Part Two, chapter 4, "The General Formula for Capital," pp. 247–57.

63 Ibid., pp. 389–416.

64 Ibid., pp. 389f.

65 See, in particular, Karl Marx, *The Class Struggles in France, 1848–1850*, in: Karl Marx and Frederick Engels, *Collected Works Volume 10*, London: Lawrence & Wishart, 1978, pp. 45–145; and *The Eighteenth Brumaire of Louis Bonaparte* (1852), in: Karl Marx and Frederick Engels, *Collected Works Volume 11*, London: Lawrence & Wishart, 1979, pp. 99–197.

66 Karl Marx, *Capital Volume 1*, pp. 390f.

67 Ibid., pp. 393f.

68 Ibid., p. 395.

69 Ibid., pp. 394f.

70 Ibid., p. 412.

71 On the highly ambivalent position of the law in this context, but also in *Capital* overall, see Georg Lohmann, "Normative und rechtsstaatliche Kapitalismuskritiken und ihre Verdrängung bei Marx," *Deutsche Zeitschrift für Philosophie*, 66.4 (2018), 429–65.

72 Karl Marx, *Capital Volume 1*, p. 415.

73 Another formula Marx likes to use is that the "working class" is "a class constantly increasing in numbers, and trained, united and organized by the very mechanism of the capitalist process of production." Ibid., p. 929.

74 Ibid., p. 409.

75 Ibid., p. 414.

76 Ibid., p. 408.

77 Here, Marx touches upon a theme that E. P. Thompson will examine almost 100 years later in his classic study "The Moral Economy of the

English Crowd in the Eighteenth Century," *Past & Present*, 50.1 (1971), 76–136. For the wider context, see E. P. Thompson, *The Making of the English Working Class*, New York: Vintage, 1963.

78 Karl Marx, *Capital Volume 1*, p. 131.

79 Ibid., pp. 126ff.

80 See, for instance, Philipp Staab, *Falsche Versprechen: Wachstum im digitalen Kapitalismus*, Hamburg: Hamburger Edition HIS, 2016.

81 Thorstein Veblen, *The Theory of the Leisure Class*, Oxford: Oxford University Press, 2009 [1899].

82 See Karl Marx, *Capital Volume 1*, pp. 132f.

83 See Charles Tilly, *Durable Inequality*, Berkeley, CA: University of California Press, 1999.

84 Karl Marx, *Capital Volume 1*, pp. 293–306.

85 See Michael Burawoy, *Manufacturing Consent: Changes in the Labor Process under Monopoly Capitalism*, Chicago, IL: The University of Chicago Press, 1979.

86 Niklas Luhmann, *Trust and Power: Two Works by Niklas Luhmann*, Chichester: John Wiley & Son, 1979, pp. 147ff. According to Luhmann, the task of such "symbiotic mechanisms" is to guarantee that the communication media of money or truth, despite their abstract nature, remain coupled to organic processes (the satisfaction of needs, physical violence, perception) and thus to preserve their general intelligibility. Of course, I employ this useful concept only by analogy, aiming to demonstrate that the economic factors that Marx discusses need to be "symbiotically" tied to lifeworld processes that can be experienced in order to be able to fulfill the functions he ascribes to them.

87 None of the social theorists after Marx was as interested in this hidden material side of the key concepts of economic theory, so closely associated with social life, as the Georg Simmel of *The Philosophy of Money*. However, amid the fervor with which he studied the complex interactions between money and social, cultural, and psychological processes, he lost sight of Marx's central thesis: that it is not money as such but capital and its inner compulsion to profitable accumulation that tends – by way of "real subsumption" – to subjugate all social spheres to its own principle.

88 See, e.g., Peter A. Hall and David Soskice (eds.), *Varieties of Capitalism: The Institutional Foundations of Comparative Advantage*, Oxford: Oxford University Press, 2001.

89 Karl Polanyi, *The Great Transformation*, chapter II.

Chapter 6: Three, Not Two, Concepts of Liberty

1 I. Berlin, "Zwei Freiheitsbegriffe," in: I. Berlin, *Freiheit. Vier Versuche*, Frankfurt am Main: Fischer, 1995, pp. 197–256.

2   On this distinction, see C. Menke, *Tragödie im Sittlichen. Gerechtigkeit und Freiheit nach Hegel*, Frankfurt am Main: Suhrkamp, 1996, ch. 4 and C. Taylor, *The Ethics of Authenticity*, Cambridge, MA: Harvard University Press, 1992, pp. 28ff.

3   In the following I am not taking up the important question of whether the outlined concept of social freedom should also have metaphysical priority over the other two concepts of freedom, which Berlin has differentiated – a claim Hegel certainly had defended. Instead, I am restricting myself here to the conceptual question whether such a concept of social freedom represents an independent value for our evaluative self-understanding. For a defense of the stronger claim, see A. Honneth, *Freedom's Right*, New York: Columbia University Press, 2014, pp. 42–6.

4   For a similar approach, see B. Crick, "Freedom as Politics," in: P. Laslett and W. G. Runciman (eds.), *Philosophy, Politics and Society: Third Series, Vol. III*, Oxford: Oxford University Press, 1969, pp. 194–214.

5   See E. Anderson, "The Epistemology of Democracy," *Episteme*, 3 (2006), 8–22. The British Neo-Hegelian Bernard Bosanquet put forward a magnificent proposal with the same intent 120 years ago. See B. Bosanquet, "The Reality of the General Will," *International Journal of Ethics*, 4 (1894), 308–21.

6   See J. Dewey, "The Ethics of Democracy," in: A. Boydston and G. E. Axetell (eds.), *John Dewey, The Early Works: 1882–1898, Vol. I*, Carbondale, IL: Southern Illinois University Press, 1969, pp. 227–49.

7   See Anderson, "The Epistemology of Democracy," pp. 9–23.

8   See, e.g., Philip Pettit, "Agency-Freedom and Option-Freedom," *Journal of Theoretical Politics*, 15 (2003), 387–403.

9   On the distinction between "overlapping" and "intertwining" ends, see D. Brudney, "Gemeinschaft als Ergänzung," *Deutsche Zeitschrift für Philosophie*, 58 (2010), 195–219.

10 On this spectrum of positive freedom, see R. Geuss, "Auffassungen der Freiheit," *Zeitschrift für philosophische Forschung*, 49 (1995), 1–14.

11 Berlin, "Zwei Freiheitsbegriffe," pp. 226–36.

12 On this reconstruction of free will, see Hegel's exemplary discussion in G. W. F. Hegel, *Elements of the Philosophy of Right*, ed. Allen Wood, trans. H. B. Nisbet, Cambridge: Cambridge University Press, 1991, pp. 25–62.

13 See R. Brandom, *Reason in Philosophy: Animating Ideas*, Cambridge, MA: Belknap, 2009, pp. 72–7.

14 F. Neuhouser, *Foundations of Hegel's Social Theory: Actualizing Freedom*, Cambridge, MA: Harvard University Press, 2003, pp. 145–74.

15 R. B. Pippin, *Hegel's Practical Philosophy: Rational Agency as Ethical Life*, Cambridge: Cambridge University Press, 2008, pp. 121–209.

16 Hegel, *Elements of the Philosophy of Right*, pp. 41–2.

17 See A. Honneth, *The Pathologies of Individual Freedom. Hegel's Social Theory*, Princeton, NJ: Princeton University Press, 2010, ch. 4.

18 P.-J. Proudhon, *Bekenntnisse eines Revolutionärs*, Hamburg: Reinbek, 1969 [1849].
19 See Brudney, "Gemeinschaft als Ergänzung."
20 See A. Honneth, *Die Idee des Sozialismus. Versuch einer Reaktualisierung*, Berlin: Suhrkamp, 2015, ch. 4.
21 Hannah Arendt, *Vita Activa oder Vom tätigen Leben*, Munich: Piper, 1967, pp. 7, 24, 25.
22 See J. R. Shook and J. A. Good (eds.), *John Dewey's Philosophy of Spirit, with the 1897 Lecture on Hegel*, New York: Fordham University Press, 2010; J. Dewey, "From Absolutism to Experimentalism," in: *John Dewey, The Later Works: 1925–1953. Vol. 5: 1929–1930*, ed. J. A. Boydson, Carbondale, IL: Southern Illinois University Press, 1984, pp. 147–61.
23 J. Dewey, *"The Public and its Problems,"* in: *John Dewey, The Later Works 1925–1953, Vol. 2*, Carbondale, IL: Southern Illinois University Press, 1984, pp. 235–372, here, p. 329.
24 See Berlin, "Zwei Freiheitsbegriffe," pp. 250ff.
25 P. Pettit, *The Common Mind: An Essay on Psychology, Society and Politics*, Oxford: Oxford University Press, 1993, pp. 271–2.
26 This contribution is a revised version of my Dewey Lecture at the University of Chicago Law School, delivered November 12, 2014.

Chapter 7: The Diseases of Society

1 In the following considerations I am building on the intentions initially developed in my essay "Pathologies of the Social," in: *Disrespect: The Normative Foundations of Critical Theory*, Cambridge: Polity, 2007, pp. 3–48. At that time, however, the theoretical conclusion that closes my reflections here was still not clear to me, namely, the inevitability of assuming a certain "organizity" of society when speaking of social pathologies.
2 Plato, "The Republic," in: *Plato, Complete Works*, ed. J. M. Cooper, Indianapolis, IN: Hackett Publishing Company, 1997, 433a–445e; A. Schmitt, *Der Einzelne und die Gemeinschaft in der Dichtung Homers und in der Staatstheorie bei Platon. Zur Ableitung der Staatstheorie aus der Psychologie*, Stuttgart: Steiner, 2000.
3 Honneth, "Pathologies of the Social."
4 S. Freud, *Civilization and Its Discontents*, in: *The Standard Edition of the Complete Psychological Works of Sigmund Freud*, ed. S. Freud et al. Volume XXI, London: Hogarth Press, 1961 [1930]; J. P. Sartre, *The Family Idiot: Gustave Flaubert 1821–1857, Volume 4*, Chicago, IL: University of Chicago Press, 1991 [1971].
5 É. Durkheim, *Socialism and Saint-Simon*, London: Routledge, 1958 [1928], pp. 8–10.

6   A. Mitscherlich, "Die Krankheiten der Gesellschaft und die psycho-somatische Medizin," in: *Mitscherlich: Gesammelte Schriften II (Psychosomatik 2)*, ed. T. Allert, Frankfurt am Main: Suhrkamp, 1983a, pp. 425–44.

7   Ibid., p. 425.

8   Ibid., p. 429.

9   S. Freud, "Civilized Sexual Morality and Modern Nervous Illness," in: *The Standard Edition of the Complete Psychological Works of Sigmund Freud*, ed. S. Freud et al. Volume IX, London: Hogarth Press, 1959 [1908], pp. 181–204.

10   H. Arendt, *The Human Condition*, Chicago: University of Chicago Press, 1998 [1958], pp. 126ff.

11   É. Durkheim, *Professional Ethics and Civic Morals*, London: Routledge, 2003 [1950].

12   J.-J. Rousseau, "Discourse on the Origin and Foundations of Inequality Among Men or Second Discourse," in: *Rousseau: The Discourses and Other Early Political Writings*, ed. V. Gourevitch, Cambridge: Cambridge University Press, 1997 [1755], pp. 111–88; see also F. Neuhouser, *Rousseau's Theodicy of Self-Love: Evil, Rationality, and the Drive for Recognition*, Oxford: Oxford University Press, 2008.

13   M. Foucault, *The History of Sexuality: Volume I: An Introduction*, New York: Pantheon Books, 1978 [1976].

14   Freud, "Civilized Sexual Morality and Modern Nervous Illness," p. 201.

15   Ibid., pp. 201–2.

16   Ibid., pp. 197–8.

17   Ibid., p. 204.

18   Ibid., pp. 196–7.

19   Mitscherlich, "Die Krankheiten der Gesellschaft," pp. 431–4.

20   Ibid., p. 440.

21   G. Simmel, *Sociology: Inquiries into the Construction of Social Forms, Volume 2*, Leiden: Brill, 2009 [1908], ch. 10.

22   Translator's note: On all other occasions in this text, "individuation" has been used as a translation of the German *Individuierung*.

23   Translator's note: On all other occasions in this text, "socialization" has been used as a translation of the German *Sozialisation*.

Chapter 8: Education and the Democratic Public Sphere

1   Immanuel Kant, "Lectures on Pedagogy (1803)," in: *Anthropology, History, and Education*, Cambridge: Cambridge University Press, 2007, pp. 434–85, p. 441.

2   Ibid., p. 484.

3   Friedrich Schleiermacher, "Über den Beruf des Staates zur

Erziehung," in: *Texte zur Pädagogik: Kommentierte Studienausgabe (Vol. 1)*, Frankfurt am Main: Suhrkamp, 2000, pp. 272–90; Émile Durkheim, *Moral Education*, Mineola, NY: Dover Publications, 2011; John Dewey, *Democracy and Education*, New York: Free Press, 1997.

4 On "re-education," see Walter Gagel, *Geschichte der politischen Bildung in der Bundesrepublik Deutschland 1945–1989/90*, Wiesbaden: Verlag für Sozialwissenschaften, 2005, ch. 2.

5 An important exception is the political philosopher Amy Gutmann, although she only accords a subordinate role to the tradition discussed here. See Amy Gutmann, *Democratic Education*, Princeton, NJ: Princeton University Press, 1999.

6 The political philosophy of Louis Althusser is one context where schools figure in this "negative" role. See Louis Althusser, "Ideology and Ideological State Apparatuses," in: *Lenin and Philosophy and Other Essays*, New York: Monthly Review Press, 1971, pp. 127–86, esp. pp. 154–7.

7 Plato, *The Republic*, Indianapolis, IN: Hackett, 1992, esp. Book V; Dewey, *Democracy and Education*, pp. 88–91.

8 Cf. Ernst-Wolfgang Böckenförde, "Freiheit und Recht, Freiheit und Staat," in: *Recht, Staat, Freiheit*, Frankfurt am Main: Suhrkamp, 2006, pp. 42–57.

9 Ibid., p. 48.

10 Cf. John Rawls, *A Theory of Justice*, Cambridge, MA: Belknap Press of Harvard University Press, 1971; Rainer Forst, *Contexts of Justice: Political Philosophy beyond Liberalism and Communitarianism*, Berkeley, CA: University of California Press, 2002 [1996], pp. 68–79.

11 Gutmann, *Democratic Education*, pp. 65, 292–303; Michael Walzer, *Spheres of Justice: A Defense of Pluralism and Equality*, New York: Basic Books, 1983, pp. 217–20. On tendencies of this sort, see especially: François Dubet, "L'égalité et le mérite dans l'école démocratique de masse," *L'Année sociologique*, 50.2 (2002), 383–408, pp. 101–4. The thought that teachers should think of themselves as agents of the democratic state and not as agents of the parents, extending the latter's original authority to a more advanced life stage of their children, is Durkheim. See Durkheim, *Moral Education*.

12 Kant, "Lectures on Pedagogy," p. 447. Almost the same thought is articulated by Schleiermacher: "Looking at the history of our modern world, we encounter certain times where entire peoples were awoken from their long-lasting stupor and crudeness only thanks to the fact that their governments took up the reins of this important business and undertook by other means to arouse in the younger generation the higher powers which the older generation, in whom these powers were lacking or had died away, was not able to awaken by the normal path of domestic education." See Schleiermacher, "Über den Beruf des Staates zur Erziehung," p. 272.

13 Kant, "Lectures on Pedagogy," p. 448.

14   Rawls, *A Theory of Justice*, pp. 440–6.
15   Kant, "Lectures on Pedagogy," p. 448.
16   Kant calls these democratic capacities "cosmopolitan dispositions."
      They are addressed in his *Pedagogy* only occasionally. Cf., e.g., Kant,
      "Lectures on Pedagogy," p. 485.
17   Durkheim, *Moral Education*.
18   Gutmann, *Democratic Education*, ch. 2.
19   On Dewey's pedagogic theory as a whole, see: Jürgen Oelkers, *John
      Dewey und die Pädagogik*, Basel: Beltz, 2009.
20   Durkheim, *Moral Education*, pp. 271ff.
21   For a defense of this idea of an "associative morality" as a goal for
      school education, see Gutmann, *Democratic Education*, pp. 59–64.
22   Cf. the exemplary studies by Dubet. See Dubet, "L'égalité et le mérite
      dans l'école démocratique de masse"; François Dubet, *Le Déclin de
      l'Institution*, Paris: Seuil, 2002, ch. 3.
23   Diane Ravitch, "Schools We Can Envy," *New York Review of Books*, 59.4
      (2012), 19.
24   Pasi Sahlberg, *Finnish Lessons: What Can the World Learn from
      Educational Change in Finland?*, New York: Teachers College Press,
      2012.
25   Colin Crouch, *Post-Democracy*, Cambridge: Polity, 2004.
26   Durkheim, *Moral Education*, Lectures 17–18.
27   Dewey, *Democracy and Education*, pp. 190–3.
28   Cf. Axel Honneth, *Freedom's Right*, Cambridge: Polity, 2014, pp. 300–3.
29   Following John Dewey, considerations in this direction are developed
      by Croft. See Richard S. Croft, "What is a Computer in the Classroom?
      A Deweyan Philosophy for Technology in Education," *Journal of
      Educational Technology Systems*, 22.4 (1993–1994), 301–8.
30   Honneth, *Freedom's Right*, p. 328.
31   On this point, see Krassimir Stojanov, *Bildung und Anerkennung:
      Soziale Voraussetzungen von Selbstentwicklung und Welt-Erschließung*,
      Wiesbaden: Verlag für Sozialwissenschaften, 2006, esp. ch. 4.
      On the significance that recognitive relations in schools have for
      the idea of a democratization of schools, see Annedore Prengel,
      "Zwischen Heterogenität und Hierarchie in der Bildung: Studien zur
      Unvollendbarkeit der Demokratie," in: Luise Ludwig et al. (eds.),
      Bildung in der Demokratie, Opladen: Barbara Budrich Verlag, 2011,
      pp. 83–94.

Chapter 9: Democracy and the Division of Labor

1   For an overview, see Robert Castel, *From Manual Workers to Wage
     Laborers: Transformation of the Social Question*, London and New York:
     Routledge, 2017.

2   See Patrick Emmenegger, Silja Häusermann, Bruno Palier, and Martin Seeleib-Kaiser, *The Age of Dualization: The Changing Face of Inequality in Deindustrializing Societies*, New York: Oxford University Press, 2012.

3   For an overview on these tendencies, see Shoshana Zuboff, *In the Age of the Smart Machine: The Future of Work and Power*, New York: Basic Books, 1988.

4   Matthew Desmond, "Why Work Doesn't Work Anymore," *The New York Times Magazine*, September 16, 2018, pp. 36–41, 49.

5   See Horst Dreier, "Vom Schwinden der Demokratie," in: Friedrich Wilhelm Graf and Heinrich Meier (eds.), *Die Zukunft der Demokratie*, Munich: C.H. Beck, 2018, pp. 29–82.

6   Agnar Freyr Helgason and Vittorio Mérola, "Employment Insecurity, Incumbent Partisanship, and Voting Behavior in Comparative Perspective," *Comparative Political Studies*, 50.11 (2017), 1489–523. For a more expansive treatment of this topic, see Philip Manow, *Die Politische Ökonomie des Populismus*, Berlin: Suhrkamp, 2018.

7   Alexis de Tocqueville [1835/40], *Democracy in America*, London: Penguin Books, 2003; Hannah Arendt, *The Human Condition*, Chicago, IL: University of Chicago Press, 1958.

8   Karl Marx, "Economic and Philosophic Manuscripts of 1844," in: Robert Tucker (ed.), *The Marx-Engels Reader*, New York: W.W. Norton, 1978; Emile Durkheim [1893], *The Division of Labor in Society*, New York: Simon & Schuster, 2014.

9   Hannah Arendt, *The Origins of Totalitarianism*, New York: Harcourt Brace, 1973.

10 Benjamin Constant, "The Liberty of the Ancients Compared with that of the Moderns," in: Biancamaria Fontana (ed.), *Political Writings*, Cambridge: Cambridge University Press, 1988. That Constant's political theory should nevertheless not be read as a defense of purely "negative" freedom has been well demonstrated by Stephen Holmes in: *Benjamin Constant and the Making of Modern Liberalism*, New Haven, CT: Yale University Press, 1984.

11 John Dewey, "Human Nature and Conduct (1922)," in: Jo Ann Boydston (ed.), *Middle Works of John Dewey*, vol. 14, Carbondale, IL: Southern Illinois University Press, 2008.

12 On the key significance of this assumption for Marx, cf. Daniel Brudney, "Community and Completion," in: Andrews Reath et al. (eds.), *Reclaiming the History of Ethics*, Cambridge: Cambridge University Press, 1997.

13 G. W. F. Hegel, *Elements of the Philosophy of Right*, ed. Allen Wood, Cambridge: Cambridge University Press, 1991. On this topic, see Hans-Christoph Schmidt am Busch, *"Anerkennung" als Prinzip der Kritischen Theorie*, Berlin: De Gruyter, 2011, ch. III.

14 See Axel Honneth, *Anerkennung. Eine europäische Ideengeschichte*, Berlin: Suhrkamp Verlag, 2018, ch. III.

15 Orlando Patterson, *Slavery and Social Death*, Cambridge, MA: Harvard University Press, 1983.
16 Marie Jahoda, Paul Lazarsfeld, and Hans Zeisel, *Die Arbeitslosen von Marienthal. Ein soziographischer Versuch über die Wirkung langandauernder Arbeitslösigkeit*, Frankfurt am Main: Suhrkamp Verlag, 1975 [1933].
17 In this connection, I'll restrict myself to mentioning two monographs, one older and one more recent, both of which contain references to further relevant literature: Carole Pateman, *Participation and Democratic Theory*, Cambridge: Cambridge University Press, 1970, ch. 3; Andrea Veltman, *Meaningful Work*, Oxford: Oxford University Press, 2016, ch. 3.
18 Didier Eribon, *Returning to Reims*, Cambridge, MA: MIT Press, 2013.
19 Pateman, *Participation and Democratic Theory*, ch. 3.
20 See, for example, Zuboff, *In the Age of the Smart Machine*, p. 395.
21 Jurgen Osterhammel, *The Transformation of the World: A Global History of the Nineteenth Century*, Princeton, NJ: Princeton University Press, 2014, ch. VIII.
22 See as an example Sven Beckert, *Empire of Cotton: A Global History*, New York: Alfred A. Knopf, 2014.
23 Cf. Siegfried Kracauer, *The Salaried Masses: Duty and Distraction in Weimar Germany*, London: Verso, 1998; Osterhammel, *The Transformation of the World*, ch. VIII.
24 Andrea Komlosy, *Work: The Last 1000 Years*, London: Verso, 2018, pp. 57–81.
25 Marx, who faced similar difficulties in his attempts to solve this problem, helped as to the concept of "use value"; but this too leads to further complications, implying as it does that any activity that fulfills any use or satisfies any need should be designated as "labor": Karl Marx, *Capital*, vol. 1.
26 Michael Piore and Charles Sabel, *The Second Industrial Divide*, New York: Basic Books, 1994; Charles Sabel, *Work and Politics*, New York: Cambridge University Press, 1984, p. 32.
27 Piore and Sabel, *The Second Industrial Divide*, p. 38.
28 See the excellent study: Ernst Michael Lange, *Das Prinzip Arbeit. Drei metakritische Kapitel über Grundbegriffe, Struktur und Darstellung der Kritik der Politischen Ökonomie von Karl Marx*, Berlin: Ullstein Verlag, 1980.
29 Durkheim, *The Division of Labor in Society*.
30 See Steven Lukes, *Emile Durkheim: His Life and Work*, London: Allen Lane-Penguin Books, 1973, ch. 7.
31 See Robert Blauner, *Alienation and Freedom: The Factory Worker and His Industry*, Chicago, IL: University of Chicago Press, 1964; *Alienation in Work: The Diversity of Industrial Environment*, Chicago, IL: University of Chicago Press, 1974.
32 Philipp Staab, *Macht und Herrschaft in der Servicewelt*, Hamburg: Hamburger Edition, 2014, esp. ch. 5.

33 See the references in Joshua Freeman's fascinating book, *A History of the Factory and the Making of the Modern World*, New York: W.W. Norton, 2018. For the German case, see Joan Campbell, *Joy in Work, German Work: The National Debate: 1800–1945*, Princeton, NJ: Princeton University Press, 1989.

34 Harry Braverman, *Labor and Monopoly Capitalism: The Degradation of Work in the Twentieth Century*, New York: Monthly Review Press, 1974.

35 Durkheim, *The Division of Labor in Society*, p. 300.

36 See van der Linden, *Workers of the World, Eine Globalgeschichte der Arbeit*, Frankfurt: Campus Verlag, 2017, ch. l; Komlosy, *Work: The Last 1000 Years*, ch. 5.

37 Cf. the results in Pateman, *Participation and Democratic Theory*. Also interesting in this connection is Michael Walzer's report on the "San Francisco Scavengers": Michael Walzer, *Spheres of Justice*, New York: Basic Books, 1983, pp. 177ff. An overview of relevant empirical findings can be found in: Alex Bryson et al., "Share Capitalism and Worker Wellbeing," *Labour Economics*, 42 (2016), 151–8.

38 On arguments of this form, see Walzer, *Spheres of Justice*, ch. 6.

39 Erik Olin Wright, *Envisioning Real Utopias*, London: Verso, 2010.

Chapter 10: Childhood

1 *The Ice Storm* (1997), script by James Schamus, director: Ang Lee.

2 Richard Ford, *Canada*, New York: Ecco, 2012.

3 Donna Tartt, *The Goldfinch*, Boston, MA: Little, Brown, 2013, p. 215.

4 Philippe Ariès, *Centuries of Childhood: A Social History of Family Life*, New York: Alfred A. Knopf, 1962.

5 See David Archard, *Children: Rights and Childhood*, London: Routledge, 3rd edition, 2014, part 2.

6 See Martin Dornes, *Die Modernisierung der Seele: Kind – Familie – Gesellschaft*, Frankfurt am Main: Fischer, 2012, esp. pp. 95–100.

7 Archard, *Children: Rights and Childhood*, pp. 37f.

8 On the normatively charged concept of "child" or "childhood," see Theodor W. Adorno, *Minima Moralia: Reflections on a Damaged Life*, London: Verso, 2005; esp. aphorisms nos. 2, 72, 79, and 146. See also my conversation with Daniela Berner-Zumpf, "Der Philosoph und das Kind im Ringen um Anerkennung: Acht Fragen an Axel Honneth: Gespräch mit Daniela Berner-Zumpf," in: Caroline Teichert, Daniela Berner-Zumpf, and Michael Teichert (eds.), *"Alle Tassen fliegen hoch": Eine Kritik der Kinderphilosophie*, Weinheim and Basle: Beltz, 2020, pp. 92–101.

9 Rousseau's educational theory, as laid out in his *Émile*, represents an interesting intermediary position. On the one hand, it

strongly advocates the isolation of the child from society; on the other, it credits the child with an ability to learn from the natural environment that is so strong that "external" teaching seems pretty much superfluous. See Jean-Jacques Rousseau, *Emile or On Education*, New York: Basic Books, 1979. On the opposite tendencies in *Émile*, namely the emphasis on the need for the rational formation of "amour propre" by the right kind of social interaction, see Frederick Neuhouser, *Rousseau's Theodicy of Self-Love: Evil, Rationality, and the Drive to Recognition*, Oxford: Oxford University Press, 2008, pp. 171–83.

10 On this radical position, see Archard, *Children: Rights and Childhood*, pp. 70–7.

11 The pressure toward sequentialization in education is most clearly reflected in the conclusions drawn from Piaget's theory of the stages of early child development. See Dieter Katzenbach and Olaf Steenbuck (eds.), *Piaget und die Erziehungslehre heute*, Frankfurt am Main: Peter Lang, 2000.

12 On the appreciation of such properties of the child as intrinsic goods of childhood, see Anca Gheaus, "The 'intrinsic goods of childhood' and the just society," in: Alexander Bagattini and Colin M. Macleod (eds.), *The Nature of Children's Well-Being: Theory and Practice*, Dordrecht: Springer, 2015, pp. 35–52.

13 See, e.g., Barbara Arneil, "Becoming versus Being: A Critical Analysis of the Child in Liberal Theory," in: David Archard and Colin Macleod (eds.), *The Moral and Political Status of Children*, Oxford: Oxford University Press, 2002, pp. 70–94.

14 A paradigmatic case of such a perspective is Tamar Schapiro, "What is a Child?," *Ethics*, 109/4 (1999), 715–38.

15 For more details, see Archard, *Children: Rights and Childhood*, pp. 153ff.

16 Immanuel Kant, *Kant On Education*, Boston, MA: D.C. Heath & Co., 1900, p. 26.

17 For more details, see Archard, *Children: Rights and Childhood*, chs. 11 and 12, and David Archard, *Children, Family and the State*, Hampshire: Ashgate, 2003, in particular ch. 3.

18 Oskar Negt, "Kindheit und Kinder-Öffentlichkeit," in: Gerd Harms and Christa Pressing (eds.), *Kinderalltag: Beiträge zur Analyse der Veränderung von Kindheit*, Berlin: FIPP, 1988, pp. 18f.

19 On the role of the school in this process, see Axel Honneth, "Education and the Democratic Public Sphere: A Neglected Chapter of Political Philosophy," in: *Recognition and Freedom*, Leiden: Brill, 2015, pp. 17–32.

20 See, e.g., Horst-Eberhard Richter, *Family as Patient: The Origin, Nature and Treatment of Marital and Family Conflicts*, London: Souvenir Press, 1974.

21 This is one of Anca Gheaus's arguments for an expansion of "nonparental care for children" provided by social institutions. Anca

Gheaus, "Arguments for Nonparental Care for Children," *Social Theory and Practice*, 37/3 (2011), 483–509; here: p. 501. I shall mention some more of her arguments in what follows.

22 For a critique of such apocalyptic visions of the family, see Dornes, *Die Modernisierung der Seele*, pp. 244–51.

23 Hartmut Tyrell, "Ehe und Familie," in: Kurt Lüscher, Franz Schultheis, and Michael Wehrspaun (eds.), *Die postmoderne Familie: Familiale Strategien und Familienpolitik in der Übergangszeit*, Constance: Universitätsverlag Konstanz, 1991, pp. 145–56.

24 One excellent example among many is Raymond Carver, "Nobody Said Anything," in: *Will You Please Be Quiet, Please?*, New York: McGraw-Hill, 1976, pp. 41–59. Among more recent films, *Boyhood* (2014; script-writer and director: Richard Linklater) is pretty much unparalleled in the impressive way in which it presents both children's suffering from the symptoms of the dissolution in the traditional family and their enormous capacity to deal with them and to master attachment uncertainties.

25 This argument can also be found in Gheaus, "Arguments for Nonparental Care for Children," here esp. pp. 498–501.

26 On the substance of the concept "class sociality," see the thought-provoking essay by Karl-Siegbert Rehberg, "'Klassengesellschaftlichkeit' nach dem Ende der Klassengesellschaft?," *Berliner Journal für Soziologie*, 21/1 (2011), 7–21.

27 See Gheaus, "Arguments for Nonparental Care for Children," here: pp. 490–2.

28 This chapter is based on my presentation at a conference organized by Ferdinand Suterlüty: "Der Streit ums Kindeswohl" [The controversy over children's well-being]. It took place in Frankfurt am Main, January 16–17, 2015. I am grateful to Monika Betzler and Barbara Bleisch, the editors of the volume in which the text originally appeared, for their extensive and valuable comments during the revision and completion of the essay.

Chapter 11: Denaturalizations of the Lifeworld

1 On this moment, see Wilhelm Dilthey, *Introduction to the Human Sciences*, Princeton, NJ: Princeton University Press, 1989. Interestingly, Dilthey names J. S. Mill as one of the authors responsible for the methodical differentiation and the introduction of the category of *Geisteswissenschaften*. See pp. 57f.

2 In the Francophone world, the role of Dilthey is played by Ernest Renan, who delimits the *science de l'humanité* from the *science de la nature*, without, however, making use of Hegel's idea of a sphere of "objectifications of the spirit." See Ernest Renan, *L'avenir de la science*

[1848], Paris: Garnier-Flammarion, 1995. (English edition: *The Future of Science: Ideas of 1848*, London: Chapman and Hall, 1891.)

3   The concept of *Humanwissenschaften*, as used during the past few decades in Germany, is, however, narrower than the much older concept of *Geisteswissenschaften*, because while it denotes those disciplines that consider the human being from various perspectives, it does not consider the human beings' objectifications of the spirit.

4   Arguably, John Stuart Mill is chiefly responsible for the differentiation between the natural and human sciences on the basis of a gradual continuum, as we find it in the Anglo-Saxon world. See John Stuart Mill, *The Logic of the Moral Sciences*, London: Duckworth, [1872] 1988.

5   This connection between understanding and "empathy" can, however, also be seen as a first step toward acknowledging that, in order to capture the meaning of a text or other cultural product, we need to comprehend not only the convictions of the author or creator but also their intentions and emotional attitudes. On this, and on the usefulness of Dilthey overall, see Wolfgang Detel, *Geist und Verstehen: Historische Grundlagen einer modernen Hermeneutik*, Frankfurt am Main: Klostermann, 2011, pp. 136–52.

6   Transl. note: Here and in what follows "intellectual" translates "geistig."

7   On this transition from an "elementary" to a "higher" form of "understanding" as a challenge, also using the example of a child, see Wilhelm Dilthey, *The Formation of the Historical World in the Human Sciences*, Princeton, NJ: Princeton University Press, 2002, pp. 228–34. A much more detailed account of this transition, drawing on more recent findings of developmental psychology and anthropology, can be found in: Wolfgang Detel, *Kognition, Parsen und rationale Erklärung*, Frankfurt am Main: Klostermann, 2014, ch. 2.5.

8   On the role of the archive as a storage space for cultural knowledge, see Maurice Halbwachs, *The Collective Memory*, New York: Harper & Row, 1980, ch. 2, and Michel Foucault, *The Archaeology of Knowledge*, New York: Pantheon Books, 1972, ch. III.5.

9   On the ontological status of intellectual-cultural objects, see John Searle, *The Construction of Social Reality*, New York: The Free Press, 1995.

10 The following is mainly based on John Dewey's *The Quest for Certainty: A Study of the Relation of Knowledge and Action*, New York: Minton, Balch & Company, 1929, and *Human Nature and Conduct: The Middle Works, 1899–1924*, Carbondale, IL: Southern Illinois University Press, 1988, vol. 14. I shall try to transpose the process of experimental research, as developed by Dewey in these two texts mainly with regard to the natural sciences, on to humanities research.

11 On the notion of "qualitative" objects, see Dewey, *The Quest for Certainty*, chs. II and III.

12 Ibid., esp. ch. VII.
13 This example, taken from Allen Silver's "Friendship in Commercial Society: Eighteenth Century Social Theory and Modern Sociology," *American Journal of Sociology*, 95/6 (1990), 1474–504, illustrates that the intrusion of science into the social is not a phenomenon that is specific to the more recent past, as claimed in, for instance, Lutz Raphael, "Die Verwissenschaftlichung des Sozialen als methodische und konzeptuelle Herausforderung für eine Sozialgeschichte des 20. Jahrhunderts," *Geschichte und Gesellschaft*, 22 (1996), 165–93.
14 See Dewey, *The Quest for Certainty*, especially ch. IX.
15 On the category of "sense of possibility" in the context of the humanities, see Peter Strohschneider, "Möglichkeitssinn: Geisteswissenschaften im Wissenschaftssystem," *Zeitblick*, 8/1 (2009). In this context, John Dewey understands the methodical category of "possibility" as a reference to the difference between what is currently "desired" and what is objectively "desirable." See *The Quest for Certainty*, pp. 259ff.
16 All these points are the result of an application to concrete cases of the reflections used by Dewey to justify his claim that the experimental method is also useful in disciplines with a normative orientation. See *The Quest for Certainty*, pp. 278–86.
17 This essay is based on a lecture I gave in Essen in 2013 on the occasion of the tenth anniversary of the *Fakultät für Geisteswissenschaften* (Faculty of the Humanities) at the Universität Duisburg-Essen.

Chapter 12: Is There an Emancipatory Interest?

1 Cf. Axel Honneth, *The Idea of Socialism: Towards a Renewal*, Cambridge: Polity Press, 2017, pp. 39–42.
2 Georg Lukács and Rodney Livingstone, *History and Class Consciousness: Studies in Marxist Dialectics*, translated by Rodney Livingstone, London: Merlin, 1971. Georg Lukács, "Geschichte und Klassenbewußtsein (1923)," in: *Geschichte und Klassenbewußtsein. Werke, Frühschriften II*, Neuwied and Berlin: Luchterhand, 1968, pp. 161–517.
3 Max Horkheimer, "Traditional and Critical Theory," in: *Critical Theory: Selected Essays*, translated by Matthew J. O'Connell and others, New York: Continuum, 2002, pp. 188–243.
4 Jürgen Habermas, *Knowledge and Human Interests*, Boston, MA: Beacon Press, 1968.
5 Jürgen Habermas, "Nach dreißig Jahren: Bemerkungen zu Erkenntnis und Interesse," in: Stefan Müller-Doohm (ed.), *Das Interesse der Vernunft. Rückblicke auf das Werk von Jürgen Habermas seit "Erkenntnis und Interesse,"* Frankfurt am Main: Suhrkamp, 2000, pp. 12–22.
6 Habermas, *Knowledge and Human Interests*, ch. II.

7   Ibid., ch. III.
8   Horkheimer, "Traditional and Critical Theory," pp. 210f.
9   Habermas, *Knowledge and Human Interests*, p. 286.
10 Ibid., pp. 198–205. A slightly different, more differentiated recon-
    struction of Kant's idea of an "interest of reason" has meanwhile
    been developed by Axel Hutter: *Das Interesse der Vernunft. Kants
    ursprüngliche Einsicht und ihre Entfaltung in den transzendentalphiloso-
    phischen Hauptwerken*, Meiner: Hamburg, 2003.
11 Habermas, *Knowledge and Human Interests*, pp. 205–10.
12 Ibid., p. 211.
13 Habermas has acknowledged some of the mistakes here identified (cf.
    especially: Thomas McCarthy, *Kritik der Verständigungsverhältnisse.
    Zur Theorie von Jürgen Habermas*, Frankfurt am Main: Suhrkamp, 1980,
    esp. pp. 112ff.) in his reactions to some critiques. However, he later
    never tried again to pursue any further the attempt to determine an
    emancipatory interest as developed in *Knowledge and Human Interests*,
    so that the consequences of these revisions for such a program cannot
    be sufficiently evaluated.
14 See, as an example: Hans-Joachim Giegel, "Normative Orientierungen
    und sozialwissenschaftliche Erkenntnis: Rückblick auf Erkenntnis
    und Interesse," in: Müller-Doohm (ed.), *Das Interesse der Vernunft*,
    pp. 42–70.
15 See my own attempt in such a direction: Axel Honneth, *Freedom's
    Right: The Social Foundations of Democratic Life*, Cambridge: Polity,
    2014.
16 I follow here the relevant determinations by Titus Stahl who lets
    himself be informed by Quine; see: Titus Stahl, *Immanente Kritik.
    Elemente einer Theorie sozialer Praktiken*, Frankfurt am Main: Campus
    Verlag, 2013, pp. 191ff.
17 Allen W. Wood, "Unsociable Sociability," *Philosophical Topics*, 19/1
    (1991), 325–51.
18 Sigmund Freud and James Strachey, *Civilization and its Discontents*,
    New York: W.W. Norton & Co., 1961, pp. 21–151, esp. ch. IV. Sigmund
    Freud, "Das Unbehagen in der Kultur," in: *Gesammelte Werke*,
    Frankfurt am Main: S. Fischer Verlag, 1948, Band XIV, pp. 419–506,
    esp. ch. IV.
19 Karl Marx and Friedrich Engels, *The Communist Manifesto*, London:
    Penguin, 2002.
20 See John Dewey, *Lectures in China, 1919–1920*, Honolulu: University
    of Hawaii Press, 1973, esp. pp. 64–81. With regard to Hegel, see: Axel
    Honneth, *The Struggle for Recognition: On the Moral Grammar of Social
    Conflicts*, Cambridge: Polity, 1994, ch. 2.
21 Georg Simmel and Kurt H. Wolff, "IV," in: *The Sociology of Georg Simmel*,
    New York: Free Press, 1964. Georg Simmel, *Soziologie. Untersuchungen
    über die Formen der Vergesellschaftung*, Leipzig: Duncker & Humblot,
    1908, ch. IV.

22   See the interpretation by Frederick Neuhouser, *Rousseau's Theodicy of Self-Love: Evil, Rationality, and the Drive for Recognition*, Oxford: Oxford University Press, 2010, esp. Part III.
23   See, for example: Marcel Mauss, *The Gift: Forms and Functions of Exchange in Archaic Societies*, Miami: HardPress, 2014.
24   Barrington Moore, *Injustice. The Social Basis of Obedience and Revolt*, Basingstoke: Palgrave Macmillan, 1978.
25   See for this and the following: Stahl, *Immanente Kritik*, pp. 380–7.
26   Among many others: Talcott Parsons, *The Structure of Social Action*, New York: Free Press, 1968, Vol. I, Part II, ch. X. Another version of this thesis is offered by John McDowell's understanding of "second nature": John McDowell, *Mind and World*, Cambridge, MA: Harvard University Press, 1994; Axel Honneth, "Between Hermeneutics and Hegelianism: John McDowell and the Challenge of Moral Realism," in: Nicholas H. Smith (ed.), *Reading McDowell: On Mind and World*, London: Routledge, 2002, pp. 246–65.
27   Examples are offered in the famous studies by Charles Tilly or James C. Scott: Charles Tilly, *Identities, Boundaries and Social Ties*, London: Routledge, 2006; James C. Scott, *Domination and the Arts of Resistance*, New Haven, CT: Yale University Press, 1992.
28   For the slave revolts, see the interesting remarks by Joshua Cohen: "The Arc of the Moral Universe," in: *The Arc of the Moral Universe and Other Essays*, Cambridge, MA: Harvard University Press, 2010, pp. 15–72, esp. pp. 43ff.
29   For such reservations, see: Robin Celikates, "Slow Learners? On Moral Progress, Social Struggle, and Whig History," Ms., 2016.
30   Kenneth R. Westphal, *The Blackwell Guide to Hegel's Phenomenology of Spirit*, Malden, MA: Wiley-Blackwell, 2009, pp. 37–53. G. W. F. Hegel, *Phänomenologie des Geistes, Werke in zwanzig Bänden, Vol. 3*, Frankfurt am Main: Suhrkamp, 1970, pp. 145–55.
31   Ibid., p. 154.
32   I dedicate this lecture to my much too early deceased friend Mark Sacks. For as long as I had the privilege to be his friend, he was a permanent source of surprising intuitions and warmest care; without his engagement, the *European Journal of Philosophy* would not exist.

Chapter 13: A History of Moral Self-Correction

1   See Claus Offe, *Europe Entrapped*, Cambridge: Polity, 2015; esp. chs. II and III. See also Philip Manow, *Die Politische Ökonomie des Populismus*, Berlin: Suhrkamp, 2018.
2   This is the position Wolfgang Streeck has come to. See his "Market and People: Democratic Capitalism and European Integration," *New Left Review*, 73 (2012), 63–71.

3 An example of this strategy is the otherwise fascinating study by Orlando Figes, *The Europeans: Three Lives and the Making of a Cosmopolitan Culture*, New York: Macmillan, 2019.

4 On this perspective, see Claus Offe, "Is there, or can there be, a 'European Society'?," in: John Keane (ed.), *Civil Society: Berlin Perspectives*, New York: Berghahn, 2006, pp. 169–88.

5 Claus Offe, *Europe Entrapped*, pp. 63ff. I owe more to Claus Offe's reflections on this aspect than I can express in my text. In effect, my presentation does no more than push further an argument suggested in his book.

6 Thomas Hobbes, *Leviathan*, Oxford: Oxford University Press, 1996. Quentin Skinner, "Thomas Hobbes on the Proper Signification of Liberty," *Transactions of the Royal Historical Society*, 40 (1990), 121–51.

7 Quentin Skinner, *Liberty before Liberalism*, Cambridge: Cambridge University Press, 1998.

8 Ibid., pp. 82f.

9 A recent proponent of this position is Robert Nozick, *Anarchy, State, and Utopia*, Oxford: Basil Blackwell, 1980 [1974].

10 See Jerome Schneewind, *The Invention of Autonomy: A History of Modern Moral Philosophy*, Cambridge: Cambridge University Press, 1977. See also Patricia Springborg, "Liberty Exposed: Quentin Skinner's Hobbes and Republican Liberty," *British Journal for the History of Philosophy*, 18 (2010), 139–62.

11 The notion of "toleration," which also developed as a moral response to the challenges of the wars of religion, followed a similar historical course, with the development of a controversy between two opposed positions. See Rainer Forst, *Toleration in Conflict: Past and Present*, Cambridge: Cambridge University Press, 2013.

12 Friedrich Engels, *The Condition of the Working Class in England*, Oxford: Oxford University Press, 1993. See also E. P. Thompson and Eileen Yeo (eds.), *The Unknown Mayhew: Selections from the Morning Chronicle 1849–1850*, London: Merlin Press, 1971.

13 See, among others, Giovanna Procacci, *Gouverner la misère: La question sociale en France, 1789–1848*, Paris: Seuil, 1993; John Roach, *Social Reform in England 1780–1880*, New York: HarperCollins, 1978; George Steinmetz, *Regulating the Social: The Welfare State and Local Politics in Imperial Germany*, Princeton, NJ: Princeton University Press, 1993; Andreas Gestrich, Steven King, and Lutz Raphael (eds.), *Being Poor in Modern Europe: Historical Perspectives 1800–1940*, Bern: Peter Lang, 2006.

14 Albert Hirschman, "Rival Interpretations of Market Society: Civilizing, Destructive, or Feeble?," *Journal of Economic Literature*, 20/4 (1982), 1463–84. On the debates over the merits of capitalist markets, see also Lisa Herzog and Axel Honneth (eds.), *Der Wert des Marktes: Ein ökonomisch-philosophischer Diskurs vom 18. Jahrhundert bis zur Gegenwart*, Berlin: Suhrkamp, 2014.

15   See Thomas Marshall, *Citizenship and Social Class*, London: Pluto Press, 1992 [1949].

16   On these economic developments, see Colin Crouch and Wolfgang Streeck (eds.), *Political Economy of Modern Capitalism: Mapping Conversion and Diversity*, London: Sage, 1997.

17   See Jürgen Osterhammel, *Colonialism: A Theoretical Overview*, Princeton, NJ: Markus Wiener Publishers, 1997, and Wolfgang Reinhard, *A Short History of Colonialism*, Manchester: Manchester University Press, 2011.

18   On the situation in France, see Lawrence C. Jennings, *French Anti-Slavery: The Movement for the Abolition of Slavery in France, 1802–1848*, Cambridge: Cambridge University Press, 2000. On the situation in England, see Howard Temperly, *British Antislavery, 1833–1870*, Columbia, SC: University of South Carolina Press, 1972. An illuminating overview is provided by Benedikt Stuchtey, *Die europäische Expansion und ihre Feinde: Kolonialismuskritik vom 18. bis in das 20. Jahrhundert*, Berlin: De Gruyter, 2010.

19   See Françoise Vergès, "Les troubles de la mémoire: Traite négrière, esclavage et écriture de l'histoire," *Cahiers d'Études Africaines*, 45, 179/180 (2005), 1143–78.

20   See, among others, Daron Acemoglu and James A. Robinson, *Why Nations Fail: The Origins of Power, Prosperity, and Poverty*, New York: Crown Publishers, 2012, ch. 9.

21   See Claus Offe, *Europe Entrapped*, pp. 76ff.

22   Marcel Mauss, *La nation, ou le sens du social*, Paris: PUF, 2013.

23   Georg Simmel, *Sociology: Inquiries into the Construction of Social Forms*, Vol. 1, Leiden: Brill, 2009, ch. 4: "Conflict," pp. 227–305.

24   Albert O. Hirschman, "Social Conflicts as Pillars of Democratic Market Societies," *Political Theory*, 22/2 (1994), 203–18.

25   See John Dewey's interpretation of the "struggle for recognition," which takes its cue from Hegel: John Dewey, *Lectures in China 1919–1920*, Honolulu: The University of Hawaii Press, 1973.

26   See Claus Offe, *Europe Entrapped*, p. 78.

27   See Albert Hirschman, *The Passions and the Interests: Political Arguments for Capitalism before the Moment of its Triumph*, Princeton, NJ: Princeton University Press, 1997 [1977].

28   On the alternatives, see Richard Bellamy, "The Challenge of European Union," in: John S. Dryzeck, Bonnie Honig, and Anne Phillips (eds.), *The Oxford Handbook of Political Theory*, Oxford: Oxford University Press, 2006, pp. 245–61.

29   Jürgen Habermas, "The Lure of Technocracy: A Plea for European Solidarity," in: *The Lure of Technocracy*, Cambridge: Polity, 2015, pp. 3–28.

30   See Jason Scott Smith, *A Concise History of the New Deal*, Cambridge: Cambridge University Press, 2014.

31   See Ira Katznelson, *Fear Itself: The New Deal and the Origins of Our Time*, New York: W.W. Norton & Co., 2013.

32   Franklin D. Roosevelt, *Presidential Nomination Address at the Democratic National Convention*, 2 July 1932. Available at: https://publicpolicy .pepperdine.edu/academics/research/faculty-research/new-deal /roosevelt-speeches/fr070232.htm.
33   This text is a revised version of the lecture I gave at one of the Conférences Marc Bloch at the Sorbonne on June 11, 2019, upon the invitation of the EHESS. I would like to give my heartfelt thanks to Julia Christ, Bruno Karsenti, and Christine Pries for their advice and helpful comments.

Index